T0358756

DO DIFFERENT

DO DIFFERENT

The Untold

DHONI

Joy Bhattacharjya & Amit Sinha

PENGUIN
VIKING

An imprint of Penguin Random House

VIKING

USA | Canada | UK | Ireland | Australia
New Zealand | India | South Africa | China

Viking is part of the Penguin Random House group of companies
whose addresses can be found at global.penguinrandomhouse.com

Published by Penguin Random House India Pvt. Ltd
4th Floor, Capital Tower 1, MG Road,
Gurugram 122 002, Haryana, India

First published in Viking by Penguin Random House India 2022

ISBN 9780670094820

Typeset in Adobe Caslon Pro by Manipal Technologies Limited, Manipal
Printed at Replika Press Pvt. Ltd, India

www.penguin.co.in

To my father, a massive Dhoni fan,
who passed away on 24th April 2021
waiting for a CSK match the next day
—Amit

To my parents Shiv and Shukla,
the best partnership I have seen
—Joy

Contents

Introduction

'A riddle, wrapped in a mystery, inside an enigma.' That's how the British Prime Minister Winston Churchill described Russia. Had he been around eight decades later, he would have probably said the same about an Indian captain, the most successful in Indian cricket history.

For Dhoni is the ultimate black box. On tour with Chennai Super Kings or with the Indian team, his hotel room door is always open, players and staff walking in and out and room service being constantly summoned. And yet none of his colleagues had even a whiff of what was to come when he announced his Test retirement. He is the symbol of the Chennai franchise, the 'Thalaiva' who they would follow to the grave, and yet they found out about his international retirement from social media. He is a joy in press conferences, speaking honestly and eloquently about the game, and yet gives nothing away beyond that. And every opposition team coach and captain has tried to decode the intent behind that bland and kindly smile. Dhoni has that frustrating ability to give you everything you ask for, and you realize you still have nothing, no better understanding of the most iconic leader in Indian sporting history.

Many have tried to decode the Dhoni story, and yet every account seems to come up frustratingly short of capturing the essence of the man.

And so we thought we'd not even try. Instead of trying to build a single narrative from the scores of different angles he can be viewed from, we decided to include those diverse narratives and also capture his most iconic moments on and off the field.

So, through this work, you'll meet the young cricketer still a fair way off from making it to the big stage as seen through the eyes of many people: from a fellow wicketkeeper and competitor; to Dhoni's first agent who managed his portfolio giving us his perspective on the brand that Dhoni became; to an international fast bowler who played with him since his first-class days and then starred for him in the Indian Premier League (IPL). There is also the Ranchi story, what the sleepy Jharkhand town gave Dhoni, and then an account of his cricketing journey from one of our leading sports journalists.

And, of course, we also have the matches and moments that defined him—in the IPL, in international cricket and even off the field. Finally, there is a detailed look at Dhoni through the unsentimental view of numbers.

These are all different views, very diverse views, and together they give us a far more complete and realistic picture of a man who is many things to many people.

You can choose to dip in and sample a specific match or perspective or let the narrative lead you along. In keeping with our approach, we've not tried to decide that for you.

Happy reading.

Joy Bhattacharjya
Amit Sinha

PART I

Dhoni's Finest Knocks

Amit Sinha
and
Joy Bhattacharjya

1

Glimpses of a Superstar

119* (134)—Nairobi, 19 August 2004 vs Pakistan A

In August 2004, two Indian teams found themselves in contrasting destinations. The senior team travelled to a rain-soaked Amsterdam to play Australia and Pakistan in a tri-series while the India A team found itself in the arid conditions of Nairobi in Kenya. The Sourav Ganguly-led senior team faced another setback, having suffered a defeat in the Asia Cup, as they failed to make it to the finals of the rain-marred tournament. In Nairobi, a bunch of India hopefuls led by spinner Sairaj Bahutule, who had already represented India at that point, gathered to play the Kenyan team and the Pakistan A team. Both the teams began their campaigns, on different days but in a similar fashion, with a loss. But the journeys of these teams were to diverge and, as a consequence, the story of Indian cricket too would change its course.

On 19 August, two days before the senior team's first match of the tri-series against Pakistan in Amsterdam, a young MS Dhoni was greeted by chants of his name in a small Nairobi ground. This was the result of a knock he had played against the same opposition a couple of days ago where he had scored 120 runs out of a total of 330 in India's first innings. Today, the situation was different as India had lost a wicket early in the innings in the pursuit of 235 runs when Dhoni walked in. For Dhoni too, who had gotten this chance largely because Dinesh Karthik had been selected to play for the senior team in Amsterdam, this was an opportunity to show that the 120 in the previous outing against Pakistan was no flash in the pan.

Waiting for him at the other end was the familiar sight of Gautam Gambhir, with whom he had stitched a 207-run partnership in the earlier match. Commentator Atul Wassan introduced him as the 'find of the tour' even before Dhoni faced his first delivery and went on to discuss his purposeful walk with fellow commentator Javagal Srinath. The Jharkhand cricketer, despite having been overlooked for the senior team promotion, was making quite an impression in Nairobi.

Facing his fourth ball of the innings, he cut fast bowler Riaz Afridi for his first runs of the innings. Javagal Srinath was just beginning to talk about how young cricketers need to be put through the 'process' despite having displayed their talents. The powerful cut seemed like an assurance sent to the commentary box. Such was the impact of the youngster on the audience that had been watching him for so long, the discussion revolved around his talent and how to ensure it didn't get wasted. On the panel was Saba Karim, a prodigy from the same region whose career didn't really blossom despite all signs of it at the corresponding age levels.

Facing Iftikhar Rao in the sixth over, Dhoni misjudged the length and edged the ball to the slips. However, luck was on his side that afternoon as Pakistan skipper Misbah-ul-Haq grassed a tough chance. In Anjum's next over, Dhoni was back to his attacking self as he picked the length early this time and pummelled the short ball to the midwicket fence. In the same over, the ball found itself in the same place again, although this time it was pitched full and on the batsman's legs.

The Nairobi Gymkhana, one of the highest cricket grounds in the world thanks to its location 5,500 feet above sea level, saw Indian cricket transform four years ago when an unheralded Indian team made it to the final of the ICC Knockout Trophy, only a few months after the match-fixing scandal. What started in that tournament reached its peak with India's success in the 2003 World Cup and on tours of Australia and Pakistan. By mid-2004, however, the wheels had stopped turning for Indian cricket as the team suffered losses in both bilateral and multilateral competitions. The mantra that had worked for John Wright and Sourav Ganguly for four years seemed to be missing the mark now and it would all culminate in all the drama that unfolded in Indian cricket in the subsequent year.

Strangely, as the senior team was giving another listless performance in Amsterdam, on the rugged grounds of Kenya, the story of Indian cricket's future was being forged by two men who would play a huge part in taking Indian cricket to its peak seven years later.

Riaz Afridi, the elder brother of current Pakistan sensation Shaheen, was a nippy customer who was the star of Pakistan's win of the U-19 World Cup that year. However, against Dhoni and Gambhir, he found the going difficult. In the 11th over, Dhoni rocked back to hit him for a 4 through covers that proved the man was more than a spinner killer. He was quick to punish any error from the fast bowlers, be it Afridi or his bowling partner, Junaid Zia. The first lofted shot from the youngster's bat came in the fifteenth over when Iftikhar made the mistake of pitching it right in the slot for Dhoni to send it flying over covers. The small crowd gathered at the stadium was overjoyed. They seemed to have come exactly to witness this kind of shot making from the long-haired batsman. Even the commentators could barely hide their excitement.

Once the half-century mark was crossed, Dhoni went after the Pakistani spinners and hit both Qaiser Abbas and Mansoor Amjad for massive 6s that went out of the ground. A mere teaser of what was to follow in the next one and a half decades. Neither pace nor spin could trouble the duo as even Gambhir crossed his half-century and took India A closer to the target. Batting on 96, Dhoni decided to go for the glory shot against Junaid Zia, a bowler who had shoulder barged him earlier in the innings. The straight hit over the bowler's head came off spectacularly and another century was reached in 124 balls, the second in two matches. With 11 runs needed of the remaining 32 deliveries and a leg-spinner bowling, even those who had not seen him before knew what was coming. Mansoor Amjad, the leg-spinner, was launched into the stands for Dhoni's fourth and fifth 6 of the innings. The match was won. With two centuries in two matches against the Pakistan A side, the required stamp of confirmation was acquired. Everyone who watched Dhoni on those two days was left enamoured by his nonchalance and power play. In the unlikeliest of places, a star was born.

Two days later, the senior team suffered a defeat against Pakistan in the tournament opener. The wheels of change had started moving again in Indian cricket.

Partial scorecard of the match on page 95.

2

The Vizag Vig Vang

148 (123)—Visakhapatnam, 5 April 2005 vs Pakistan

On 11 January 1992, as captain Mohammad Azharuddin walked back to the pavilion, in came a young Sourav Ganguly to make his international debut in front of a West Indies bowling attack that had reduced the Indian batting line-up to 35/4. Batting alongside Sachin Tendulkar, this youngster's 13-minute-long stint at the crease was cut short by a contentious LBW decision. It would take four more years for this young boy from Bengal to take guard at the highest level once again, which he marked with a glorious ton at Lord's.

Those four years away from national reckoning, however, shaped a lot about Sourav Ganguly, the cricketer. And that was evident in the hunger with which he scored runs in the first half of his career. But it was only when he took over as the captain of the Indian team in 2000 that the impact of that time spent in the wilderness become clearer in relation to Ganguly, the captain.

In an interview given to Rediff's Faisal Shariff, a day before assuming charge of the Indian team officially against South Africa in March 2000, Ganguly laid out his road map for the future of the

Indian team, much of it based on his experiences as a youngster. He said, 'When you pick a player, give him five Tests, five one-dayers, before you close the chapter.'

Five years later, when Pakistan arrived in India for a full-fledged series, the Indian skipper's captaincy was on its last legs. Worse, even his form was whittling away. On 2 April 2005, Ganguly got out for a golden duck coming in at number 3 in the first ODI of the series. While India comfortably won the match, thanks to Tendulkar's heroics with the ball, the match had also seen the new Indian wicketkeeper accumulate his fourth score of less than 15.

In the next ODI held at Vishakhapatnam's Dr Y.S. Rajasekhara Reddy ACA-VDCA Cricket Stadium, the wicketkeeper got his fifth chance to play in Indian colours. When a throw from Yousuf Youhana claimed Sachin Tendulkar in the fourth over of the match, much to everyone's surprise, the stockily built Mahendra Singh Dhoni walked out to bat to join a swashbuckling Virender Sehwag at the crease. Unfazed by the change of partner at the other end, Sehwag waited for only one ball after Tendulkar's dismissal to dispatch Naved-ul-Hasan into the stands before adding another 4 on the next delivery. Another Sehwag special was on the cards, it seemed.

But that was until Dhoni took strike. The first delivery of the next over, and also the first one which he faced, was met with a straight bat before it disappeared behind the bowler for a 4 in no time. If the innings that followed could be defined by one shot, then it would have to be this one. There was not an iota of stage fright in this man who had chosen to take on the pace of Mohammad Sami with a straight bat. If there were any doubts that it was a pinch-hitter who had been sent to get a few quick runs to make the most of the fielding restrictions, they were dispatched in the coming overs with some ferocious hitting against the leg spin of Shahid Afridi.

That Afridi over also gave us the first glimpses of the coolness that was going to define this boy from Ranchi. After his leg-before appeal was turned down, Afridi didn't enjoy being hit inside out over extra cover for 4 by this 23-year-old. And neither did he hold himself back from letting the batsman know what he thought of him. In response, Dhoni smiled ever so slightly as he walked up to his partner at the non-striker's end. But whoever thought that smile was going to be his only response was proved wrong when the strength of Dhoni sent the next delivery several rows back into the stands.

The Sehwag–Dhoni blitz had brought up India's 100 by just the 11th over, but Sehwag left soon, trying one shot too many. With Ganguly clearly struggling against the Pakistan pace battery, the long-haired wicketkeeper cut down the risks himself. When a more fluent Rahul Dravid joined him after Ganguly's dismissal, the shots came out again. Offie Arshad Khan was sent over extra cover for 4 and then for a maximum over midwicket in the twenty-sixth over, and the attack continued when Hafeez came on to bowl. Having developed a reputation of butchering spinners, MS Dhoni was now putting on an exhibition of how to do it on the big stage. The century was reached with a single down the ground and off came the helmet to reveal the full extent of the coloured locks and a smile that had something honest about it. In 30 overs, Dhoni had made the journey from 0 to 100 with little fuss, but the smile, it seemed, was about the journey he had made from the platforms of Kharagpur to this moment, where everyone in the crowd and the dressing room applauded at the sign of the arrival of something special.

The heat and humidity of Visakhapatnam meant that there was little energy left in the batsman to run between the wickets after having spent 30 overs in the middle. But that translated into more trouble for the Pakistani bowlers as the flashing blade of Dhoni blasted them to smithereens. The way Afridi was taken apart in the fortieth over with 16 runs from 3 deliveries showed that not only did this Ranchi boy have the nonchalance of an elephant but also the memory of one. The Pakistani all-rounder finished the match with figures of none for 82 from his 9 overs.

By the time Dhoni was out in the forty-second over, he had not only accumulated 148 runs for himself but had also put the failures of the first four matches of his career far behind him. As he walked off to a standing ovation, it was clear that all that lay ahead of this supremely confident young man was a bright future.

Ganguly's captaincy lasted only two more games after the win at Visakhapatnam, but history will be kind to him for not closing the chapter on Mahendra Singh Dhoni before his fifth game in his last act of Dadagiri as Indian captain.

Partial scorecard of the match on page 96.

3

Bigger Bang on Diwali

183* (145)—31 October 2005 vs Sri Lanka

The year 2005 was a long one for Indian cricket. It began with great expectations for the team with a captain who had identified his set of match-winners and seemed ready to begin preparing for the next World Cup, which had slipped from their grasp the last time. The only missing piece of the puzzle was a wicketkeeper-batsman. That hot and humid morning in Visakhapatnam, made hotter by a scorching MS Dhoni century, seemed to have answered that puzzling question for Team India.

But by the time November knocked on the doors, that morning seemed like a memory from the distant past. The tide had begun to turn from the next match itself and for the longest part of 2005 that 148 seemed to be the only bright spot in India's cricketing year. For starters, Sourav Ganguly and John Wright were no longer with the Indian team. Greg Chappell had taken charge of the team and Rahul Dravid had ascended from being the vice captain to the captain of the Indian side. Even Sachin Tendulkar had changed his jersey number from 10 to 33! Dhoni's position in the batting line-up had also changed. India's losing

11

form, however, showed no signs of changing. A series loss from a dominant position of 2–0 to an eventual scoreline of 2–4 in favour of Pakistan immediately following that Vizag match was further followed by two tri-series losses leading to a very different-looking Indian team taking on the visiting Sri Lankan side in October.

With some confidence regained after winning the first two matches, India had a mountain to climb when their chase of 299 began in Jaipur. The loss of an in-form Sachin Tendulkar in the first over didn't help matters much but just like in Visakhapatnam, MS Dhoni, this time with slightly longer hair, came out to join Virender Sehwag at the crease. The team needed some quick runs at the top of the order to ease the pressure on a slightly inexperienced middle order and the boy from Jharkhand, wielding his bat like a lumberjack, seemed like the man for the job.

A cautious Dhoni took some time to get his eye in but when a Chaminda Vaas delivery angling away from him was sent over extra cover for a 6, the carnage had well and truly begun. In Vaas's next over, Dhoni did an encore, sending it for a flatter 6 this time. Unlike Visakhapatnam, in this partnership between Sehwag and 'Naya Sehwag', as some used to call Dhoni for his free-flowing strokeplay after the Visakhapatnam knock, the latter had turned the aggressor. His first three boundaries were all 6s. Although Sehwag too played at more than a run-a-ball, his partner raced to his half-century when he was on 32 with a slap down the ground for 4 off Vaas. This clearly was no 'Naya Sehwag'. This man, as it became evident on that October afternoon, was a different beast. If Sehwag was the guitar in a team of sarods, Dhoni was the electric version. And the electric guitar wasn't ready to stop even after the guitar stopped playing on that day. An over after Sehwag's departure, Dhoni was busy hitting leg-spinner Upul Chandana into the stands.

After having demolished Vaas, Dhoni, now wearing a cap that lent the coloured mane some more character, took on Murali. On most days, a lofted shot against the spinner would get people talking but with this man, it wasn't about how far he sent the ball but how hard he hit it. And how hard he hit the five-and-a-half-ounce sphere was clear when, in the twenty-first over, he drove one straight at Muralitharan that raced to the boundary like a tracer bullet, despite meeting the bowler's hand on the way.

Although there was still much left to chase at the midway mark of the Indian innings, the Dhoni demolition had visibly left the islanders deflated and demoralized in the Jaipur heat. Ironically, it wasn't much different from the treatment meted out by Sanath Jayasuriya's blade a decade ago to teams around the world, who, interestingly was the one bowler skipper Atapattu didn't turn towards when the Indian wicketkeeper-batsman went ballistic.

The century was brought up in the twenty-fifth over and along with the smile, came the Assault Rifle celebration, where he wielded the bat like a rifle and fired a shot towards the dressing room. The helmet came off too, curiously, for one last time as the more mature version of him never indulged in similar theatrics again in the years that followed.

But there was still a job at hand. This wasn't the first innings of the match but a chase and that too a steep one. With the ever-reliable Rahul Dravid gone soon after Dhoni's 100, the Lankans sensed a chance as a frail middle order appeared only a wicket away. The in-form batsman, though, dug his heels in and continued the attack on whoever came on to bowl. A certain self-belief that had by now come to be identified with this man was on full display in Jaipur. In the twenty-eighth over of the chase, Atapattu consulted with the bowler to put a fielder at long-on for an aerial shot from Dhoni. The aerial shot happened on the next ball and in the direction of long-on, but the fielder had no chance! This was exactly the kind of fireworks a crowd waiting for Diwali had come to watch. And they lapped up every bit of it.

On the score of 148, he finally mistimed a skier but there was no man underneath the swirling ball and he hit the 150 milestone along with his highest personal score. With the contest effectively killed by the Dhoni special, what remained to be seen was whether he would also go on to claim the record of the highest score by a wicketkeeper. Adam Gilchrist had held that honour with his mammoth 172 against Zimbabwe scored in 2004's VB series. A visibly tired Dhoni, now batting with a runner, allowed first Yuvraj Singh and then-newcomer Venugopal Rao to do the bulk of the scoring.

Twenty-two runs were required from the final 6 overs when the 24-year-old decided enough was enough. The leg spin of Upul Chandana was all that a tired Dhoni would have liked, and he didn't break a sweat in hitting his eighth and ninth 6s of the innings to go past Gilchrist's 172. With 2 required to go three up in the series, he launched another one into the stands to take his score to 183.

India had seen that score before. The man who had scored it, coincidentally against the same opposition six years ago, went on to lead Indian cricket for five years. Not many at that time could connect the dots but they did a couple of years later. And they did better six years down the line.

On that evening, though, after months of appearing listless, the team for once radiated the confidence of the man who was refashioning its destiny.

Partial scorecard of the match on page 97.

4

Can Do It in Whites Too!

148 (153)—Faisalabad, 21–25 January 2006 vs Pakistan

Any sentence that has 'India–Pakistan cricket' in it is unlikely to have the word 'dull' anywhere close to it. However, when India visited Pakistan in 2006, there was no other way to describe the action in the first couple of Test matches. The pitches were so flat and the criticism so strong that at the end of the second Test, the Pakistan Cricket Board itself announced that it was taking initiatives with international assistance to improve the conditions of the pitches that were proving to be a graveyard for the bowlers. The rain-marred first Test in Lahore saw 1089 runs being scored for the loss of just 8 wickets. The next Test in Faisalabad saw 1702 runs being scored with only 28 wickets falling over five days of Test cricket.

Yet, 148 out of those 1702 runs stood out on one gloomy January afternoon. In fact, for the first time in seven days of cricket in the series, when MS Dhoni took on the Pakistan bowlers, the action was anything but dull.

By 2006, Pakistani bowlers knew what MS Dhoni was capable of. Only nine months ago, he had blown them off with a thunderous 148 in only his fifth ODI. The history of limited-overs cricket, however, stands testament to the fact that not all big hitters of the white ball find the going easy against the red cherry. And so, when MS Dhoni arrived on the pitch in only his fifth Test with his team in a precarious situation, Pakistan's instinct was to press harder.

After posting a mammoth 588, Pakistan began to see an opening develop on the third afternoon when India collapsed from 236/1 to 281/5. Sachin Tendulkar had just been sent back by Shoaib Akhtar, and as always, Akhtar, after taking Tendulkar's wicket, had turned into Akhtar Pro Max. Even before sending the Little Master back into the hut, he had tried to get under the skin of a youngster who almost shared his hairstyle and gave it a tinge of brown too. The mercurial pacer probably took offence to that. It would be revealed in the hours that followed, however, that the Indian with an impressive mane also shared another trait of Akhtar's—jazbaa!

Dhoni had been welcomed to the crease with a vicious bouncer from Akhtar with some words on the side. Dhoni couldn't duck it the way he would have liked, and the ball almost kissed his helmet on its way to Kamran Akmal's gloves. By the time Dhoni could find his balance, Akhtar stood two metres away, giving the young man some valuable lessons on the art of ducking a bouncer. The next ball bowled at 153.6 kmph was another bouncer but this time it was sent over the slips by Dhoni. Shoaib had a smile on his face for he knew it was a battle now, unlike in the morning when nothing he said or did could rattle the calm and collected Rahul Dravid. The next one at 152 kmph was directed at the ribcage and Dhoni managed to keep it down. Another Akhtar stare saying, 'How long are you going to survive, kid?' followed.

An over later, Akhtar steamed in again and bowled another one aiming for the helmet. This time though, the ball met the blade on the way and in seconds was flying across the square leg boundary for the first 6 of the innings. Things were heating up on that cold afternoon.

But having been brought back to earth with that flat-batted 6, Akhtar had his tail up in the same over again as he managed to get Tendulkar to glove one to the keeper to leave India staring at a possible follow-on scenario. As the crowds erupted when a timid-looking Irfan Pathan played another Akhtar bouncer awkwardly, Dean Jones quipped on air, 'Don't think there's a boring draw here on the cards. Shoaib Akhtar has brought this Test to life.' Of course, Jones knew a thing or two about the Rawalpindi Express's ability to bully the lower order into submission.

It looked like the plan in the following overs as Akhtar hurled one bouncer after the other at both Dhoni and Pathan. The left-hander remembers the baptism by fire, 'I asked MS how's the pitch behaving upon my arrival, and he said "Kuch nahi ho raha" (Nothing is happening). Then when I began batting, one ball flew close to my right ear and another close to my left ear. I went up to him again and asked, "Mahi, what's happening?" He responded with a smile and said, "Ab asaan ho jaaega" (Now, it will be easy).'

The two also devised a strategy to counter Akhtar. Pathan remembers, 'Shoaib was bowling fast and making the ball talk on a flat surface. He was the only one who looked like he could take wickets as he was able to get some swing. He was also throwing verbal volleys at us. We decided that to rile him up, I'd respond to whatever he says, and MS would laugh at it.'

The plan worked. Even with the bat, Dhoni didn't back down. He pulled and cut with the same ferocity with which Akhtar was bowling at him. After the Akhtar challenge, Mohammad Asif seemed way too easy to face as he was dispatched to the boundary ropes thrice in an over. Abdul Razzaq too was treated with similar disdain. Suddenly, the narrative had turned from the Indian lower order being bullied to a counter-attack brewing. Pathan adds, 'As soon as Shoaib got tired, we knew we had won half the battle and felt confident about avoiding the follow-on.'

Pakistan had only themselves to blame for the narrative changing so quickly. Their actions fed into the counter-attack. When Danish Kaneria was brought into the attack, the man facing him was MS Dhoni. Dhoni quietly pushed the first ball towards Kaneria with a proper front-foot defence to give evidence of his Test batting credentials. Kaneria's response was to hurl the ball back in the direction of the batsman and then pepper him with words. In typical Dhoni style, the response didn't come immediately and definitely not in the form of words. The next 2 deliveries, however, were sent flying out of the ground as Dhoni brought up his half-century in just 34 deliveries with seven 4s and three 6s.

On the other side of tea, Pathan meted out similar treatment to the leg-spinner, showing how well he had grown in confidence in the company of Dhoni. When the leg-spinner turned to bowl round the wicket, one knew that the bully had been bullied. If there was any doubt, it was laid to rest when Dhoni played one of the most audacious shots seen in the match. As Kaneria slipped in a faster one that would have been a wide had Dhoni let it go, he slapped it towards the boundary behind him. Another 6 right over his head a few overs later was evidence enough that Kaneria had tickled the dragon with his actions.

As the day came close to an end, Shoaib Akhtar returned to the attack with the hope of changing the script of the game. Instead, he became the bowler Dhoni drove uppishly to bring up his maiden Test hundred off just 93 deliveries. The Faisalabad crowds had been treated to a 97-ball century by Shahid Afridi in the first innings and not many would have thought then that it could be bettered. But not only had Dhoni bettered Afridi's effort, but he had also driven India to safety in the match.

The Shoaib–Dhoni contest didn't end with the day though as the next day brought a re-energized Akhtar determined to get his team a breakthrough. But the results were disastrous this time around. He was driven straight down the ground for

4 when he for once decided to pitch it up to Dhoni. When he went back to bowling short, it was sent over the slips in a way similar to the shot which helped Dhoni open his account in the innings. Quite predictably, Akhtar came round the wicket as if to intimidate the batsman. At this point though, Dhoni wasn't going to be intimidated. He pulled it for another 4 to the mid-wicket boundary. The next delivery was a shocker. Bowled from the same angle, Akhtar hurled a beamer at Dhoni at 156 kmph. The ball missed the wicketkeeper and went for 4. And there was no apology from the bowler either.

That beamer, if anything, was an admission that the battle was over. There was only one winner. It was the jazbaa of MS Dhoni, who once again ended with 148 versus Pakistan and helped India to a 15-run lead with a 210-run partnership with Pathan.

Partial scorecard of the match on page 98.

5

Pakistan Pummelled, Again!

72* (46)—Lahore, 13 February 2006 vs Pakistan

Where should MS Dhoni bat for India in the ODIs? This question has walked alongside the gloveman throughout the length of his career. With his knocks in Vizag and Jaipur in 2005, Dhoni had shown a rare streak of hunger for big runs to go with his belligerent style of batting. Strangely though, those knocks didn't result in Dhoni getting a fixed position in the batting line-up. Such was the craze for flexibility under new coach Greg Chappell that within weeks of finishing as India's highest run-getter against Sri Lanka in the team's 6–1 win, he was batting at number 8 against the visiting Proteas. The decision clearly didn't pay off as South Africa registered wins in both the matches.

The next ODI series India was to fight for was against Pakistan in Pakistan. The first match saw Dhoni earning himself a promotion. Coming in to bat at number 4, he left the crease with 68 against his name when the scorecard read 226 at the end of the thirty-third over. What followed revealed the problem in pushing the swashbuckler up the order. Despite the solid foundation, India couldn't play the full quota of overs and managed only 103 more, losing 7 wickets in the process. The match, too, was given away. The fireworks of Dhoni, the team decided, would serve it better if reserved for later. They were not needed when India levelled the series in Rawalpindi courtesy a collective effort by the top order in the second ODI. The action then moved to Lahore for the third ODI.

Shoaib Malik's big bat had taken a liking for the Indian bowling attack and after having missed out on centuries in Rawalpindi and Peshawar, he finally got one in Lahore as Pakistan piled up 288. In Umar Gul and Mohammad Asif, Pakistan had two bowlers to make the chase a difficult proposition for the Indian batting line-up, especially with the clouds hovering above the ground. And within the first 5 overs of the chase, Asif, who had tormented Indian batsmen in the Test series, showed everyone what he was capable of. In a tall chase, India had been struck early blows and it was left to the senior pros Rahul Dravid and Sachin Tendulkar to pull India out of the ditch. They did the job expected of them but when India lost their fifth wicket at 190, 95 of them coming from the Little Master's bat, the match looked evenly poised as the required run rate inched closer to 7.

Enter MS Dhoni with the walk of a butcher and the calm of a monk on his face. If one were to replace MS Dhoni with Dragon in the previous sentence, it wouldn't make much of a difference for on that overcast afternoon when Asif and Gul were making the ball talk, Dhoni breathed fire in the next 45 minutes. India had already seen some classy batting from Tendulkar while Yuvraj Singh, who had already notched up his 50 when Dhoni arrived on the crease, had treated the crowd to some sublime timing. But the Dhoni blast blew it all to smithereens.

Umar Gul, bowling his final over, was launched over extra cover for 4 in the same way that Vaas had been in that knock of 183. Power and authority. The show had just begun. With Gul's quota finished and Asif left with only 2 overs, Inzamam-ul-Haq turned to the backup consisting of Rana Naved, Abdul Razzaq and Yasir Arafat. Shahid Afridi had all the overs left but based on evidence, throwing a spinner in front of Dhoni wasn't an idea Inzamam seemed to like a lot.

But to Dhoni's Mjolnir, it didn't matter much. Razzaq was deposited over long-off with disdain when he tried to pitch it up. Naved was pulled for a 4 off a short one. Another length delivery was slapped through cover with such ferocity that it left no time for any fielder to move. With another boundary from the next delivery, Dhoni raced to his half-century off 36 deliveries. The aerial fist bump with Yuvraj, the most famous of which we would come to see in Durban on 19 September after the latter's big feat, made its first appearance in Lahore. For a country that had warmed up to the gentle fist bump of Sourav Ganguly and Sachin Tendulkar, this new version reeked of the beginning of a special partnership.

Interestingly, the left-handed Yuvraj, who had been joined by Dhoni when his score was 53, had moved to only 68 in this period. As opposed to the wicketkeeper-batsman's nine boundaries (in fact, he added another one on the next ball) in that time, Yuvraj had sent only one to the fence in this period. Just like the crowd, the southpaw too seemed to be enjoying this gem of a knock although from the best seat in the house.

The show wasn't over yet. By taking 16 from Naved's over, Dhoni had effectively killed the contest, forcing Inzamam to turn to his best bowler, Mohammad Asif, as the last roll of dice. Yuvraj respectfully turned the strike over to Dhoni on the first ball. Asif pitched it slightly short of length, but Dhoni rocked back to send it whizzing through the cover region. Proper cricket against a proper bowler. Two balls later, Asif pitched it slightly up, and once again Dhoni sent it racing through the same part of the ground. Not all fire and brimstone. Sometimes, he also inflicted paper cuts so deep that they could bleed the opposition to death.

The effect could be seen on the Pakistan supporters who had begun to make their way back as the Indian contingent in the crowd roared at the prospect of a certain victory. Dhoni's thirteenth 4 of the innings gave India the match with 14 deliveries to spare. Forty-five minutes before that moment, Pakistan had sensed an opening. That moment now looked like one that had transpired in fourth century AD.

When the time came for the Man of the Match award, the right-hander's match-turning 72 off 46 balls edged out three higher scores on the day, that of Malik, Tendulkar and Yuvraj. This was also the first time that Dhoni had crossed the 50 mark and hadn't hit a single 6. The strike rate still stood at 156.52. On that overcast afternoon in Lahore, Dhoni had set a template for how to finish matches. It was impossible for the management to not zero in on this man for this role in the future. And so began the story of Dhoni the finisher by enthralling the crowds at Lahore.

One man among the thousands present was so impressed by this youngster that during the presentation ceremony he broke protocol to make a request to the smiling Dhoni. He said, 'I saw a placard asking you to have a haircut. But if you were to take my opinion, you look good in this haircut. Don't have a haircut.'

That man was none other than Pakistan President Pervez Musharraf.

Partial scorecard of the match on page 99.

6

In a Different Avatar!

96 (106)—Jamshedpur, 12 April 2006 vs England

Under the stewardship of Rahul Dravid and Greg Chappell, the words 'unpredictability' and 'experimentation' came to be associated with Indian cricket more than usual. Chappell's idea was to keep the opposition guessing with frequent changes in the batting order, which he also thought would make the batsmen more dynamic. Chappell was the same man who had made MS Dhoni bat at number 8 against South Africa in 2005 right after he had blazed his way to glory at number 3 against Sri Lanka in the home series. A few months later, Dhoni was back in the middle order against Pakistan. And when England came visiting in 2006, the Dravid–Chappell duo put the wicketkeeper-batsman right at the top of the order. Opening the batting was a job Dhoni knew inside out, having done it for various teams in the past. However, his stints at the top of the order before this hadn't yielded much. In fact, after his blitz against Pakistan in Visakhapatnam, it was a dream for the Indian fans to watch Sehwag and 'Naya Sehwag' blow the opposition away right at the start of the innings. But it was a dream unrealized for Indian fans.

However, almost a year after his Visakhapatnam knock, Dhoni showed us glimpses of one of the biggest 'what ifs' in Indian cricket in the last few decades. The venue this time was Jamshedpur, and the opposition was England. But the conditions were not much different from Visakhapatnam. What had changed in the twelve months though was Dhoni, the batsman. Not only had the past twelve months catapulted him into the league of most exciting batsmen around the world, but they had also matured him. The basher had not given up his attacking instincts but had developed a style of batting that suited his team better.

And that's how Dhoni took up the challenge of opening the batting in the absence of Rahul Dravid, a challenge that had been made more difficult with the loss of his opening partner Sehwag in the innings. But the instructions from the management were to send the team off to a flier and the Jharkhand batsman was in no mood to spare Matthew Hoggard bowling his first over of the game. A full-pitched delivery with a bit of width was pounced on by the batsman. The next ball also got the same treatment but only brought him a couple of runs thanks to a silly misfield by Liam Plunkett. Seeing how severe the batsman was to pitched-up balls, Hoggard decided to pull the length back only for Dhoni to send it from right between the legs of the square-leg umpire for a boundary. If anyone needed evidence that this youngster had all the shots, they were getting it. The final delivery was walloped to the point boundary to end Hoggard's first over with 14 runs. In the next over, the same bowler was driven straight down the ground and expectations of a special knock by the local boy were beginning to soar in Jamshedpur. Although it was just the fourth boundary of the innings, the right-hander just seemed to be in a ruthless mood that morning. Attack was the only option he knew, it seemed. Or maybe that's what the sight of Hoggard was bringing out of him.

A young James Anderson beat his bat with a fastish one in the sixth over, but the blazing willow of Dhoni had an answer on the very next ball. Just a little room outside the off stump, and in no time, the ball was running past the cover boundary. This was some spectacular hitting by the wicketkeeper, made more special by the struggle of the batsmen at the other end. Before the fifteenth over, Dhoni had seen four of his batting partners get out. Dhoni was still attacking from the other end, lifting a Sajid Mahmood delivery over the covers to add another boundary to his name.

With the fall of India's fifth wicket for the score of 52 with more than 30 overs left in the innings, the responsibility had changed for Dhoni. While he began on an attacking note, the ask had changed with Romesh Powar coming in to bat at the other end. Having won the series easily before this match, India was looking set to embarrass themselves with a mediocre performance. Moreover, the conditions were beginning to get more challenging as the day progressed towards noon.

But Dhoni, knowing well how difficult it would be to run in these conditions, kept going after the English bowlers whenever he sensed a chance. He moved into his 50s with a slap to the cover boundary against the left-arm spin of Ian Blackwell. Plunkett pulled a muscle in trying to stop that ball, showing how difficult it was to survive in the Keenan heat.

Support from the burly off-spinner at the other end gave Dhoni more confidence as the duo helped India claw their way back in the contest. The rebuilding had been going well as the partnership was inching towards 50. The sight of Hoggard once again excited Dhoni and he was treated with equal disdain in the first over of his second spell as he was in the first one. First Dhoni cut him away and then hit one of the flattest 6s over the bowler's head to get the crowds involved in the proceedings again. Even though the team was struggling, Dhoni was piling on the misery single-handedly for the English bowlers.

But the heat had to take a toll at some point; as Dhoni moved into the 70s and the cap replaced the helmet at the top, he was erring on timing more frequently. The amount of power he had poured in to his shots as well as the running between the wickets had clearly exhausted him. But India had only managed 150 and if the team had to reach a respectable total, their best bet was a big Dhoni innings. Out came the helicopter against Vikram Solanki in the thirty-second and the thirty-fourth overs to announce that he wasn't going to allow the heat to dictate terms to him, the second one going over the boundary rope for Dhoni's second maximum of the day.

With running between wickets becoming more and more difficult, it became a matter of when the big shots would be coming from Dhoni's bat. In the thirty-fifth over, as a restless Dhoni now wearing a hat scratched around, Dean Jones in the commentary box could sense that anything pitched up by the part-timer Solanki would get the treatment. And that's exactly how it panned out. Solanki floated one up to Dhoni and had to see it vanish out of the ground once Dhoni stepped out and made contact.

The English team had lost their way in the heat, as it seemed that Dhoni in the company of Powar had brought India back into the match. A full toss on the leg stump by Mahmood that Dhoni put away with ease to bring up the 100-run partnership suggested a break was much needed. The pace of the English bowlers had dropped drastically, and in a rare sight on a cricket field, Dhoni was batting with an ice pack inside his shirt. As odd as it looked, it was quite an intelligent decision for a man who had to keep wickets in the same heat after some time.

But the drinks break meant a halt in the proceedings and a half-hearted shot by the right-hander on Mahmood's bowling proved to be his undoing. Dhoni lost his wicket just 4 short of his century when the scoreboard read 186. Post that, it was India's turn to lose their way in the heat, which they duly did by allowing England to get their first win of the series by 5 wickets after putting up a mere 223 on the board.

India lost their first match of the series that day, but Dhoni's knock gave us a glimpse into the man's mental fortitude. A century would have been a cherry on the top. A longer stint at the top would have been, well, who knows!

Partial scorecard of the match on page 100.

7

Dhoni the Basher, Who?

76* (159)—Lord's, 23 July 2007 vs England

Several months after it began in Chennai, MS Dhoni's Test career reached the home of cricket in England in July 2007. He had taken a long route to reach there having played Tests in India, Pakistan, the West Indies, South Africa and Bangladesh. Not to forget the bitter but life-changing experience of the World Cup in the Caribbean. England, however, was a different ball game for more than one reason for the stumper. The conditions in England were waiting to test Dhoni the wicketkeeper as well as the batsman. Behind the wicket, the challenge was to cope with the ball that moves after passing the bat. In front of the wicket, his home-grown technique looked too agricultural to buy him runs in the seaming conditions. There was also the little matter of Dinesh Karthik who was to travel with the team as a batsman after tasting success in the role of an opener in India's last series against Bangladesh. While the numbers justified Dhoni's inclusion, there was something about Karthik that made him such an irresistible talent that the selectors found it difficult to look away.

Both were drafted into the XI when Rahul Dravid led the team out at the Lord's Cricket Ground for the first Test of the series.

The match didn't begin on the most auspicious note for both as Karthik grassed a sitter off Strauss, while later in the day, Dhoni claimed a catch off Pietersen, which the replays suggested wasn't clean. It didn't cost India much though as Pietersen eventually edged one to Dhoni 10 runs later. After inflicting a collapse on the English batting line-up, the famed Indian batting order with the Fabulous Four in the middle order failed to put up an impression either, getting all out for a paltry 201. Karthik made 5. Dhoni made five less to get out for a blob on his fifth delivery. Worse, the manner in which he got out seemed to confirm those doubts about the efficacy of his technique.

On the morning of the fifth day, his team was in dire straits in pursuit of a tall target when Dhoni walked in with the scoreboard reading 145/5. The batsman who had just departed was Dinesh Karthik who had contributed 60 out of the total score of 145 before falling to the guile of James Anderson. If Dhoni's first innings stay at the crease was anything to go by, England were looking at an early finish to the game, despite the constant threat that the clouds seemed to present to the fate of the match.

Batting alongside Laxman, Dhoni had the job of steadying the ship first. This wasn't a job he was best suited for as the numbers suggested. In his first twenty-eight outings at the Test level, only twice had Dhoni lasted beyond 100 deliveries. And when he began, the attack was on. Vaughan had employed the services of three slips, a gully and a short leg to play with the mind of a man who was on a pair.

But a job was a job. And it had to be done. So, Dhoni put his head down and got to it, taking 14 balls to open his account. There were no major technical adjustments made to counter the pacer trio and the bowlers did look very close to taking a wicket every time they bowled to the Indian wicketkeeper initially. The first boundary off Anderson came off the top edge as Dhoni awkwardly played a half shot close to his body against a rising delivery from Anderson. A shot like that, irrespective of the result, adds more confidence to the opposition side than it does to the batsman. But Dhoni held his own and in the company of the veteran V.V.S. Laxman, he grew in confidence with every passing minute spent on the crease.

As the session progressed, the duo negotiated better, hitting some attractive shots every time pushed too far back and ensuring that they never got into a shell. Laxman, the man with a reputation for rescuing India in tricky second-innings situations, seemed to be doing it yet again for them until Tremlett was thrust into the attack post lunch. The debutant gave exactly what the captain would have wanted of him by removing Laxman with a peach of a delivery. This left India with only Dhoni, and his half-baked technique, with just the tail for company, to try and save the match.

When the match began, the English bowling attack with just thirty-seven Tests between them looked to be the one who'd be under pressure when bowling to the Fabulous Four with the experience of 419 Tests between them. But in a matter of five days, the tables had turned and how! With the backdrop of dark clouds and a glorious Lord's pavilion, the only man standing between England and an Indian defeat was a man who with his long hair looked more like an oddity on the hallowed turf of the 'Home of Cricket'.

With the departure of Laxman, any hopes of an Indian win disappeared. The new job of the wicketkeeper was to bat out the overs with the tail. Senior pro Anil Kumble, who'd later go on to make the only ton of the series for India, found the going tough as the light began to fade and Monty Panesar found his rhythm. Dhoni, at the other end, had played out more than 100 deliveries scoring only 41 from them. His defence didn't always look the most elegant, but it was doing a job which was making England wait longer for the next breakthrough.

The wait came to an end soon, as Kumble was stuck plumb in front of the wicket to Sidebottom, probably the only man with a mane game as head-turning as Dhoni at Lord's that day. As Zaheer Khan emerged from the long room, it became clear that it was only a matter of time before England went 1–0 up in the series. The skies looked threatening, but the India tail didn't seem like it could resist for too long.

Dhoni brought up his half-century with a hastily taken single off Tremlett. The half-century consumed 120 deliveries, making it a painstakingly slow one by his standards. But the team knew what the youngster was up to in the middle, and they stood up in applause in the dressing room. On air, Mark Nicholas described him as an 'exciting and popular' cricketer as he raised his bat to acknowledge the cheer.

The clouds had begun doing their thing and the two umpires began to reach for their light meter more frequently, making Vaughan frown more as the session progressed. Like Kumble, Zaheer soaked the pressure for 21 minutes before edging one to the keeper. R.P. Singh's stay was even shorter as Panesar bowled the tailender before going on one of his trademark ecstatic celebrations. England sniffed a win.

With the light fading quickly, Vaughan was forced to bring himself on to bowl his off-spinners in an attempt to prise out a wicket. Dhoni, now with a cap on, decided to attack the captain while shielding the number 11 Sreesanth, who had danced on the pitch after hitting Andre Nel for a 6 only a few months ago. No such shenanigans this time for the Kerala paceman though. When Dhoni failed to get a single off the last ball of Vaughan's final delivery, the mercurial bowler had the task of negotiating 6 deliveries from Panesar unless he could eke out a single. Sreesanth did negotiate well with some help from umpire Steve Bucknor who turned down a vociferous appeal against the number 11. To make up for his mistake from the previous over, Dhoni pinched a single off the final delivery of Vaughan's next over to ensure he retained the strike.

At this point though, the umpires converged to discuss the light as a roar went around the stadium. The Indian squad looked on anxiously at the two umpires from the famed balcony of Lord's.

Eventually, Taufel and Bucknor offered light to the two batsmen in the middle and in no time Dhoni and Sreesanth marched off. The English fans waited for close to three hours for their team to get at least one over to topple that lone wicket remaining in the Indian innings. That, however, didn't happen.

The last man one would have expected to save India the blushes on the final day of a Test at Lord's had done it, facing 159 deliveries and occupying the crease for more than 200 minutes. No Indian batsman had faced as many deliveries in the match as their wicketkeeper. Dhoni had once again proved his detractors wrong.

Eight months ago, in Durban against South Africa, Dhoni had arrived on the pitch in a similar situation. He attacked as wickets around him fell. But just on the verge of tea, an attempt at an expansive drive cost Dhoni his wicket and India the match. He had emerged as the highest run scorer for India in the innings and the match but that was little consolation for him. After the match-saving knock at Lord's, Dhoni revealed that loss in Durban still rankled him. 'Playing this kind of a game is very different for me. I tried that in the second Test in South Africa but couldn't save the match. I'm glad that we saved the match. It's as important as winning a match', said the 26-year-old about his efforts.

Several years later after scoring a double 100 against Australia, when asked to talk about his favourite innings, Dhoni pointed to his knock at Lord's as special because it helped the team to win the series 1–0.

Special indeed!

Partial scorecard of the match on page 101.

8

The Captain-Batsman Takes Centre Stage

124 (106)—Nagpur, 28 October 2009 vs Australia

A juicy full toss on the leg stump. A half-volley under the bat. A half-tracker at a pace that invites dispatching. These are some of the answers one can get when batsmen are asked what they would like to receive as the ideal first delivery in an innings. The list will surely have more answers but none of them is likely to be a hit on the helmet by a delivery bowled at 135 kmph.

On 28 October 2009, that's exactly the kind of first ball that MS Dhoni faced. The bowler was Ben Hilfenhaus, who had his tail up after dismissing Yuvraj Singh and the score was 98 for the loss of 3 wickets in the second ODI of the 2009 home series against Australia. India had lost the first ODI of the series, a fact that must have been playing on the captain's mind when he went out to bat in the sixteenth over because despite getting hit on the back of the head on the first ball, he kept his composure and stole a run through a leg bye.

And then he smiled as he assessed the damage caused to his helmet. Not many would have seen what followed. The captain was still on 0 from the solitary ball he had faced.

But it soon began. In operation were Nathan Hauritz and Adam Voges, both unable to extract either turn or enough bounce to trouble two of India's better batsmen of spin. Both Dhoni and Gambhir picked regular boundaries on either side of the wicket and steadied the ship. Both were particularly harsh on the off-spinner Hauritz, and one of the straight drives hit by the captain off his bowling was so straight that it almost kissed the stumps at the other end before crossing the boundary rope a few seconds later.

After Gambhir reached his second half-century of the series, it was time for his captain to take over. However, before he took over, Dhoni had to tumble.

In the twenty-seventh over, facing Mitchell Johnson, Dhoni went on the back foot and set off for a quick single, presenting Ricky Ponting with a chance to take a shy at the stumps at the non-striker's end. A rampaging Dhoni, however, found the bowler in his way as he made a final dash to reach the crease. Ponting missed the stumps. The Indian skipper tumbled in an ungainly fashion.

He got up. He stared at the bowler but didn't offer any words. The crowds at Nagpur didn't like the sight of their captain down and quickly got behind him, chanting 'Dhoni, Dhoni' in unison. The Indian captain was on 36 off 42 balls at that point. This was a very typical Dhoni-the-captain knock at this point, where the end goal determined his approach to the innings. Dhoni the batsman, who crowds would throng the stadiums to watch but had disappeared behind the captaincy role, emerged soon after the incident of the twenty-seventh over.

Shane Watson replaced Johnson in the next over and the right-hander managed to find a small gap between extra cover and mid-off with an unconventional-looking cover drive. The result was 4 runs which placed India close to 190 at the 30-over mark. The conventional wisdom with regards to ODI cricket says that a team should try to double the score that they have managed in the first 30 overs if wickets have been preserved. With 7 wickets in hand, India needed to do that.

Soon after the 200-run mark was breached, the captain brought up his half-century as well. The innings had been stabilized by the partnership which had now gone beyond 100. Gambhir, who had dominated the partnership, looked set for a century when overenthusiasm got the better of him and he ran from the non-striker's end in search of a quick single without realizing the ball had not crossed the mid-on fielder. The partnership was over.

With one set batsman gone, it was up to the other set batsman to steer the innings towards a big score. The captain took the responsibility. The assault began in the thirty-fourth over with a back foot punch against Hauritz that raced to the cover boundary. Just when it seemed that the Australian bowlers were getting on top of the Indian batsmen by stitching together a few tight overs, he flexed his muscles again in the fortieth over and blasted a length ball outside off by Peter Siddle to announce his plan of action for the final 10 overs.

Mitchell Johnson was welcomed back into the attack with back-to-back boundaries that came right off the middle of the bat. Whether Dhoni was still miffed at the bowler or not was unclear but the ferocity with which the two shots were hit would force anyone to think that the batsman had still not forgotten what had panned out some 15 overs ago. Ben Hilfenhaus was next in line and got hit for a 6 that barely found any elevation but did definitely get the legs to travel over the long-on boundary. Dhoni now had the highest score by an Indian captain against Australia but there was more to come as Shane Watson realized soon. Dhoni hit him over his head for another maximum to bring up his fifth century in just 94 deliveries. There was no expression to suggest that the 100 was brought up by the captain, except for a raise of the bat towards the dressing room.

While the broadcasters were still showing the distance covered by the previous 6, Dhoni hit another one on the next delivery.

Although the evening was bringing the temperature down in Nagpur, Dhoni was taking it up with every assault of his. In the next over of the all-rounder, after India had overhauled its highest total against Australia, the captain hit a full toss in the direction of the bowler so hard that he had to take evasive action despite it hitting the ground on its way to the bowler and then to the boundary.

By the time he fell to a flying catch by Tim Paine for 124, Dhoni had done the damage by taking India to a score in excess of 350, which had seemed a far cry when he had arrived at the crease with the score at 97/3 and got hit on the head on his first ball. The crowds at the Jamtha were treated to something special that afternoon. They had seen Dhoni the basher wearing the captain's cape after a long, long time.

At the end of the match, which India won comfortably by 99 runs, Dhoni articulated his approach towards batting post captaincy. He said, 'Earlier when you went for a big shot, you backed yourself and went for it. It's not the same as I was three or four years ago, less responsibility and more flair. But now I have more responsibility every time I turn up on the field. A lot depends on what kind of pressure you are handling.'

Partial scorecard of the match on page 102.

9

Dial D for a Clinical Chase

101* (107)—Mirpur, 7 January 2010 vs Bangladesh (Tri-Series)

Despite a home series win over Sri Lanka, for India, the year 2009 in white-ball cricket ended as badly as well it had begun. After series wins in New Zealand, the West Indies and Sri Lanka, India's frailties were left exposed when the team failed to qualify for the knockout stages of the Champions Trophy held in South Africa. The visiting Australian side also flexed their muscles to beat India 4–2 right after the Champions Trophy humiliation. There was also the failed campaign to defend the T20 crown in June. This was far from ideal for a team that was hosting the World Cup in about fifteen months. India's streak of six series wins before the Champions Trophy was forgotten and questions were now raised about the missing 'Midas Touch' of MS Dhoni.

The knives only came closer when India began 2010 with a 5-wicket loss against Sri Lanka in a tri-series that also featured Bangladesh. Dhoni's 70-ball 37, which stalled India's progress in the innings, gave his doubters more fodder.

And that's why when two days later the man walked out at 51/3 in a chase of 298 for victory, it was so much more than just another contest against Bangladesh in Mirpur. With about a year left for the World Cup campaign, there were several things to resurrect for MS Dhoni on that evening apart from India's innings which was down in the dumps.

India had lost Sehwag first, who fell short of his ground after running off a misfield from Razzak off his own bowling. Then Gambhir played onto a Rubel Hossain away swinger and was bowled. Yuvraj followed Gambhir almost immediately into the pavilion as he too saw his stumps shatter after playing inside the line to a Syed Rasel off-cutter.

Granted that India were a markedly different team from the one that lost to Bangladesh in the 2007 World Cup. Yet, an area where India had stumbled in the recent past was in chasing formidable targets. In the past year, India had faltered in chases, most notably in chasing the target of 303 that Pakistan had set in the Champions Trophy.

Fans of the Indian team, therefore, were understandably nervous when Dhoni walked in. Facing a steaming Rubel Hossain, the crafty seamer Syed Rasel and the left-arm spin of Abdul Razzak and Shakib Al Hasan, India was staring at a familiar nemesis. The home team was on top and the crowds at Mirpur were letting that be known to the two Indian batsmen in the middle. They could sense an encore of the 2007 World Cup result where India's defeat to Bangladesh proved more than just costly for the team.

The man who Dhoni joined though, was riding a wave of confidence. The young Virat Kohli, who had made his way to the team a couple of years ago on the back of leading India to a win in the U-19 World Cup, had only recently been part of a 300-plus chase against Sri Lanka in Kolkata (a match that Dhoni was suspended for due to a slow over rate). Not only did he successfully guide India to the finish line but also notched what would be the first of many international centuries.

An advantage that Dhoni and Kohli had when they met at 51/3 was that the Indian run rate matched the required rate, thereby allowing Dhoni and Kohli to get settled. Dhoni got off to a sedate start, scoring 4 off 14. Most of the deliveries that Dhoni faced in this period came off Syed Rasel's bowling. While Rasel did not have the pace to trouble batters, he was extremely consistent with his lines and lengths. His natural left-arm angle just outside off stump and good length did not give many run-scoring opportunities for Dhoni.

Rubel Hossain, on the other hand, presented a different challenge and opportunity. Unlike Rasel, Hossain regularly touched the 130 kmph mark and was keen to test the pitch. While this would present more run-scoring chances for Dhoni, it would also mean that Dhoni would have to be on his toes and couldn't just defend him with the same ease.

Hossain started with a bang when he hit Dhoni's thigh pad on an attempted pull shot. He then induced a thick edge which sped away to the third man boundary. Hossain followed this up with a back of a length in-dipper that kept low and beat Dhoni's cut shot. At this stage, the score was 76/3 after 14 overs. Dhoni had proceeded to 11 from 20 balls but Hossain looked good for another breakthrough.

It was at this critical juncture that captain Shakib Al Hasan made the decision to remove Hossain, who had only bowled 4 overs and was bustling with gusto. Shakib decided to deploy only spin between the fifteenth and twenty-sixth overs. India managed to stay within the touching distance of the run rate as they reached 138/3. The key to India's ticking score was Dhoni, the removal of his helmet signalling the end of his ordeal against the pacers. He looked free without the helmet and he played with a sense of freedom too. From 11 off 20 balls, he had gone to 36 from 47 at the beginning of the twenty-seventh over. He scored only one boundary in this duration, a boundary deposited beyond deep long-off from Mahmudullah's flat, almost yorker length off break.

Another shot that had Dhoni's cleverness written all over it was a late cut for 3 off Naeem Islam.

By the time Hossain was brought back onto the attack in the twenty-seventh over, Dhoni was settled. He greeted the pacer on his return with a half pull/half hook shot towards the deep midwicket boundary for 4. In his next over, Dhoni unleashed his trademark cover drive as he picked Rubel's length ball in a jiffy and sent the ball to the extra cover boundary. By the end of the twenty-ninth over, India was at 158/3. Dhoni had accelerated to 50 from 59 balls while Kohli was on 64 from 82 balls.

But Bangladesh had runs on the board and knew that one breakthrough at this stage could change the momentum of the game. This crucial stage arrived in the thirty-third over. India had moved to 185/3 when Dhoni hit the ball back to Shakib Al Hasan. But Al Hasan failed to hold onto this precious chance.

Shakib would soon atone for this mistake in his next over. He created a similar caught-and-bowled opportunity, and this time held onto the chance offered by Kohli who was dismissed 9 short of a century. India was at 203/4 after 35 overs. India not only had a tricky required run rate to maintain, but they also needed to ensure that they would suffer no further damage. After Suresh Raina, India had a relatively inexperienced Ravindra Jadeja followed by a longish tail of Harbhajan Singh, Zaheer Khan, Ashish Nehra and S. Sreesanth.

Dhoni relaxed the frayed nerves of the Indian fans with his aggressive batting post Kohli's departure. With the required run rate still hovering above 6, he knew that there would be pressure on the new batter and therefore it was important for him to fire. And fire he did. He cut the first ball after Kohli's dismissal off Abdul Razzak for 4. He then followed this with a dominant pull shot in the direction of deep midwicket for another boundary. Thanks to Dhoni changing gears, India was suddenly at 225/4 by the end of the thirty-eighth over and in control.

The Indian captain recommenced his attacking display as the required run rate dropped below 6. The returning Syed Rasel was greeted by a majestic cover drive through extra cover while Abdul Razzak was met with a late cut off the front foot for another delightful boundary. India was now at 261/4 in 43 overs with victory in sight. Any further doubts of an Indian victory were assuaged following a flurry of boundaries from Raina. The only question that remained was whether Dhoni would make it to his seventh ODI century. Dhoni answered this too in the affirmative as he brought up a century with a flick down fine leg off a Rasel full toss.

With Dhoni as the anchor, ably supported by Kohli and Raina, India reached their target of 297 with 15 balls and 6 wickets in hand. Dhoni was awarded the Man of the Match for his efforts. Dhoni's innings not only helped India avoid an upset, but also proved to be a masterclass on how to pace a run chase, something the fans would see happen in fourteen months' time again on a bigger stage.

Partial scorecard of the match on page 103.

10

Ice Catches Fire in Dharamshala

54* (29)—Dharamshala, 18 April 2010 vs Kings XI Punjab

When Team India boarded the flight to South Africa for the inaugural World T20, there was little expectation from the young team and its captain. As the seniors of the team decided to give the tournament a miss, the selectors took a punt on a young team. That was also the last time MS Dhoni the skipper had to deal with fewer expectations. Twenty days and a glittering trophy later, everything changed for the man from Ranchi. If Dhoni was at the helm, the cup was the only option.

No trophies, however, came his team's way in the subsequent two years. Despite having arguably the most compact side in the IPL, Chennai Super Kings (CSK) had faltered at the knockout stage in the first two editions. The team was faring worse in the third edition and at the end of the fifth over of the chase in the do-or-die match against Kings XI Punjab, it seemed that, for once, the IPL knockouts wouldn't feature a team wearing yellow. The loss of openers Matthew Hayden and Murali Vijay was far from ideal for a start for a team that was chasing 193 in a match they had to win if they were to sneak into the top four. The ever-reliable Suresh Raina stepped up and provided some momentum to the innings with Subramaniam Badrinath before his dismissal left his team with 104 to score from 62 deliveries.

Apart from the sight of the Dhauladhar in the background, there wasn't much that was pleasant for the next batsman walking in. In fact, the MS Dhoni that walked in at Raina's dismissal wasn't only under pressure as a captain but also as a batsman. Apart from a match-winning 66 against the Kolkata Knight Riders (KKR), the remaining scores against his name throughout the tournament didn't present for great reading. Moreover, for some, big hitters like Justin Kemp and Albie Morkel in the dugout would have been better choices to replace Raina at the crease considering the required run rate still stood over 10.

But there's a world of calculations in the head of MS Dhoni that would have probably stumped even Alan Turing and his mates had they come across it. He got down to the task from ball one as he got off to the mark with a 4, courtesy a fumble at the boundary by his good friend Yuvraj Singh. The Punjab bowlers, who had been pasted throughout the tournament, seemed to have found their mojo. While the occasional boundary did come in the next 5 overs, the two batsmen found themselves mostly stifled which allowed the required run rate to climb beyond 12 as the final 5 overs of the match began.

Badrinath, whose availability was in doubt on the morning of the game, reached his half-century with a boundary off Piyush Chawla. His strike rate of 151 made his captain's knock of 22 from 18 deliveries look terribly inadequate. But a ball after reaching the milestone, Badrinath's innings came to an end.

The captain remained there, now joined by the left-handed Albie Morkel. Not too long ago the South African all-rounder had proved his credentials as a finisher when playing against Australia in their own den. He produced two jailbreak knocks in the series to give his team wins that not many saw coming à la

Lance Klusener. In Dharamshala too, Morkel opened fire, scoring two boundaries from the first 7 deliveries he faced. That was as many boundaries as Dhoni had managed during his 8-over stay at the crease. Worse, when V.R.V. Singh bowled a no-ball in the eighteenth over, Dhoni failed to capitalize on the free hit. The final delivery of the same over was sent over the long-on boundary by Morkel, making many wonder whether the decision to hold back the all-rounder was the correct one.

29 off 12. They say in the shortest format, you turn to your best bowler in the nineteenth over to ensure the chase becomes unachievable by the time it reaches the twentieth over. Skipper Kumar Sangakkara sought out the services of Rusty Theron, who, just a few weeks earlier, had bowled a super over against the same opposition hours after landing in India and conceded only 9 runs. Seemed like the perfect choice with 29 runs left to defend.

Theron pitched the first one halfway down the track only to see it get dismissed by a powerful pull from Dhoni. A short ball outside off wasn't such a bad strategy for Dhoni, especially with a packed field on the offside. But the bowler clearly underestimated the CSK captain's power. He met the ball where the seventh stump would have stood and sent it racing towards the midwicket boundary. The fielder at midwicket made a dive, but it had whizzed past him before he knew it.

The engines of that calculating brain had started to whirr. 25 from 11 made for better reading than 29 from 12. It only got better when Theron compensated with his length on the next delivery. Pitching it up in Dhoni's arc in the death overs is inviting trouble but it was the impact of what had been done to the previous delivery. Dhoni did the needful by smashing it down the ground for another boundary. The man who had been hailed as Punjab's new Iceman was coming off as the second best in this battle of Icemen. The equation now read 21 from 10. To his credit though, the Potchefstroom-born pulled things back to leave Chennai with 16 to get from the final 6.

16 to get to squeeze into the top four and keep the hopes of a trophy alive. 16 to get to prove the calculations still worked. 16 to get to stave off forgettable form for the captain.

Irfan Pathan, devoid of the pace to trouble Dhoni, relied on his guile when it came to the final over. The first delivery, in fact, was just what any captain would want from his bowler bowling the twentieth over—a wide yorker. On that day though, it wasn't good enough. Dhoni reached out and made contact, that too with the middle of the bat. 4 off 16 gone. More guile from Irfan up next. A short ball on the middle stump line and the right-hander mistimed it. Still no luck for Punjab as it landed just short of the fielder, allowing the Indian–South African duo to scamper back for the second.

And then Pathan erred. As Dhoni swung his bat up and down in anticipation, the left-hander landed one right in the spot for him to send it out of the ground. Next delivery. Same length. Different line. Even easier for Dhoni to send it into the orbit. Game over. As everyone looked at the ball flying out of the ground, Dhoni let the veneer of calm come down for a few seconds. He shouted a few words to himself. He gave his right cheek a Tysonesque punch. More importantly, though, he had prevailed. And so had Chennai Super Kings in IPL 2010. In a season which saw four teams finish with 14 points at the end of the league stage, Dhoni's effort that night ensured that the men in yellow remained at the top of that pack and played in the knockouts.

A few days later, Dhoni lifted the trophy for CSK for the first of many times.

Partial scorecard of the match on page 104.

11

The Biggest Night

91* (79)—Mumbai, 2 April 2011 vs Sri Lanka

On the eve of the 2011 World Cup final, a wicketkeeper-batsman who was also leading his team in the tournament had scored 427 runs from 7 innings. He had notched up a ton as well as three half-centuries in the quadrennial event and was in the running for the Man of the Tournament award. They say leading by example is the best way to lead a side and to be doing that in a World Cup at home made what Kumar Sangakkara had managed incredibly special.

Oh, yes. Those were Kumar Sangakkara's numbers on the eve of the final. The other wicketkeeper-batsman leading his side into the final had anything but flattering numbers to show on his report card as a batsman. 151 runs from an equal number of innings played by Sangakkara told a sad story of MS Dhoni, the batsman ahead of the most important day in his life as a captain. This was, after all, a Cricket World Cup final being held in Mumbai. Can it get any bigger for an Indian captain? Surely not.

And that's why concerns regarding the form of the Indian captain were legitimate. Not that it bothered the man much.

When questioned about it ahead of the semi-final against Pakistan, Dhoni gave the logic behind the dismal numbers. 'I have been batting quite well but some of the situations have not really been good for playing flamboyant cricket.' He added, 'When you are batting at five, six or seven, if the top order scores well, it does not give much opportunities to the lower order.' There was some rationale to that statement as India's top order as well as middle order were firing on all cylinders throughout the tournament and had orchestrated the team's rise to the final in the campaign. It would have all seemed like a good excuse had it not been for that evening of 2 April.

Chasing 275 in the final, India had lost Virender Sehwag on the second ball of the chase and saw Sachin Tendulkar leave early too after a few attractive shots. Gautam Gambhir along with Virat Kohli resurrected the innings and took India past the 100-run mark when India suffered another blow. Tilakaratne Dilshan's gentle off-spinner and a not so gentlemanly send-off to Virat Kohli after dismissing him for 34 gave India another bump in the road.

MS Dhoni came out, much to the surprise of everyone watching the proceedings. The man who had been held back as a result of this ploy was Yuvraj Singh, whose confidence was sky-high on account of having a stellar tournament with the bat and the ball. But like most of the times in his career, Dhoni knew what he was doing. He was taking the bull by its horns.

In the first six years of his career, Muttiah Muralitharan had claimed MS Dhoni's wicket six times. Most famously, he had caught him plumb in front with a doosra on a sunny afternoon in the Caribbean when much of India was looking up to the long-haired youngster to bail them out and help his team survive one more day in the World Cup. Dhoni flunked the test, getting out for a golden duck and killing India's hopes in the do-or-die encounter of the 2007 World Cup.

But such was his confidence on that evening of 2 April that the moment he decided to walk out to bat instead of Yuvraj Singh,

Paddy Upton, the team's mental-conditioning coach, knew that the contest was going India's way.

In an interview to Firstpost in 2014, Upton said, 'When Dhoni tapped on the glass window and indicated to Gary (Kirsten) that he was batting ahead of Yuvraj and then when he walked down the stairs at Wankhede, I turned to Gary and said that MS is going to win us the World Cup. These were my exact words.'

As Dhoni completed his routine—resting the willow between his legs, raising both his elbows, the thumb of the left hand flicking the eye from inside the helmet followed by him loosening and then tightening the gloves, then picking up the bat and punching the handle while assessing the field, and going on to hit the top of it on his right thigh followed by another flick of the thumb on his eye as the bowler got ready to deliver—Nasser Hussain in the commentary box said, 'This is a big test for MS Dhoni. All eyes on him. Everything that he's touched has turned into gold. Number 1 in the world in Tests and ODIs, IPL, Chennai Super Kings won it. Champions League, they won it. World T20 they won under Dhoni. Can they win the World Cup under Dhoni?'

But what made Dhoni do what he did? Maybe it was a long con or maybe it was just things falling into place, but back in 2008 when Dhoni led CSK in the IPL, his team also recruited his long-time on-field nemesis Muttiah Muralitharan. Three seasons of the league saw Dhoni face Murali in the nets and by the time fate brought them on the World Cup final stage in different jerseys, the Indian captain was well equipped to take on the guile of Muralitharan.

First, he assessed the situation and allowed Gambhir to take on the bowling attack while taking his own sweet time to settle. He faced 24 deliveries before finding the ropes for the first time but the style in which he did find the ropes on the twenty-fifth ball spoke volumes of a man in command. The required run rate had just crept past 6 as the chase crossed the thirtieth over mark and Murali's economy rate was hovering around half of that. Once again, he had come around the stumps to Dhoni, the way in which he had dismissed him in the 2007 World Cup fixture. This time though, the right-hander slapped him past cover emphatically. The difference that shot made to the team's morale was more than the 4 runs it contributed to the scorecard. Dhoni had hit bigger 6s but this shot was so emphatic that it seemed to create a dent in the opposition's confidence. Having been at the receiving end of some big Dhoni knocks, the last thing the Sri Lankans would have wanted was for the Indian captain to find his feet.

Next over though, the fear seemed to be coming true as he sent a Thisara Perera bouncer over point for his second boundary. The required run rate was still over 6 but the partnership was growing between the left-handed Gautam Gambhir and the captain. More than 100 runs were required in the chase but with Yuvraj waiting in the wings, the islanders began to look uncomfortable at the sight of this duo getting comfortable at the crease. So comfortable that Gambhir came down the track to smash Kulasekara to the midwicket boundary despite the keeper being brought up to curb his tendency to advance down the track. This could easily have been the shot of the night had it not been for the almost perfect straight drive that Tendulkar played during his short stay and the one with which the match was going to end.

The confidence of Gambhir was rubbing off on his partner as well as he too slapped a Suraj Randiv delivery for 4 through the offside to bring the required run rate under 6 after a long time. As victory appeared closer on the horizon, Wankhede began buzzing with a different energy, A.R. Rahman's Vande Mataram being played by the stadium DJ adding to the atmosphere. The crowds chanting it also had an impact on the men in the middle. The skipper, known for his ability to walk out of fire unfazed, would later remember that as a moment which gave him goosebumps.

For skipper Sangakkara, the desperation was rising and that meant pressing his two trump cards—Malinga and Murali—back into action as the last roll of the dice. The duo played Malinga with dexterity but at the end of Malinga's over Dhoni appeared to be in pain to give his billion countrymen a bit of a frown. But few moments later, he was back to going on the back foot to Murali and hitting it through the offside for 4, this time to get to his half-century. The frown had disappeared.

Though not off of the face of the Sri Lankans, particularly Muralitharan. Having tasted a lot of success bowling round the wicket to Dhoni, the off-spinner playing his final ODI stuck to the angle, perhaps in the hope of bamboozling the right-hander with his clever mixing of doosras with the off-spinners. Unfortunately for the master cricketer, it wasn't a battle he was destined to win that night. He finally did switch to bowling over the wicket after Dhoni clobbered him for another powerful drive through the offside to bring the deficit to less than 60. With only 15 deliveries left in his spell, it was a case of too little too late.

Nerves left frayed after Gambhir's dismissal for 97 were soothed by the sight of Yuvraj and Dhoni, easily the most reliable middle-order duo in the past half decade, coming together to finish the job. And finish they did in one of the most spectacular ways a World Cup final could have been finished. Irrespective of whatever Nuwan Kulasekara goes on to do with his life, the average Indian fan who was glued to the television screen on 2 April 2011 would always remember him as the man who sent down the delivery that MS Dhoni sent into the Mumbai sky leading Ravi Shastri to utter, 'Dhoni finishes off in style. A magnificent strike into the crowd. India lift the World Cup after twenty-eight years. The party starts in the dressing room, and it is an Indian captain who has been absolutely magnificent on the night of the finals.'

Magnificent Mahi was relieved. As his eyes followed the trajectory of the white ball, he must have thought of the innumerable countrymen who in the past two months kept goading him to win the World Cup wherever they encountered him. He had finally won it with a captain's knock to send them into frenzy before calmly going back to collect the stump as a memory of an unforgettable evening in the lives of a billion Indians.

Oh yeah! In the end, there was only one wicketkeeper-captain the world was talking about. And that was not Kumar Sangakkara!

Partial scorecard of the match on page 105.

12

The Formula Works, Again!

44* (58)—Adelaide, 12 February 2012 vs Australia

There is something about the Adelaide Oval. Not only do its immediate surroundings make it one of the most picturesque stadiums of the world, but its shape also elicits curiosity. Among all the cricket grounds that have 'Oval' in their name, there is no cricket ground as true to its name as the one in Adelaide. It's as oval in its shape as it can be. And the peculiarity in its shape means that hitting 6s square of the wicket is far easier for batsmen than to hit big ones straight down the ground.

When India took on Australia in the fourth match of the Commonwealth Bank tri-series, the dimensions of the Adelaide Oval were the last thing on their mind. After having lost the Border–Gavaskar Trophy comprehensively, they had made an unsuccessful start to the ODI series too. MS Dhoni, the man who had led India to a win in the format's World Cup less than a year ago, was flayed for his captaincy and batting, most severely by the Australian media. *The Australian* wrote of Dhoni in a piece titled 'India's Pillar of Strength Reduced to Useless Rubble'.

'Worst of all, Dhoni has failed with the bat. The Indian captain is no thunderer at the best of times—neither is coach Duncan Fletcher, which may be part of the problem—but how can he demand more of his batsmen when he has nowhere to hide behind scores of 6, 23, 57, 2, 12 and 2?'

When Dhoni arrived at the crease with India needing 92 in a chase of 270 from more than 15 overs, it seemed like a match made for him to finish. India still had 6 wickets in hand and on the other end was Suresh Raina. But it's never that easy when the opposition is Michael Clarke-led Australia. Pup, as they called him, sensed that with two new batsmen at the crease, India would find the going slightly tougher after the departure of a well-set Gambhir.

He opted for the third powerplay immediately and ensured that there were no easy singles for the duo. Dhoni the ODI batsman, however, was quite the master at manipulating fields. Four years ago, at the same ground when India was 4 down for 70 in a chase of 203, Ricky Ponting had challenged MS Dhoni with a peculiar field. There were eight men on the offside and only three on the leg side. Mitchell Johnson speared the ball way outside off stump as was expected with that field. Dhoni, however, was up to the task and stepped out and made contact with the ball where the eighth stump would be. He nudged it towards square leg and forced wicketkeeper Adam Gilchrist to chase it down as he completed 3 runs with Yuvraj Singh as Ricky Ponting looked absolutely flummoxed. Four years later at the Adelaide Oval, in the thirty-seventh over of the match, Dhoni did an encore off the bowling of Dan Christian. With the mid-on at the boundary, Dhoni nudged one to the edge of the circle and by the time both the mid-off fielder and the long-on fielder could converge on the ball, the Indian captain had galloped for a couple of runs with Raina.

But Clarke and his men tightened the screws. Dhoni's score stood at 8 from 25 deliveries at one stage despite his teammate going at more than a run a ball. For a while, it seemed that Dhoni was doing exactly the opposite of the job that was expected of him. While Raina went for the big shots to ensure the deficit didn't go out of control, Dhoni struggled to find the gaps. The required run rate inched closer to 8 now with less than 8 overs to go.

Unable to find the boundary rope, Dhoni fell back on his second greatest strength—quick running between the wickets. In the company of Raina, another Indian batsman famed for his running, he regularly stole doubles to keep his team in the hunt. Even Ponting's direct hit at the beginning of the forty-fifth over turned into a mistake that allowed Dhoni his sixth double of the inning. Then came the twist, however, as Raina stepped out to take on Xavier Doherty's left-arm spin in the next over, only to see the ball squeezed under his bat before disturbing the stumps. The equation read 31 required from 23 balls with 5 wickets in hand. Manageable.

Another left-hander, Ravindra Jadeja, joined Dhoni in the middle but the pressure of the chase seemed to be mounting on the Indians. Dhoni's scratchy stay in the middle seemed to be hurting India's cause after Raina's loss as he just couldn't seem to find the boundary. To make matters worse, Doherty managed to summon up his all to deliver possibly the best over of his career when India could take only 4 off his forty-ninth over. The 4 runs had come from the first 3 deliveries but when Jadeja went for a big hit and could only find the fielder at deep midwicket, Dhoni changed ends and much to everyone's surprise, played two dot balls. Not only did that mean that India would need 13 from the final over, but it also meant that taking the strike against Clint McKay would be new to the crease batsman Ravichandran Ashwin.

The Victoria-born bowler had a terrific match till this point. In his 9 overs, he had picked 3 wickets—Sehwag, Kohli and Gambhir. Captain Clarke trusted him over a young Mitchell Starc and his job seemed easier when he ran in to bowl the first ball with Ashwin at the crease. All that he needed was to put together a couple of good balls to starve the Indian captain off the strike. He didn't even have to bowl a good delivery first up to keep Dhoni off-strike as Ashwin tried a Mibah-esque scoop but failed to connect. He did better on the next delivery, giving the ball a trademark tailender thump towards the leg side. A second run was on the cards, but Dhoni knew that Ashwin had done his part of the job. It was now up to him. He needed to do something in this over that he had failed to do in his 15-over-long stay at the crease—find boundaries.

The right-arm medium-fast bowler, who had a golden chance at winning the Man of the Match at this point, ended up landing the ball on what is called the 'slot' in cricket. Dhoni pulled the trigger and the ball travelled more than 100 metres in the air before finding itself deep in what's called the hill at the Adelaide Oval. Earlier in the day, both Rohit Sharma and Virat Kohli had gotten out trying to cross the longest boundary on the ground. Dhoni had fetched a 6 and brought the equation down to a manageable 6 runs from 3 balls.

The match had now been reduced to the experience of the two men in the middle. Dhoni's 199 ODIs versus 18 ODIs of Clint McKay. The bowler's inexperience came to the fore on the next delivery as he nervously slipped one too high at Dhoni. The ball was deemed a beamer and although David Warner caught it at deep square leg, the two batsmen in the middle had crossed for a double. 3 runs required off 3 balls. Dhoni pulled again and this time Warner's attempt to cut the boundary resulted in him giving Dhoni enough time to come back for a third run.

As if knocking 13 off the final over to win India a match was something he had been doing every day, Dhoni quietly picked up a stump at the non-striker's end and acknowledged a jubilant crowd who had once again been left Mahi-smerized!

Partial scorecard of the match on page 106.

13

Magician Mahi's Rescue Act

113* (125)—Chennai, 2012 vs Pakistan

Seven years is a long time in the life of an Indian cricketer and longer if that period has been punctuated by the player's ascension to the role of a captain. When MS Dhoni walked out to bat against Pakistan in his fifth ODI at Visakhapatnam, his hair was long and brown and his shoulders broad and free. The 148 that followed in the subsequent hours, many say, was always on the cards once he walked in that way. Almost eight years later in Chennai, on a chilly December morning, when the fall of a Mumbaikar brought Dhoni to the crease early in the innings, it was a very different sight. While the walk was defiant, there was a tension in the air which on that day could also be seen on the man's face. Tension and responsibility were spelled out by the streaks of white visible in Dhoni's hair peeping through the helmet. It's unclear how many of them went white in the 9 overs he sat in the dressing room watching Indian batsmen capitulate against the Pakistani opening bowlers but what's certain is that the man who walked in to bat seemed nothing like the one who had walked out in Visakhapatnam more than seven years ago.

But it was Mahendra Singh Dhoni then and it was Mahendra Singh Dhoni this time too. In the mood for a masterclass, albeit of a different kind.

In at 29/5 on a tricky Chennai pitch with more than 40 overs to go and only 25 runs away from India's lowest score in the format, the captain had his task cut out. The familiar sight of Suresh Raina amidst the ruins must have brought some relief. Too often the duo had joined forces to bail their IPL franchise out of hellholes on the same ground. But what was staring at them on that day was a challenge of a different nature. The challenge was to bat close to 40 overs—double the length of a T20 innings.

While the majority of the damage had been done by Junaid Khan and the 7-foot Mohammad Irfan, the bowlers backing them up were no less a threat. Umar Gul and the spin duo of Saeed Ajmal and Mohammad Hafeez kept the pressure on the Indian duo even at the end of the opening pacers' first spell. Such was the dominance of the spin duo on that day that it took 14 overs for batsmen of Dhoni and Raina's calibre to eke out a boundary. The Chennai crowds, who had been put on mute by the destruction caused by opening bowlers, had been put to sleep by the ensuing proceedings.

The captain, however, had a job to do and that was to resurrect the innings. It's not every day that half the team is sent back to the pavilion with 40 overs still left in the innings. Surviving the entire length of the innings in the company of lower-order batsmen was a challenge, especially on a pitch that had seen some rain the previous day and against bowlers who seemed possessed in the first spell. But with his Zen-like calm, Dhoni stuck to the task. Suresh Raina took the occasional risks while Dhoni did the ugly job—of playing the waiting game.

Thanks to the grit on display, India crossed the 100-run mark in the thirtieth over but the joy was short-lived. Mohammad Hafeez, who had been stripped of the captaincy in the ODIs, showed his utility with the ball and snuck one in through Raina's defences. On the other end, Dhoni's immediate reaction was that of a grimace. He knew how crucial Raina was to the plan for the remaining overs of the match. In the incoming R. Ashwin, Dhoni still had a man he could trust to not throw his wicket away and when the local boy joined his captain at the crease, he showed why Dhoni had that kind of faith in him.

But Dhoni's numbers still remained a mystery to most. Despite being in the middle for close to 30 overs, his score was just over 30 without a single boundary. While the plan to hold one end up to prevent a collapse was clear, there was a bit of fear about the final flourish not coming from the man. After all, bowlers need one good ball, and sometimes even a bad ball, to rain on the well-thought-out plans of the batsmen. The Indian captain finally gave a teaser of what was to come when he pulled one from Gul to square leg boundary in the thirty-eighth over of the innings. This was his first boundary in 79 deliveries. In the next over, Junaid Khan erred in a fashion that has become a sin if you're a fast bowler in the twenty-first century. His front foot landed way ahead of the white line demarcating the bowling crease. Captain Misbah had a quick word with his bowler before Junaid delivered the next ball. The instructions were either lost in translation or were not good enough. Dhoni walloped Khan down the ground for a 6. It wasn't a length ball and for once it seemed as if the batsman had played a mistimed pull, but the power took it beyond the long-on boundary.

The next ball didn't yield a 4 or a 6 for the spectators but it gave them a glimpse of an angry MS Dhoni. After nudging the ball behind, Dhoni set off for a single seeing Ashwin taking a couple of steps. Umar Gul, however, was quick to cover ground and get to the ball at fine leg. If the throw had hit the stumps, it would have been curtains for the captain who had already given up. Luckily, Gul's throw wasn't good enough and, in an instant, Dhoni turned to give Ashwin an earful over his indecisiveness. The pressure of an India–Pakistan affair!

The schooling didn't distract Ashwin from his job, which was to turn the strike over to the skipper every time he got the opportunity. And why wouldn't he when the exercise came with the reward of getting the best seat in the house to a Mahi masterclass? After the assault on Khan, it was Gul's turn as Dhoni whipped one in the air towards the cow corner to accrue another 4 runs that took him past the 50-run mark in the fortieth over of the innings.

Slowly and steadily, India was moving on from that horrific start. But staying on the pitch for more than 30 overs had stretched Dhoni physically. As a result, the running between the wickets bore the brunt. So did Pakistan as a result of that. With limited opportunities available to convert 1s into 2s, Dhoni decided to set his shoulders with just 6 overs left in the innings.

The power of Dhoni came to the fore in the first of the 24 deliveries remaining in the innings. Against the left-arm pace of Irfan, Dhoni pulled hard but since the ball made contact with the edge of his flashing blade, it ran down to the point boundary instead of going to the square leg boundary. Mohammad Irfan was surprised. That was not all. The left-armer was welcomed in the next over with one of the most ferocious straight drives down the ground the Chennai crowd would have seen. With that shot, the 200 was brought up, a score that not many would have anticipated when half of the team was back in the hut for 29.

A boundary and a 6 followed and suddenly the day that had seemed to begin with Irfan's name written on it was quickly moving away from it. His debut figures had been spoiled, even if by something special. Irrespective of the result of the match, the day belonged to the Indian captain who had reached his eighth ODI century from 118 deliveries. He had also crossed 7,000 ODI runs in the process.

India finished their innings with 227 runs courtesy of a Dhoni double on the final ball of the innings. Pakistani wicketkeeper Kamran Akmal, who had run up to the stumps to collect the ball, couldn't help but pat his counterpart on the back after he completed that double. The partnership with Ashwin had yielded 125 runs which came in just 101 deliveries. A knackered but proud Dhoni walked back to the pavilion to applause from the Chennai crowd to return in a while for 50 overs of wicketkeeping duties.

India went on to lose the match by 6 wickets. However, nothing that happened post-India's innings could take the sheen away from the effort that the Indian captain had put on that December morning. Interestingly, it was the first ODI India was playing after Sachin Tendulkar retired from the format. Moments before Rohit Sharma's dismissal, something which brought Dhoni to the crease, the broadcasters played a clip of the Little Master's entry to the crease. Little did they know that MS Dhoni would end up paying such a fine tribute to the resilience shown by the Mumbaikar over the years as he held one end up while seeing wickets tumble on the other end.

Partial scorecard of the match on page 107.

14

Thala Enthrals Chennai in Whites!

224 (265)—Chennai, 23–24 February 2013 vs Australia

The years 1983 and 2011 were very similar for Indian cricket. Besides the joy of winning a World Cup, the years also witnessed some of the most disappointing performances by the team in the longest format of the game. For Dhoni and his men, things didn't get better in 2012 either. Having suffered 0–4 defeats in both England and Australia in 2011–12, the hopes were high of India dishing the two teams the same result on their return tours to the subcontinent. The English team rained over those hopes by claiming a rare series win against the home side under the leadership of Alastair Cook. After three major series defeats including one at home, Dhoni's hold over the Test captaincy seemed to be slipping away.

There were more than murmurs in the media that Dhoni needs to step aside. Sunil Gavaskar led the chorus saying that Virat Kohli's century in the Nagpur Test showed that he's ready to take on the responsibility. Another former India skipper went even harder at the man who had taken India to the number 1 spot in Test rankings not too long ago. Bishen Singh Bedi questioned

Dhoni's place in the side, saying, 'He's not a Test skipper. You need a skipper who's worthy of his place in the eleven.' In response to the criticism, Dhoni remained stoic. 'The easiest thing for me to say right now is "I quit captaincy" and be a part of the side. But that's like running away from the responsibility', said the skipper after India's defeat in the Kolkata Test against England.

That's how dark the clouds were over Dhoni's head when the Border–Gavaskar series commenced in Chennai, the city where the skipper had made his Test debut eight years ago. Michael Clarke had no hesitation opting to bat when the coin fell in his favour. Nor did he have any hesitation in continuing his love affair with Indian bowling which had begun in his first Test innings in Bengaluru almost a decade ago. At the end of day 1, centurion Clarke walked back to the pavilion with pride after helping Australia accrue more than 300 runs on the first day itself. No mean feat.

Local boy Ravichandran Ashwin's 7-wicket haul ensured Australia didn't run away with the contest in the first innings of the series. Even then Australia's 380 looked impressive for a team that had two 0–2 series defeats in India to stave off. What could the Indian captain under fire conjure up in reply?

At the post-match press conference, Dhoni told the media that he had dodged all the fire that was thrown at him by choosing to avoid reading the sports page of the newspaper. It didn't seem so though when he walked out to bat on the third day morning with the scoreboard reading 196/4. Almost 200 runs behind the Australian total, the skipper with the heir apparent had his task cut out.

The first task was to deal with the now roaring Nathan Lyon. Having dismissed Sachin Tendulkar with a dream delivery that landed on the rough to disturb the master's furniture, the off-spinner now had a spring in his steps. If Ashwin could get 7 wickets, it was only natural from Australia to expect similar returns from their premier spinner. Skipper Clarke backed his bowler's attacking line and length with an equally attacking field. The new batsman, already under pressure, could be broken if more pressure was applied, so thought Clarke and co. Little did they know what was going to hit them.

Probably that explains the spinner's expression of 'Where did you pull that out from?' when the Indian captain bashed him over midwicket for his first 4 of the match. Clarke responded by taking the leg slip out. The short-leg fielder still lurked in the vicinity though. One delivery later, Dhoni swept from outside the off stump for another thunderous 4. The plan was clear. The attack was on with the objective being to not allow Lyon to grow more powerful. The onus now was on the bowler to think out of the box. He had built considerable pressure bowling that tempting line outside the off stump and the length that invited batsmen to drive but suddenly those deliveries were getting dispatched to the boundary. Clarke decided to let Lyon rest only to see Kohli attacking his replacement, Moises Henriques.

Bad move. Back came Lyon for one last spell before lunch. And once again Dhoni put him to the sword in the second over of his spell. The power in those forearms seemed superhuman when the bowler missed the length to offer a full toss. Lyon did just that to see the ball race to the cover boundary, forcing him to change his angle. This time Dhoni cut it for 4. Lyon, who was looking ominous half an hour ago, seemed to not have any answers to the counter-attack.

As Kohli strode confidently towards a well-deserved ton in the second session of the day, Dhoni quietened down for a bit before going berserk. Mitchell Starc's left-arm pace got him 3 boundaries. Debutant Henriques was welcomed to his second spell with a dismissive 6 followed by a 4. Pattinson, Siddle and Lyon got hit for a boundary each and suddenly Dhoni was on 85 off 79. Only a few months ago, when his team needed him at 29/5 in an ODI against Pakistan on the same ground, Dhoni had curbed his attacking instincts so much that at one point he was on

38 off 79 deliveries. He finished with an unbeaten 113 from 125 eventually. Today, though, the need was for him to attack. And here he was, making a mockery of the Australian bowling attack in whites on the third day of a Test match.

But once again the situation needed him to alter his approach. Kohli, after completing a superb ton, fell shortly and was followed into the pavilion by Jadeja and Ashwin in quick succession. In the company of Harbhajan Singh, Dhoni brought up his own ton in just 119 deliveries when, keeping up with his continued assault on the first delivery of the bowler's spell, Dhoni advanced down the track to Siddle to move from 98 to 102 with a boundary.

Harbhajan's dismissal now made things tricky. At 406, India's lead was just 26 with 2 wickets left and the two men left to bat included the debutant Bhuvneshwar Kumar and number 11 Ishant Sharma. For the next couple of hours, the Meerut born, a keen learner of the game, put a premium on his wicket while watching his captain do some tremendous things with the bat.

With the pitch offering turn, Lyon was called back. Only to be hit for a gigantic 6 on his second ball of the over. Next over. Another lofted shot for 4. It was as if Dhoni had picked out the man from South Australia for special treatment. Despite picking up 3 wickets, including those of Tendulkar and Kohli, Lyon only seemed to register his presence to get clobbered by Dhoni on that afternoon. It came to a point where the Indian captain refused to take a single off him when there was one for the taking. The next ball was invariably deposited into the stands. Years later, Lyon's teammate David Warner, himself capable of tearing down bowling attacks, admitted that he had not seen anyone take down a bowler the way Dhoni took Lyon down that day. This was carnage. And there was absolutely no let-up even when he inched towards his double hundred. For years, the Chennai crowd had seen Thala turn up the heat in the yellow jersey. This onslaught in white was a bonanza for them.

Slowly but steadily, Dhoni in the company of Bhuvneshwar, was taking the match farther away from Australia as the shadows lengthened in the final session. And on the way, he was breaking records, answering everyone who questioned his place in the side in his own way. He went past Budhi Kunderan's tally of 192 late in the day to make the highest individual score by an Indian wicketkeeper in a Test on his own. But those were not records Dhoni probably cared about. His innings was a statement. Nothing more. Nothing less. When he finally reached the double 100, there was nothing more than the standard raising of the bat to the crowds. As the decibel levels soared at M.A. Chidambaram and his teammates applauded with pride, Dhoni remained focused on his task.

And the task didn't come to an end at the end of the day's play. It didn't come to an end when he finished his innings at 224, the second-best score by a wicketkeeper in Test cricket. It even didn't come to an end when India cantered to an emphatic win on the fifth morning of the Test riding on Dhoni's double.

It came to an end when a few weeks later in Delhi, Dhoni swept for a boundary to complete India's clean sweep of the Aussies, the first time ever that India won a series 4–0 under a captain who was not thought to be good enough to be in the XI.

The bowler was, of course, Nathan Lyon.

Partial scorecard of the match on page 108.

15

The Caribbean Heist

45* (52)—Port of Spain, 11 July 2013 vs Sri Lanka

Cricket in the Caribbean ceased to be the kind to keep people up and glued to their television screens late into the night post the nineties which saw a remarkable decline of West Indian cricket. The nature of the pitches barely allowed much exciting cricket anyway. And that's why when almost twenty days after winning a thrilling final in the ICC Champions Trophy in Birmingham, India played Sri Lanka in the final of a tri-series in the Caribbean, the buzz was missing. After all, Sri Lanka were too familiar foes for the Indian audience now and most importantly what could the two teams possibly dish out to better the experience of the final of the World Cup a couple of years ago. There was also the small matter of the Ashes getting off to a brilliant start courtesy a number 11 Ashton Agar scoring 98 on debut.

MS Dhoni, however, had other plans. Making a comeback into the team for the final of a series in which his deputy had led the team for the most part in his absence, he made sure those in India following the game late into the night were left with a story to tell. A story for everyone who fell asleep at the halfway mark of the game. A story that would begin with, 'But you know what, he wasn't even supposed to be there for he had been ruled out of the series in the first match itself.'

Those who fell asleep though cannot be blamed. Put into bat by Dhoni, Sri Lanka looked on course for a solid total when they reached 171 in the thirty-eighth over for the loss of 3 wickets. When it seemed the foundation for a final flourish had been laid, the duo of Ravi Ashwin and Ravindra Jadeja spun a web in the next 12 overs. For 30 runs, the Islanders lost their 7 wickets and were all out for 201.

In Shikhar Dhawan, Rohit Sharma and Virat Kohli, India had a top order that had not only shone in the Champions Trophy but had also enjoyed good form in the series. 202 didn't seem like a total that would stretch the batting line-up of the World Champions. Just like the Sri Lankan innings, the Indian chase too seemed to be on autopilot mode when Sharma batted with Raina to take the score to 139/3. When left-arm spinner Rangana Herath removed the opener, though, and Raina edged one to the keeper soon after, the pendulum began to swing to the other side.

With the required run rate still below 4, Dhoni decided to cut down on the risks and stitch partnerships with the lower order. But it didn't go quite as planned. The men who had allowed India the luxury of chasing such a small total—Jadeja and Ashwin—went back on successive deliveries in Herath's final over. A collapse after a good start against Sri Lanka, of course, wasn't a story that many Indian cricket fans were unfamiliar with. At 7 down and with 50 still to make, Port of Spain smelled of Kolkata 1996, minus the burning down of the stands, of course.

Those in the stands in 2013 knew one thing that their counterparts from 1996 didn't—that it ain't over until MS Dhoni is in the middle. In his typical style, he looked divorced from the hara-kiri that was panning out at the other end. Because of him, those watching the game in India still didn't give in to their bodies that demanded sleep as he began chasing the last 50 runs with only the tail for company.

Out of the remaining 12 overs to get those 50 runs from, one-third were to be bowled by Lasith Malinga. For a man who had taken 4 wickets in 4 deliveries, 24 deliveries against the tail were way too many. As the lights began to fade in Port of Spain, Malinga licked his lips in anticipation.

But before having a go at India's tail, he had to square off against an old nemesis. After being carted around by the batsman in the 2011 World Cup final, Malinga had clawed back some territory when Dhoni could manage only a tie against him in the Commonwealth Bank tri-series fixture in Australia a year later in Adelaide.

A full toss outside the off stump was the first offering by Malinga and Dhoni placed it perfectly to reduce the target by 4 runs. Never the one to give up, Malinga beat his bat a ball later with the kind of delivery that deserved an edge. A similar delivery next up did get the edge but there was no slip to pouch it. Four more shaved off the target. Advantage Dhoni in the battle of two death over veterans.

In round two of the battle, the Indian made the mistake of exposing Bhuvneshwar Kumar to Malinga when 9 overs were still left in the chase. 4 deliveries were all that it took for the slinger to leave MS Dhoni one less tailender to play with. With 35 to get from 8 overs with 2 wickets left, the scores in this contest of Ms were level.

Just like the Sri Lankan captain had calculated that Sri Lanka's best chance at winning the contest was by trying to dismiss the other batsmen, the Indian captain had also understood that India's best chance lay in trying to score runs off bowlers other than Malinga. And that's how 8 runs were squeezed out of the forty-third over of the innings bowled by Angelo Mathews before Malinga was given the respect he deserved and allowed to get a maiden against his name.

At the other end, Sri Lanka tightened the noose around Vinay Kumar, whose selection ahead of Umesh Yadav had raised some eyebrows. The resistance shown by the Karnataka man with the bat at this point of the match, however, did well to tilt the balance in his favour. The resistance also brought 5 runs for the team. The balls consumed though made the equation tighter. In the last 4 overs of the match, India needed 21. The breathing space was diminishing quickly.

And it had its effect on the course of the match. After having seen Kumar negotiate 14 deliveries, Dhoni felt confident enough to turn over the strike to him at the beginning of the forty-seventh over. The calculation backfired as the number 10 tried to hoick one on the leg side and gave away his wicket. When Malinga came back for his final over, India needed more runs than balls remaining for the first time in their chase. Facing all the 6 deliveries of the over, the batsman let the bowler win their mini duel between the two. At the end of the over though, Dhoni hadn't been snared but the task that stood ahead of him only grew taller, even taller than the number 11 who had joined him.

Ishant Sharma, never the least reliable number 11, had one job to do—survive the second-last over to be bowled by Angelo Mathews. He tried to self-sabotage twice but eventually came out luckier on both the occasions to leave his captain with 15 to get from the last 6.

99 overs gone. 19 players dismissed. The last man standing was the chasing team's best bet in front of a Herculean task. This was ODI cricket at its finest. Yet the drama that unfolded in the 100th over surpassed it all.

Before it began, Dhoni rearmed himself. In a 2012 interview he had revealed that in the death overs, he likes to play with a heavier bat more suited to slogging. So, out came Ambati Rayudu and Murali Vijay with a number of bats for the captain before Shaminda Eranga started the final over. The first ball gave no indication of how good the new bat was. It kept low and missed

Dhoni's bat by miles. Sangakkara applauded the bowler's presence of mind from behind the stump.

Sadly for his skipper, the presence of mind deserted the youngster playing only in his tenth match when he bowled a length ball next. Now, there was little doubt about the efficacy of the willow Dhoni had summoned. It was a 6 the moment the ball made contact with the bat which made a perfect arc on its follow-through. And in no time, it landed in front of the Media Centre. The dressing room finally afforded a smile as Dhoni walked down the pitch with the bat under his arm, somewhat like that night in Mumbai.

9 from 4 soon became 5 required off the last 3 as Dhoni crunched the next delivery over point for a 4. Suddenly, it was India in the driver's seat. The pendulum had resigned. It had done enough swinging for the day. As his teammates applauded and supporters danced in the stands, in the commentary box Ian Bishop quipped, 'Isn't he something under pressure?'

But there were still 5 runs to get from the last 3 balls of the match in Port of Spain where the length of the shadows now threatened to be dwarfed by the ever-growing tensions. A few months ago, it was the same equation against Malinga in Adelaide when the match ended in a tie. Three off those 5 came off the final delivery. But it was Eranga with the ball in his hand today. And all that Eranga needed to vanquish the memories of the last 2 deliveries was to get a wicket somehow. A wicket that would give Sri Lanka the Celkon Cup.

Not this time though. A rattled Eranga had little better to offer as the fourth delivery of the over. The swinging blade of the Indian captain threw his all at it and sent it sailing over the cover boundary. Six runs. Game over. Match won. Series done. A series he had been ruled out from. Who would have thought!

Back in his homeland, the tired eyes had now a big smile to accompany them as well as a story for those who had chosen sleep over a cracking final.

Partial scorecard of the match on page 109.

16

Standing Tall amidst the Ruins

71 (133) and 82 (140)—2014 vs England in Fourth and Fifth Tests, India's Tour of England

Mahendra Singh Dhoni's tours to England always came at interesting times in his career. In 2007, he was the contender, having almost cemented his place across formats in Team India, but yet, not quite fully in Tests. In 2011, he was at the other end of the spectrum, ruler of all he surveyed, barely a couple of months after hitting that shot for 6 at Wankhede, so much so that despite a disappointing outcome, the 2011 Test series verdict in England barely registered on the collective consciousness of fans, still giddy with the hangover of being 50-over world champions as they were.

But by 2013, the knives were out. Not only had a team under Dhoni lost to England at home but MS Dhoni had nothing to offer but a smile when asked about the difficult waters his franchise team's owners had apparently dipped their toes into in his presser ahead of Team India's departure for the Champions Trophy. There were no such questions though when he returned home with the trophy that made him the only captain to win all three ICC tournaments.

The year 2014 though, presented an interesting scenario. There were some doubts creeping in as to where Team India was headed in red-ball as well as white-ball cricket, the heady days of 2011 long gone by then. Particularly in red-ball cricket, having gotten the World Cup-sized monkey off their collective backs, born-again Indian cricket fans with fresh enthusiasm and vigour flowing through their veins started eyeing newer challenges. And no challenge was bigger than India winning in red-ball cricket in the SENA (South Africa, England, New Zealand, Australia) countries, away from home.

From 2011 to 2014, India had not only failed but failed terribly in that pursuit. 2011 saw India lose to England and Australia while 2013 and 2014 had seen South Africa and New Zealand prove to be unconquerable for Dhoni's men.

2014 didn't end up being that different in eventual outcome. But something about what MS Dhoni did that summer possibly left in its wake the seeds from which future Indian sides were able to do much better in foreign conditions. Seeds of grit, gumption and resilience, hand in hand with self-belief. And so, the summer of 2014 found MS Dhoni in England, almost at the end of an undeniably solid, if not entirely spectacular career in Test whites. It's interesting to note that by this time, general expectations of Dhoni the batter in Test matches had started to wane, but the series gave a memorable snapshot of some qualities Dhoni carried as a batter, enhanced further by all that situational experience garnered over the years. He began with a formidable 82 in India's first innings of the series.

By the time the fourth match of the series began, the scenario had started to look ominous for India, albeit a situation not yet completely irretrievable. From the heady days of drawing the first Test and even winning the second, the Indians had come crashing down in the third match. And even as Dhoni took the brave call of batting first at Manchester in the fourth Test, it seemed all over barely an hour into the match, when Dhoni walked out with the team tottering at 8/4.

It makes for a grim visual if one tries to imagine the moment. The batting gone for all practical purposes, seaming conditions enabling the ball to swing prodigiously from opposition players at their peak and a despairingly familiar sense of 'Here we go again' settling in amongst the supporters. Bleak, to say the least. Especially when one considers that for a stroke maker like Dhoni, the ideal situation would have been to stride to the crease to build on top of a solid foundation which would hopefully have been laid by those above him, which he had done in the first match. But the reality was quite the opposite in Manchester on that cold morning. At this point, it's easy to mumble words like resolve, fortitude, etc., but another thing to actually live it. Dhoni did live it though, single-handedly playing strokes and adding to the runs, even as others kept falling around him. A lucky slash over slips which led to many an 'ooh' emanating from the crowd, a loud appeal for a somewhat fortuitous bat-pad edge to the boundary through mid-off-cover (that's right!). Hooking a rising ball from Stuart Broad to the boundary, riding his luck through the afternoon sun, leaning into glorious cover drives in the 40s and 50s and through it all, not giving in. So much so, that with a 133-ball 71, he single-handedly dragged the team from the pits of despair past the 150-run mark, which as we all know, is the anointed mark of lower-middle-class cricketing respectability on English pitches.

In the end, it wasn't enough to save India from eventually succumbing to a heavy defeat in the match, but heading into the final Test still just 2–1 down, India would have looked at their captain's innings to think that it wasn't all over yet.

But a short while into the final Test match, it was all over. Or at least, it definitely seemed that way, when Dhoni was put in to bat, and had to walk out to hold the side tottering at 28/4 under perfect conditions for seam and swing bowling, and as coincidence would have it, England once again, had players by the name of Broad and Anderson steaming in.

But mixing sturdy defence with dollops of luck and strokeplay, stepping forward to drive through the covers now and then, Dhoni did what he had almost gotten used to through that series. Pull his team out of trouble and then look up a little at times to see if a measure of respectability could be attained, and then maybe, just maybe, one could start thinking of putting the opposition under some pressure.

And so, the strokes flowed, the hard-hit cover drives, the punch through the offside, the pull to the rising ball, all carried with the trademark whirlwind economy of Dhoni's movements when at the crease—swift, sudden and deceptively violent. It's a testament to the attitude and ability of the man, that he almost doubled the team score even though the eighth wicket had fallen before India even crossed 80. He played with the calm needed to stabilize the innings, and in the company of number 11 Ishant Sharma, he stitched a 58-run partnership before becoming the final man to get out on 82. 82 out of India's total of 148.

When the dust settled, the stats were unexpected and startlingly positive for Dhoni the batter, even though Dhoni the leader had to contend with another series loss in England. He finished as the second-highest scorer for India through the series, with four fifties from 10 innings, putting in a solid contribution of 349 runs along the way. It spoke much of how the rest of the batting had fared, but more importantly, it also spoke as to how a leader of a team failing to put up performances that fans expected of them tried his best to lead by example and stood tall amidst ruins.

Partial scorecard of the match on page 110.

17

The Second Lead to the Second Lead

85* (76)—Auckland, 14 March 2015 vs Zimbabwe

Mahendra Singh Dhoni was in his late teens when on a hot summer evening in 1999 he saw India succumb to one of their most mysterious World Cup defeats. In Leicester, India had the match in their grasp with 7 runs to chase down from 11 balls with 3 wickets in hand when Henry Olonga stood at the top of his run-up. However, in a flash, their 1999 World Cup campaign came crashing down as Olonga ended up taking 3 wickets in those 5 deliveries.

Sixteen years later, when MS Dhoni walked out to bat under the lights at Auckland against Zimbabwe in a World Cup fixture, the threat of getting knocked out wasn't looming large. India had won all their five matches before their final group match against Zimbabwe but a defeat against the African nation would have been embarrassing as they had only managed to win a single group match and that too against the UAE. More importantly, for a lot of Indians watching the game, it would have evoked bitter memories of the Leicester loss.

The task ahead of Dhoni and his batting partner Suresh Raina was a huge one. Not only had India not chased down a total as big as 288 in World Cup history before, but they were also now languishing at 92 for the loss of their top four. Raina was on 10 from 23 deliveries, playing a fairly sedate knock by his standards. But on that evening, that was the need of the hour. The pitch wasn't the easiest to bat on as the ball wasn't coming onto the bat. Moreover, Zimbabwe's bowlers just didn't produce enough pace for Indian batsmen to play with.

Such was the caution on display that India still hadn't crossed the 100-run mark in their chase after 25 overs. But then Raina began to open his arms, first stepping out to spinner Sean Williams in the twenty-fifth over and then hitting back-to-back 6s against the same bowler in the twenty-ninth over. At the other end, Dhoni still played the waiting game as the required run rate hovered above 8. India still needed a whopping 161 runs from their final 20 overs in the chase with only the all-rounders and the tail to follow. Was this going to be the wake-up call for the team before the knockouts?

Skipper Dhoni had other ideas. He pulled one from Solomon Mire for his first boundary in the thirty-first over and then found the boundary on the other side to ensure 8 runs of the over were collected easily. The acceleration had begun. To celebrate his twenty-sixth 50-run partnership with his trusted ally Raina in their sixty-sixth inning batting together, Dhoni danced down the track to dispatch a fastish Sikander Raza full toss to the square leg boundary in the next over. Brendan Taylor, who had played the innings of his life in what was supposed to be his last ODI for Zimbabwe, began to sense that a special comeback was being mounted against his team. Although the required run rate still stood over 8 and the Indian tail wasn't too many wickets away, the shoulders began to drop. They dropped further after his most experienced Hamilton Masakadza dropped Raina at the end of the thirty-fourth over bowled by Raza. That was just the slice of luck Raina needed. There was no looking back by the left-hander from that point on as his right-handed batting partner continued finding boundaries at the other end to keep the scoreboard moving. For the Zimbabwean bowlers, the line and lengths kept deteriorating and the balls kept finding a way to miss the fielders.

The change in gears was evident as the 100th run in the partnership came on the 103rd delivery. The early caution from Dhoni had also changed to a more offensive approach as he made full use of the offerings on the leg stump from off-spinner Raza whose control on the ball declined as the pressure rose. With 91 runs left to get from the last 10 overs, those big forearms were put to good use when Dhoni pulled a short ball from Raza for another boundary on the first ball of the fortieth over. A couple of overs later, we saw the big 'Spartan' bat of Dhoni rise as he brought up his fifty-seventh half-century. But the job was still not done.

The boundary balls kept getting more frequent as the deficit came down, as everyone from Tendai Chatara to Tinashe Panyangara kept losing their radar at least once in an over. Suresh Raina brought up his fifth ODI century from 94 deliveries, an effort that should count as one of the better centuries by an Indian middle-order batsman in a World Cup. To have done it in front of a man whom he immensely respects must have made the moment extremely special for the Ghaziabad-based southpaw.

The crowds who had come to the ground to see India record their tenth consecutive World Cup win, all of them under Captain Dhoni, were now beginning to realize that it wasn't too far away. They had their hearts in their mouths when one from Raina's bat seemed to be heading to Raza's hands at long-off, but the Zimbabwean generosity ensured that the *oohs* soon turned to *ahs*. With 31 runs needed off 23 deliveries, even Raina's dismissal wouldn't have worried Dhoni a lot at the other end who kept on pinching singles. With less than 30 runs to get, the skipper brought out the big shot to send the Indian fans at the ground into celebration mode. He thumped a length ball straight over the bowler's head for a flat 6. After erring in length, Mupariwa erred in line and gifted a full toss outside leg stump for Dhoni to add 4 more to his burgeoning tally. This was proving to be yet another masterclass in batting under pressure from the skipper. He played the waiting game when the team was under pressure and then gradually began to transfer the weight of pressure to the other side. Finally, when the opposition found its feet shaky under the weight of the pressure, Dhoni brought out the big shots to deliver the knockout punch.

With 8 left to get from the remaining 10 deliveries, Dhoni drove hard at a full toss but was denied a boundary by a scintillating fielding effort at deep cover. Too bad for Zimbabwe that it meant that a 6 was all that India needed to wrap up their sixth consecutive win of the World Cup. Nothing is a more tempting invitation for Dhoni to hit it out of the ground than 6 required to win the match. And when Panyangara banged it halfway down the pitch next delivery, there was only one destination for the white ball—out of the ground. While Raina went home with the Man of the Match effort and Taylor got all the love for a century in a losing cause in his final Zimbabwe outing, Dhoni quietly reaffirmed his place among the world's best finishers with a contribution of 85 from 76 deliveries in a record-breaking 196-run stand.

Partial scorecard of the match on page 112.

18

Tiger Abhi Zinda Hai!

92 (86)—Indore, 14 October 2015 vs South Africa

The subplots underpinning the second ODI between India and South Africa in the 2015 ODI series rivalled a film script written by Quentin Tarantino and at the centre of it all was the home team's captain—MS Dhoni.

After losing the T20I series 2–0, India suffered defeat in the first ODI at Kanpur by 5 runs despite Rohit Sharma's 150 off 133 balls. Social media and critics held one man responsible for the loss, India's finisher supreme MS Dhoni, who couldn't dispatch South Africa's young gun Kagiso Rabada to the boundary in the last over. Add to this the residual frustration of the loss in the World Cup semi-final to Australia, the metaphorical knives were ready to skin Dhoni alive.

In the simmering heat of such subtext, the second ODI was set to be a cracker with Messrs A.B. de Villiers and co. looking to put yet another dagger into the hearts of the Men in Blue.

India's man-in-form Rohit Sharma was given a rude shock by Rabada, who cleaned him on the fourth delivery of the second over. Ajinkya Rahane and Shikhar Dhawan rebuilt the innings after Rohit's departure, but the southpaw was outfoxed by Morne Morkel in the 13th over, handing an easy catch to J.P. Duminy, leaving India wanting for more at 59/2. The imperious Virat Kohli walked into bat with the stage set for him to shine on a wicket tailor-made for a big one. However, the batting gods had written despair on Kohli's fortune cookie for the day, and following an embarrassing mix-up with Rahane, he returned to the pavilion after making just 12 off 18 balls. India's fortune cookie, like the baked good itself, was crumbling; Rohit, Shikhar and Virat were all back in the pavilion.

His team reeling at 82/3, skipper MS Dhoni joined Rahane at the crease with some massive repair work to do. The two struck a mini stand to address the fall of wickets with Rahane taking charge while Dhoni lightly nudging the ball around. Just when it was looking like a partnership was building. Imran Tahir produced a delivery that spun from around Rahane's leg stump to clip the bails, sending him packing for a well-made 51 off 61 balls.

India was in absolute tatters—102 for 4 in the twenty-third over—when MSD's old faithful partner in crime, Suresh Raina, came into bat next. The plot and ending of Raina's innings were as predictable as a Sooraj Barjatya film. Skipper de Villiers handed the ball to Morkel for the next over and asked him to bang it in short. The tall pacer banged one into Raina's midriff and a faint edge following a tentative shuffle was enough to hand a catch to Quinton de Kock.

India's score? 104/5 in 23.4 overs with only one recognized batsman left at the crease—MS Dhoni. If there was ever a situation on a cricket field that could be characterized as a crisis—it was this one—staring MSD and his men in their faces.

The plan for South Africa was simple—get Dhoni and the match was in the bag. One wonders what must have been going through Dhoni's mind as he watched his team implode on a wicket that had no recognizable demons.

Going for the jugular, de Villiers brought in Rabada with a young and meek Axar Patel there for the taking but he managed to survive the first two deliveries and gave MSD the strike. Everyone knew the next ball was going to be fast and short from Rabada, who had dismissed Dhoni in the first ODI.

Rabada banged it in short and fast (142.9 kmph) but MSD, quite intelligently, tucked it away to the fine leg for a boundary. It was a quiet message from Dhoni to the Proteas that he was prepared to tackle anything thrown at him that day.

Patel (13 off 27 balls) was the next man to go when Dale Steyn struck his pads with a fast, back-of-the-length delivery and Aleem Dar raised his finger. The Indian innings was skating on thin ice, and it was all up to MS Dhoni to conjure up a saving grace and propel them to a fighting total. The thirty-seventh over, bowled by JP Duminy, was Dhoni's chance to put some pressure back on the visitors. However, only two deliveries remained when he came on strike. Showing great intent, Dhoni came down the wicket and even though Duminy tried to fire it down the leg side, the ball was promptly dispatched to the stands as the crowd welcomed the 6 like a drought-hit village celebrated rainfall.

Even as Dhoni reached 40 off 49 balls, an innings that was typical of him in its construction but alien in its approach and circumstantial execution, Tahir sent Bhuvneshwar Kumar packing in the fortieth, and India were down to 165/7.

The forty-first over was handed to Rabada and the plan was to bowl short again to see if MSD goes for it or fends. First delivery, as expected, was banged into the wicket but Dhoni was batting in his zone and favourite phase of play. The result—a pull shot for 4 with excellent control and timing. It was almost as if Dhoni was sending a signal to the Proteas—bring it on. Rabada then bowled a length ball wide of the off stump and Dhoni, having forced the bowler to change his tactics, beautifully placed the ball between point and third man for another 4.

de Villiers had to use his bowlers carefully, given how MSD was capable of murdering length ball bowlers at death. Almost as a gift to India, the forty-third over was handed to Duminy and South Africa were looking a bit flummoxed by the home skipper's counter-attack. What happened next could have been predicted by anyone present at the ground, on either side of the boundary.

The first delivery of the forty-third over, a half-tracker, was sent soaring over long-on by the brutal bottom hand of Dhoni, who brought up his 50 with a maximum. Dhoni's batting partner Harbhajan Singh attacked Duminy and forced an error from Farhaan Behardien at the midwicket boundary, resulting in a 4. The next ball was in Harbhajan's slot and awfully poor from an out-of-sorts Duminy. Result? A 6 over long-on to nudge India closer to 200.

Imran Tahir had conceded only 26 runs from 9 overs before he faced the daunting task of bowling to Dhoni in the forty-fifth over. The first delivery was flat and fast at 96.4 kmph but a minor error in the line proved costly as Dhoni's deft touch guided the ball to the fine leg boundary. Just like he had done with Rabada, Dhoni had unsettled Tahir, forcing him to rethink the line of attack.

The next delivery was much slower and given some amount of flight, bowled outside the off stump, and Dhoni came down the track to send the ball flying for a thumping 6. He had forced Tahir to play into his hands and that had reaped rewards. The crowd roared on as their talismanic captain put on the vintage hat when it mattered the most and India crossed 200 with that hit.

MSD had quickly gone from 31 off 40 balls to 72 off 69 balls, scoring 41 runs in just 29 balls to set the base for an assault in the final overs as India needed a total closer to 250 for them to have any sort of chance.

The captain had breathed a new lease of life into his team's batters, albeit not the specialist ones and a bit too late. Harbhajan dazzled briefly but Steyn's pace proved to be too much for him as he was dismissed for 22 off 21 balls, leaving only Umesh Yadav and Mohit Sharma to bat.

In the forty-eighth over, Rabada was given the Dhoni 'death destruction' treatment as the Indian skipper hit him for a 6 and 4 to take India past the 220 mark. The young gun returned for the last over and what happened on the last ball of the innings was a statement that many won't forget. Rabada went to the most trusted weapon in his arsenal—the short ball—and bowled a 135-kmph delivery that Dhoni nonchalantly clobbered for a 6. It was an 'over and out' message from the Indian captain as he walked back to the pavilion.

Dhoni's 86-ball 92 was worth way more than its value on the scoreboard. The skipper had dragged an ailing team by the scruff of its neck on his shoulders to prevent them from a catastrophe.

The captain's unbeaten knock didn't go in vain as an excellent bowling effort from the bowling attack ensured India levelled the series. Not to anyone's surprise, MS Dhoni was named Man of the Match for his stellar knock. For the hundredth time in his career, Dhoni had chosen to let the bat talk and silence the detractors who were writing obituaries of his finishing abilities after the first ODI.

Partial scorecard of the match on page 113.

19

Marvellous at the G!

87* (114)—Melbourne vs Australia 18 January 2019

In 2008, a rookie MS Dhoni was India's captain when they triumphed in Australia by winning the Commonwealth Bank series that also featured Sri Lanka. The historic triumph, led by Sachin Tendulkar's unforgettable masterclass in the two finals, ushered a new dawn in India's limited-overs history and Dhoni was the flagbearer of this group, which produced scintillating cricket and was a dominant force.

Over a decade later, in 2019, India was on the cusp of writing yet another historic chapter in its book of limited-over triumphs Down Under. This time, MS Dhoni was a seasoned veteran playing under the captaincy of Virat Kohli, whom he had nurtured and guided to take over the mantle of possibly the toughest job in India after being prime minister—captain of the men's cricket team.

The series was tied 1–1, with the decider set to take place in Melbourne on 18 January 2019. Unlike most ODI series played in the second decade of the twenty-first century, this one hadn't been a high-scoring affair with a 300+ score being on par. Bowlers had dominated in the series with the likes of Jhye Richardson and Bhuvneshwar Kumar making life difficult for batters in the first two matches.

Another thing that couldn't have been ignored was the fact that 2019 was a World Cup year and several critics were questioning Dhoni's place in the ODI side. The signs of slowing down and a decrease in hitting prowess were there but both selectors and captain Kohli were convinced that MS Dhoni's place in the team, both as a batsman and senior player, was unquestionable.

Kohli won the toss and without any hesitation decided to bowl first, meaning India would chase for the third consecutive time in the series. The Australian innings survived on several small partnerships with Peter Handscomb scoring a well-crafted 58 of 63 balls to help the home side cross 200, which, at one point, looked a little dicey. In the end, Australia set India a target of 231 after being dismissed within 48.4 overs.

Rohit Sharma and Virat Kohli had smashed hundreds in the first and second ODIs, respectively, and with chasing being India's preferred modus operandi, this total didn't look like a daunting one. However, India was put on the back foot immediately when Sharma was dismissed by Peter Siddle in the sixth over, leaving the Indian skipper exposed to the new ball.

Shikhar Dhawan and Virat went about repairing the innings, but the former was dismissed by an innocuous delivery from Marcus Stoinis, who caught the Indian opener off his own bowling. Two wickets down, Indian fans probably expected Vijay Shankar or Dinesh Karthik to walk out at number 4, but it was MS Dhoni, who had batted at number 5 in the first two matches.

The total was not humongous but there was work to be done and winning this game wasn't going to be a walk in the park. On a sticky and slow Melbourne wicket, shots were not easy to play, and the size of the boundaries meant that going for a big shot could run the risk of being caught out in the deep.

Dhoni's intelligence, prowess and the ability to read the game was unparalleled but on a wicket like this, he needed to bring out the best in him. It was like a snooker player of Stephen Hendry's class playing in his last years, relying on staying in the game till the predator turned into prey. Runs were not coming easy but since the required rate wasn't even 5 when the innings started, India always knew wickets were crucial. Jhye Richardson, in the thirtieth over, beat Virat Kohli for pace on a delivery outside off stump and he was caught behind, following a knock of 46 of 62 deliveries, off which only 12 were scored via boundaries.

Kedar Jadhav walked into bat at number 5 to partner his former captain and the onus was now on Dhoni to anchor the chase. At the thirtieth-over mark, Dhoni was 38 off 60 balls, his strike rate being an uncharacteristic 63.3 but he knew that it was the need of the hour.

The required rate had climbed up to cross 6 and Australia were slowly but steadily strangling India in this game and a wicket at this stage would mean the momentum shifting in the home side's favour. Jadhav, too, not surprisingly, got off to a slow start and had made only 5 runs off 14 balls but a boundary off Billy Stanlake helped him take the pressure off both himself and the team.

While the Australian team's strategy seemed to be containment, MS Dhoni was turning the chase in his favour by just hanging around. Dhoni brought up his half-century in the thirty-eighth over off 74 balls—it was an innings that oozed class, control and character. Not once had Dhoni been tempted to use his mercurial and powerful bottom hand to go for a boundary.

Like a master artisan at work, Dhoni quietly went about his business on a day when runs were hard to come by for the batters. India's plan was clear: Dhoni would bat till the end and others would stay around him, playing shots and scoring runs.

Jadhav, another cool customer whose demeanour and size make him look innocuous, had got his eye in and was given the nod to go for shots. With India needing 77 off 69, Jadhav went after Stoinis and scored a boundary to raise a loud roar from the crowd.

Not only was Jadhav able to sneak in the odd boundary, but Dhoni's immense ability to run fast between the wickets also allowed him to pick up several doubles. In the forty-second over, Jhye Richardson struck Dhoni's pads and the Australians appealed loudly, only to be turned down by the umpire. A desperate Australia reviewed and unfortunately for them, the ball was going over the stumps. Dhoni, looking as assured as someone sitting in a bulletproof Range Rover, went about his innings unperturbed and in a characteristically calm manner.

Boundaries were hard to come by and the required rate had crept up to 9+ with Stanlake, Stoinis and Richardson bowling tight spells. India needed 50 off 33 balls and the innings had reached the stage when Dhoni had to start making his moves. Stoinis, bowling his eighth over, banged it in short as he saw Dhoni coming down the track, but the batter cleverly guided it to the boundary, the first for India in 6 overs.

The next over saw Jadhav coming into his own and going after Peter Siddle, who conceded 7 runs off his first 2 deliveries. A healthy forty-sixth over meant India needed 33 from 24 balls and a couple of boundaries would do the trick. However, Richardson gave only 6 runs away, bringing down the equation to 27 from 18 deliveries.

Stoinis was called upon to bowl the forty-eighth over and the pressure was on Dhoni to produce a boundary on a slow wicket at the death to bring India closer. A slow and low full toss was worked away by MSD to the boundary and Jadhav's 4 off the last delivery meant India needed only 14 from the last 2 overs.

The Australians were deceptively made to believe that they were in the driver's seat, but they didn't realize that it had been MS Dhoni's plan all along to stay till the end and take his team home. Even the crowd supporting India at the Melbourne Cricket Ground (MCG) was not the least bit bothered about the result because they knew who was batting—the same man who delivered the World Cup for them in 2011.

The forty-ninth over, or we could call it the 'Happy Hours of Dhoni Time', forced Australia to bring up the fielders and both batsmen just needed one marginal mistake from the bowler. First Jadhav lofted the bowler over covers for 4 and then, in almost a sense of stamping his authority on the chase, Dhoni smashed Siddle to the boundary off the penultimate delivery to bring the scores level. Jadhav promptly scored the winning runs and India had won the series in style with the chase master, MS Dhoni, unbeaten on 87 off 114 deliveries, guiding them to history.

This inning was a symbol and an indication from Dhoni that he was still India's best finisher and an indispensable force while chasing in limited-overs cricket. And the 'Old-Timer' was promptly named the Man of the Series.

Partial scorecard of the match on page 114.

20

2.0

84* (48)—Bangalore, 21 April 2018 vs Royal Challengers Bangalore

Long-time fans of the IPL may have been forgiven for expecting a routine Chennai win against Bangalore when they faced off for their return fixture at the Chinnaswamy Stadium in the 2019 season. On the one hand, defending champions Chennai had been motoring along ever so smoothly in the tournament, with seven wins from nine fixtures, the first of which came against Bangalore.

On the other, Virat Kohli-led Bangalore, despite their wealth of batting talent, had gotten off to the worst possible start with six losses in their opening six games. Having not beaten the team in yellow since 2014, and with only two wins from nine games, Kohli's men were at a stage wherein every match assumed a must-win status. To stand a chance, the team would have to overcome their long-time nemesis: Chennai. But it began on a wrong note for Kohli as the coin fell in his counterpart's favour who inserted the men in red and black to bat.

After the end of the first innings, it seemed as if Dhoni's decision to field was vindicated as his team restricted Bangalore to 161/7. As expected, Dhoni didn't take the fixture lightly despite being in a position of strength on the points table and was as shrewd as always with his bowling changes. Barring Parthiv Patel, who scored 53 from 37, none of the Bangalore batters could convert their starts and thereby enable a late innings acceleration in the death overs.

When Chennai's chase began, Kohli needed his talisman Dale Steyn to deliver, and he delivered in spades. Charging in, and with a roaring Chinnaswamy Stadium cheering him on, Steyn kick-started proceedings by dismissing Shane Watson with an outswinger that carried straight to slip. He then beat Suresh Raina for pace and clean bowled him for a duck with the very next ball. Chennai was 6/2 after the end of the first over. The confidence rubbed off on the other pacers too and the top order of the Chennai batting line-up was blown to smithereens by Kohli's men.

At 28/4 in the sixth over, the team required their captain to play a typical knock of genius. He had done that a year ago against the same opposition when he had struck 70 off 34 balls to take Chennai over the line in a chase of 206. But despite the target being smaller, this was a trickier chase in front of a stronger bowling attack and on a pitch that wasn't giving much to the batsmen. And then there were other questions hovering over the man beyond the realm of the league. Not only was Dhoni entering the game in an extremely tricky situation, but he was also facing questions about his finishing capabilities. Was Dhoni still the batter of yore? Did he merit a place in the World Cup squad that would travel to England in the summer? Could he demolish attacks the same way he used to when he burst on to the scene?

It wasn't the smoothest of starts for Dhoni. He managed to angle the first ball he faced from Umesh Yadav in the direction of backward point for a 4, but his footwork was tentative. In the next over he was again slow to react and was rapped on his pads by a Saini in swinger. With the score at 39 for 3 from 7 overs and the scoreboard pressure mounting, Pawan Negi and Marcus Stoinis entered the attack.

The drop in pace allowed Dhoni to settle in, as he collected a boundary each from their overs. He first guided Negi's delivery to deep fine leg and then swivel pulled Stoinis for 4. Following a terrific tenth over from Yuzvendra Chahal which cost only 4 runs, the Super Kings were at 57/4. The required rate was over 10 and for Chennai to have a good chance, the Dhoni–Rayudu partnership needed to go big while taking calculated risks.

Dhoni began proceedings by charging Stoinis and depositing his back of a length medium pace over the long-off boundary for 6—a shot that reminded one and all that the vintage Dhoni wasn't lost. On the other end, though, Rayudu was struggling on 17 from 23 balls as Chahal bowled another economical over for 4 runs. But the captain stood unfazed and trusted his reliable soldier to turn things around which Rayudu did with a 6 and a 4 in the next over.

But Chahal, who had been consistently troubling Rayudu with his mix of googlies and straighter ones, finally had his man against the run of play. Just when Chennai was poised to mount their chase, they were forced into another period of stabilization with the left-handed Jadeja now at the crease. The aforementioned Chahal over would only cost 3 runs while Stoinis snuck in another over for the cost of 6 runs only. The required run rate had now escalated to 14 as Chennai needed 70 runs from 30 balls. The match had reached 'the Dhoni time'.

With 5 overs to go, Chahal was called upon to bowl his final over. It seemed as if both Jadeja and Dhoni were intent on seeing him off safely as they took only 7 off the first 5 deliveries. Dhoni, though, signalled a change in intent and smashed Chahal's final ball over the long-off boundary for a flat 6. There was a look of resignation on the face of Chahal, similar to that of an aspiring magician who had put together his entire repertoire in front of the master only to be blown away by the master's final act.

But there was still a lot to do in the chase. The Chennai fans would have hoped for Jadeja and Dhoni to carry them home, but they suffered another setback when Jadeja was run out after a mix-up with Dhoni in the seventeenth over.

Now with Jadeja gone, if Chennai were to have any chance from this stage, it had to be the Dhoni Solo Act. Dhoni almost took the situation as a cue and slashed Saini's next ball through the empty slip region for 4. The solo act had begun. With the equation at 49 runs required from 3 overs, Kohli brought on Steyn for his final over. The Dhoni–Steyn face-off used to be the main act of IPL rivalries in its initial years. The batsman had come on top often, plundering him for 24 in one over five years ago. Even in 2019, the two men, now on the other side of 30, dished out an exciting contest. The winner in this one final contest was again Dhoni as he managed to squeeze 13 runs from the over with a stand and deliver 6.

Navdeep Saini charged in with the penultimate over with the Chinnaswamy crowd right behind him. The first delivery went whizzing past to the deep point fielder, but Dhoni decided to not go for the single. He dispatched the next ball to the deep long-on boundary but again refused to give the strike to Bravo. It was as if Dhoni had taken the mantle of scoring all the runs himself since he was the only one who had seemed to gauge the movement and pace of the wicket. He hit an uppercut on the third ball, which was also a no ball, for 6. He couldn't optimize the resultant free hit though and could only run a couple. Dhoni yet again refused a single on Saini's fourth legal delivery. Bravo, waiting on the other end, finally received strike after Dhoni ran a single off the fifth ball. Facing the last ball, Bravo aimed for the boundary but could only edge the ball to the keeper. Saini had done his job and conceded only 10 runs. His opening partner Yadav now had 26 runs to defend in the final over.

Three years ago, Punjab's spinner Axar Patel couldn't save 23 runs in the final over against MS Dhoni when the latter was turning out for Rising Pune Supergiant, the only other team that he has been a part of in the tournament's history. Could he do it three years later in front of a pacer?

Dhoni began by pulling Yadav's first ball for 4 towards the deep square leg boundary. The next ball was similar in line and length but got an even more expansive response. Dhoni picked the length of the ball very early, stood his ground and hit the ball outside the stadium in the same deep square leg direction for 6. 26 from 6 became 16 from 4. The fans of Dhoni's team now had cause for hope.

Dhoni then unleashed his famed 'helicopter' shot on the third ball as he picked the fullish length and smashed it with the uncorking of his wrists beyond the despairing hands of a jumping A.B. de Villiers at long-off for 6. 10 runs were now needed from 3 balls. Yadav's next delivery was a low full toss which Dhoni slogged towards midwicket for 2. Yadav continued the strategy of bowling full and went for the yorker for the fifth ball. This time though, Yadav failed to get the ball to land or dip, and thereby delivered a juicy full toss which Dhoni slogged past square leg for a flat six. Two runs were needed from 1 ball. All Dhoni needed was to get bat on ball to take the game to a super over at the minimum.

For the final delivery, Yadav decided to roll his fingers and bowl an off-cutter. This change of pace worked wonders. Dhoni couldn't get bat on ball and ran for the bye. Parthiv Patel, though, had prepared for the eventuality of a sneaked bye to tie the innings and immediately threw the ball at the stumps, dismissing the non-striker, Shardul Thakur. Bangalore had eventually survived Dhoni's onslaught and kept their dreams of a play-off berth alive with a victory by the slimmest of margins.

Chennai, who were down and out in multiple stages of the match, had come to the brink of an extraordinary victory thanks to Dhoni's innings. Through the course of the innings, Dhoni not only showcased that he retained his big-hitting ability, but also reiterated the maxim that no target is out of the realm of possibility when Chennai's Thala is at the crease.

Partial scorecard of the match on page 115.

Scorecards

Glimpses of a Superstar
(Target: 235 runs from 50 overs)

INDIA A		R	B	4s	6s	SR
Gautam Gambhir	c Misbah–ul–Haq b Qaiser Abbas	79	100	9	0	79.00
Dheeraj Jadhav	run out (Riaz Afridi)	0	2	0	0	0.00
MS Dhoni †	not out	119	134	9	5	88.80
Sridharan Sriram	not out	21	40	2	0	52.50
Extras	(lb 3, nb 5, w 9)	17				
TOTAL	45 Ov (RR: 5.24)	236/2				
Did not bat: Venugopal Rao, Ambati Rayudu, Sairaj Bahutule (c), Ramesh Powar, Shib Paul, Amit Bhandari, Aavishkar Salvi						
Fall of wickets: 1–8 (Dheeraj Jadhav, 1.2 ov), 2–177 (Gautam Gambhir, 34.4 ov)						

BOWLING	O	M	R	W	ECON	0s	4s	6s	WD	NB
Iftikhar Anjum	7	1	33	0	4.71	0	0	0	0	1
Riaz Afridi	8	1	22	0	2.75	0	0	0	2	0
Junaid Zia	10	0	63	0	6.30	0	0	0	6	1
Mansoor Amjad	10	0	68	0	6.80	0	0	0	1	4
Qaiser Abbas	10	0	47	1	4.70	0	0	0	0	0

Result: India A won by 8 wickets

The Vizag Vig Vang

INDIA		R	B	M	4s	6s	SR
Virender Sehwag	c Salman Butt b Naved–ul–Hasan	74	40	67	12	2	185.00
Sachin Tendulkar	run out (Yousuf Youhana)	2	8	17	0	0	25.00
MS Dhoni †	c Shoaib Malik b Mohammad Hafeez	148	123	155	15	4	120.32
Sourav Ganguly (c)	b Mohammad Sami	9	22	24	1	0	40.90
Rahul Dravid	c Shahid Afridi b Naved–ul–Hasan	52	59	83	3	0	88.13
Yuvraj Singh	lbw b Arshad Khan	15	10	21	2	0	150.00
Mohammad Kaif	lbw b Naved–ul–Hasan	0	1	2	0	0	0.00
Harbhajan Singh	b Arshad Khan	11	16	20	1	0	68.75
Lakshmipathy Balaji	not out	17	13	19	0	1	130.76
Zaheer Khan	c Abdul Razzaq b Mohammad Hafeez	17	9	11	0	2	188.88
Extras	(lb 2, nb 1, w 8)	11					
TOTAL	50 Ov (RR: 7.12, 214 Mts)	356/9					
Did not bat: Ashish Nehra							
Fall of wickets: 1–26 (Sachin Tendulkar, 3.2 ov), 2–122 (Virender Sehwag, 13.4 ov), 3–140 (Sourav Ganguly, 19.2 ov), 4–289 (MS Dhoni, 41.2 ov), 5–300 (Rahul Dravid, 42.1 ov), 6–301 (Mohammad Kaif, 42.4 ov), 7–318 (Yuvraj Singh, 45.5 ov), 8–325 (Harbhajan Singh, 47.2 ov), 9–356 (Zaheer Khan, 49.6 ov)							

BOWLING	O	M	R	W	ECON	0s	4s	6s	WD	NB
Mohammad Sami	9	0	65	1	7.22	27	7	2	3	0
Naved–ul–Hasan	10	0	54	3	5.40	35	6	1	1	1
Abdul Razzaq	10	0	55	0	5.50	29	6	0	0	0
Shahid Afridi	9	0	82	0	9.11	20	9	3	2	0
Arshad Khan	5	0	43	2	8.60	10	2	2	1	0
Mohammad Hafeez	7	0	55	2	7.85	10	4	1	0	0

Result: India won by 58 runs

Bigger Bang on Diwali
(Target: 299 runs from 50 overs)

INDIA		R	B	M	4s	6s	SR
Virender Sehwag	lbw b Muralidaran	39	37	67	3	0	105.40
Sachin Tendulkar	C †Sangakkara b Vaas	2	3	2	0	0	66.66
MS Dhoni †	not out	183	145	210	15	10	126.20
Rahul Dravid (c)	c & b Muralidaran	28	34	55	2	0	82.35
Yuvraj Singh	b Dilshan	18	24	48	3	0	75.00
Venugopal Rao	not out	19	39	40	1	1	48.71
Extras	(b 5, lb 3, nb 5, w 1)	14					
TOTAL	46.1 Ov (RR: 6.56, 213 Mts)	303/4					

Did not bat: Jai Prakash Yadav, Irfan Pathan, Ajit Agarkar, Harbhajan Singh, Suresh Raina

Fall of wickets: 1–7 (Sachin Tendulkar, 0.5 ov), 2–99 (Virender Sehwag, 14.5 ov), 3–185 (Rahul Dravid, 27.2 ov), 4–250 (Yuvraj Singh, 36.5 ov)

BOWLING	O	M	R	W	ECON	WD	NB
Chaminda Vaas	6	0	43	1	7.16	0	0
Dilhara Fernando	8	0	38	0	4.75	1	4
Farveez Maharoof	7	0	50	0	7.14	0	0
Muthiah Muralidaran	10	1	46	2	4.60	0	0
Upul Chandana	10	0	83	0	8.30	0	1
Tillakaratne Dilshan	5.1	0	35	1	6.77	0	0

Result: India won by 6 wickets

Can Do It in Whites Too

INDIA 1ST INNINGS		R	B	M	4s	6s	SR
Virender Sehwag	c sub (Imran Farhat) b Abdul Razzaq	31	43	57	6	0	72.09
Rahul Dravid (c)	run out (sub [Imran Farhat])	103	220	342	16	0	46.81
VVS Laxman	c †Kamran Akmal b Danish Kaneria	90	208	268	11	0	43.26
Sachin Tendulkar	c †Kamran Akmal b Shoaib Akhtar	14	33	64	3	0	42.42
Yuvraj Singh	c Danish Kaneria b Mohammad Asif	4	21	28	0	0	19.04
MS Dhoni †	st †Kamran Akmal b Danish Kaneria	148	153	229	19	4	96.73
Irfan Pathan	lbw b Abdul Razzaq	90	170	269	9	2	52.94
Anil Kumble	st †Kamran Akmal b Danish Kaneria	15	60	86	1	0	25.00
Harbhajan Singh	lbw b Shahid Afridi	38	48	49	5	2	79.16
Zaheer Khan	not out	20	32	45	2	1	62.50
RP Singh	c & b Shahid Afridi	6	29	23	0	0	20.68
Extras	(b 3, lb 15, nb 23, w 3)	44					
TOTAL	165.4 Ov (RR: 3.63, 733 Mts)	603					

Fall of wickets: 1-39 (Virender Sehwag, 11.3 ov), 2-236 (VVS Laxman, 75.3 ov), 3-241 (Rahul Dravid, 78.3 ov), 4-258 (Yuvraj Singh, 83.4 ov), 5-281 (Sachin Tendulkar, 86.3 ov), 6-491 (MS Dhoni, 131.4 ov), 7-529 (Irfan Pathan, 144.5 ov), 8-553 (Anil Kumble, 152.1 ov), 9-587 (Harbhajan Singh, 159.1 ov), 10-603 (RP Singh, 165.4 ov)

BOWLING	O	M	R	W	ECON	WD	NB
Shoaib Akhtar	25	7	100	1	4.00	1	4
Mohammad Asif	34	6	103	1	3.02	1	3
Abdul Razzaq	28	1	126	2	4.50	0	13
Danish Kaneria	54	6	165	3	3.05	1	3
Shahid Afridi	24.4	0	91	2	3.68	0	0

Result: Match Drawn

Pakistan Pummelled, Again!
(Target: 289 runs from 50 overs)

INDIA		R	B	M	4s	6s	SR
Gautam Gambhir	b Mohammad Asif	2	8	9	0	0	25.00
Sachin Tendulkar	c sub (Imran Farhat) b Abdul Razzaq	95	104	157	16	1	91.34
Irfan Pathan	c †Kamran Akmal b Mohammad Asif	0	2	2	0	0	0.00
Rahul Dravid (c)	run out (Umar Gul)	22	42	74	4	0	52.38
Yuvraj Singh	not out	79	87	135	10	0	90.80
Mohammad Kaif	lbw b Umar Gul	0	2	4	0	0	0.00
MS Dhoni †	not out	72	46	60	13	0	156.52
Extras	(lb 11, nb 5, w 6)	22					
TOTAL	47.4 Ov (RR: 6.12, 223 Mts)	292/5					

Did not bat: Suresh Raina, Zaheer Khan, RP Singh, Sreesanth

Fall of wickets: 1–12 (Gautam Gambhir, 2.1 ov), 2–12 (Irfan Pathan, 2.3 ov), 3–84 (Rahul Dravid, 18.2 ov), 4–189 (Sachin Tendulkar, 33.6 ov), 5–190 (Mohammad Kaif, 34.4 ov)

BOWLING	O	M	R	W	ECON	0s	4s	6s	WD	NB
Mohammad Asif	10	0	47	2	4.70	42	8	0	2	1
Umar Gul	10	1	42	1	4.20	41	7	0	2	0
Naved-ul–Hasan	8	0	72	0	9.00	24	12	1	1	3
Yasir Arafat	9	0	53	0	5.88	25	7	0	0	1
Shahid Afridi	3	0	24	0	8.00	4	3	0	1	0
Abdul Razzaq	7.4	0	43	1	5.60	28	6	0	0	0

Result: India won by 8 wickets

In a Different Avatar!

INDIA		R	B	M	4s	6s	SR
Virender Sehwag (c)	c Solanki b Anderson	4	5	2	1	0	80.00
MS Dhoni †	c Solanki b Mahmood	96	106	174	10	3	90.56
Mohammad Kaif	lbw b Mahmood	15	21	26	2	0	71.42
Yuvraj Singh	b Plunkett	4	11	15	0	0	36.36
Suresh Raina	c †Prior b Plunkett	2	7	12	0	0	28.57
Venugopal Rao	c †Prior b Anderson	10	11	11	2	0	90.90
Ramesh Powar	c Hoggard b Collingwood	54	83	118	4	1	65.06
Harbhajan Singh	b Pietersen	4	8	10	0	0	50.00
RP Singh	c Blackwell b Mahmood	7	20	23	0	0	35.00
Vikram Singh	c Blackwell b Anderson	8	13	18	1	0	61.53
Munaf Patel	not out	1	3	5	0	0	33.33
Extras	(lb 4, w 14)	18					
TOTAL	**48 Ov (RR: 4.64)**	**223**					

Fall of wickets: 1–4 (Virender Sehwag, 0.5 ov), 2–46 (Mohammad Kaif, 7.1 ov), 3–58 (Yuvraj Singh, 10.3 ov), 4–63 (Suresh Raina, 12.3 ov), 5–79 (Venugopal Rao, 15.3 ov), 6–186 (MS Dhoni, 38.1 ov), 7–196 (Harbhajan Singh, 40.2 ov), 8–209 (Ramesh Powar, 43.2 ov), 9–216 (RP Singh, 46.3 ov), 10–223 (Vikram Singh, 47.6 ov)

BOWLING	O	M	R	W	ECON	0s	4s	6s	WD	NB
James Anderson	9	2	28	3	3.11	40	4	0	1	0
Matthew Hoggard	8	0	59	0	7.37	21	7	1	2	0
Sajid Mahmood	8	0	37	3	4.62	29	3	0	6	0
Liam Plunkett	5	0	22	2	4.40	21	3	0	2	0
Ian Blackwell	10	0	33	0	3.30	38	1	1	0	0
Vikram Solanki	4	0	25	0	6.25	14	1	2	0	0
Kevin Pietersen	1	0	4	1	4.00	3	0	0	0	0
Paul Collingwood	3	0	11	1	3.66	12	1	0	1	0

Result: England won by 5 wickets

Dhoni the Basher, Who?

(Target: 380 runs)

INDIA 2ND INNINGS		R	B	M	4s	6s	SR
Wasim Jaffer	c Pietersen b Anderson	8	32	47	0	0	25.00
Dinesh Karthik	c Collingwood b Anderson	60	135	210	7	0	44.44
Rahul Dravid (c)	lbw b Tremlett	9	12	18	2	0	75.00
Sachin Tendulkar	lbw b Panesar	16	35	42	3	0	45.71
Sourav Ganguly	lbw b Sidebottom	40	65	86	6	0	61.53
VVS Laxman	b Tremlett	39	90	132	5	0	43.33
MS Dhoni †	not out	76	159	203	10	0	47.79
Anil Kumble	lbw b Sidebottom	3	19	29	0	0	15.78
Zaheer Khan	c †Prior b Tremlett	0	15	20	0	0	0.00
RP Singh	b Panesar	2	8	13	0	0	25.00
Sreesanth	not out	4	7	15	1	0	57.14
Extras	(b 13, lb 5, nb 1, w 6)	25					
TOTAL	96 Ov (RR: 2.93, 414 Mts)	282/9					

Fall of wickets: 1–38 (Wasim Jaffer, 10.3 ov), 2–55 (Rahul Dravid, 13.5 ov), 3–84 (Sachin Tendulkar, 24.5 ov), 4–143 (Sourav Ganguly, 44.6 ov), 5–145 (Dinesh Karthik, 47.2 ov), 6–231 (VVS Laxman, 75.6 ov), 7–247 (Anil Kumble, 82.6 ov), 8–254 (Zaheer Khan, 87.5 ov), 9–263 (RP Singh, 90.6 ov)

BOWLING	O	M	R	W	ECON	WD	NB
Ryan Sidebottom	19	4	42	2	2.21	0	0
James Anderson	25	4	83	2	3.32	2	0
Chris Tremlett	21	5	52	3	2.47	0	1
Monty Panesar	26	7	63	2	2.42	0	0
Paul Collingwood	1	0	6	0	6.00	0	0
Michael Vaughan	4	0	18	0	4.50	0	0

Result: Match Drawn

The Captain–Batsman Takes Centre Stage

INDIA		R	B	M	4s	6s	SR
Virender Sehwag	c Hilfenhaus b Johnson	**40**	31	49	6	1	129.03
Sachin Tendulkar	c White b Siddle	**4**	8	14	1	0	50.00
Gautam Gambhir	run out (Hauritz)	**76**	80	136	6	0	95.00
Yuvraj Singh	c & b Hilfenhaus	**23**	24	24	2	1	95.83
MS Dhoni (c)†	c †Paine b Johnson	**124**	107	141	9	3	115.88
Suresh Raina	c †Paine b Johnson	**62**	50	68	6	1	124.00
Harbhajan Singh	not out	**1**	1	3	0	0	100.00
Praveen Kumar	run out (Siddle/†Paine)	**1**	1	1	0	0	100.00
Extras	(b 1, lb 6, nb 2, w 14)	**23**					
TOTAL	**50 Ov (RR: 7.08, 223 Mts)**	**354/7**					

Did not bat: Ravindra Jadeja, Ashish Nehra, Ishant Sharma

Fall of wickets: 1–21 (Sachin Tendulkar, 3.3 ov), 2–67 (Virender Sehwag, 10.1 ov), 3–97 (Yuvraj Singh, 15.1 ov), 4–216 (Gautam Gambhir, 33.6 ov), 5–352 (MS Dhoni, 49.3 ov), 6–353 (Suresh Raina, 49.5 ov), 7–354 (Praveen Kumar, 49.6 ov)

BOWLING	O	M	R	W	ECON	0s	4s	6s	WD	NB
Ben Hilfenhaus	10	0	83	**1**	8.30	24	9	2	4	1
Peter Siddle	10	0	55	**1**	5.50	33	7	0	3	0
Mitchell Johnson	10	0	75	**3**	7.50	23	7	1	5	1
Nathan Hauritz	10	0	54	**0**	5.40	26	4	1	0	0
Adam Voges	5	0	33	**0**	6.60	5	1	0	1	0
Shane Watson	5	0	47	**0**	9.40	5	2	2	0	0

Result: India won by 99 runs

Dial D for a Clinical Chase
(Target: 297 runs from 50 overs)

INDIA		R	B	M	4s	6s	SR
Gautam Gambhir	b Rubel Hossain	**18**	24	37	2	0	75.00
Virender Sehwag	run out (Abdur Razzak)	**13**	8	17	2	0	162.50
Virat Kohli	c & b Shakib Al Hasan	**91**	102	136	7	0	89.21
Yuvraj Singh	b Syed Rasel	**1**	4	5	0	0	25.00
MS Dhoni (c) †	not out	**101**	107	167	9	0	94.39
Suresh Raina	not out	**51**	43	57	5	1	118.60
Extras	(lb 6, nb 3, w 13)	**22**					
TOTAL	**47.3 Ov (RR: 6.25)**	**297/4**					

Did not bat: Ravindra Jadeja, Harbhajan Singh, Zaheer Khan, Ashish Nehra, Sreesanth

Fall of wickets: 1–28 (Virender Sehwag, 3.1 ov), 2–49 (Gautam Gambhir, 7.3 ov), 3–51 (Yuvraj Singh, 8.1 ov), 4–203 (Virat Kohli, 34.6 ov)

BOWLING	O	M	R	W	ECON	0s	4s	6s	WD	NB
Syed Rasel	9.3	0	58	**1**	6.10	33	8	0	2	2
Abdur Razzak	9	0	66	**0**	7.33	20	7	0	4	0
Rubel Hossain	9	0	60	**1**	6.66	23	5	1	3	1
Shakib Al Hasan	10	0	45	**1**	4.50	26	1	0	1	0
Naeem Islam	2	0	16	**0**	8.00	1	1	0	0	0
Mahmudullah	7	0	38	**0**	5.42	15	2	0	1	0
Mohammad Ashraful	1	0	8	**0**	8.00	1	1	0	0	0

Result: India won by 6 wickets

Ice Catches Fire in Dharamsala

(Target: 193 runs from 20 overs)

CHENNAI SUPER KINGS INNINGS		R	B	4s	6s	SR
Murali Vijay	st †Sangakkara b Powar	13	11	2	0	118.18
Matthew Hayden	c †Sangakkara b Powar	5	8	1	0	62.50
Suresh Raina	c Goel b Theron	46	27	5	3	170.37
S Badrinath	st †Sangakkara b Chawla	53	36	7	2	147.22
MS Dhoni (c)†	not out	54	29	5	2	186.20
Albie Morkel	not out	14	8	2	0	175.00
Extras	(lb 5, nb 1, w 4)	10				
TOTAL	19.4 Ov (RR: 9.91)	195/4				

Did not bat: Justin Kemp, Ravichandran Ashwin, Shadab Jakati, Doug Bollinger, Sudeep Tyagi

Fall of wickets: 1–13 (Matthew Hayden, 2.5 ov), 2–27 (Murali Vijay, 4 ov), 3–89 (Suresh Raina, 9.4 ov), 4–148 (S Badrinath, 16.4 ov)

BOWLING	O	M	R	W	ECON	0s	4s	6s	WD	NB
Ramesh Powar	4	0	28	2	7.00	11	3	1	1	0
Irfan Pathan	3.4	0	44	0	12.00	7	6	2	0	0
Vikram Singh	3	0	40	0	13.33	5	4	2	2	1
Piyush Chawla	4	0	28	1	7.00	11	3	1	0	0
Rusty Theron	4	0	43	1	10.75	4	5	1	1	0
Yuvraj Singh	1	0	7	0	7.00	2	1	0	0	0

Result: Super Kings won by 6 wickets

The Biggest Night
(Target: 275 runs from 50 overs)

INDIA		R	B	M	4s	6s	SR
Virender Sehwag	lbw b Malinga	0	2	2	0	0	0.00
Sachin Tendulkar	c †Sangakkara b Malinga	18	14	21	2	0	128.57
Gautam Gambhir	b Perera	97	122	187	9	0	79.50
Virat Kohli	c & b Dilshan	35	49	69	4	0	71.42
MS Dhoni (c)†	not out	91	79	128	8	2	115.18
Yuvraj Singh	not out	21	24	39	2	0	87.50
Extras	(b 1, lb 6, w 8)	15					
TOTAL	48.2 Ov (RR: 5.73, 230 Mts)	277/4					

Did not bat: Suresh Raina, Harbhajan Singh, Zaheer Khan, Munaf Patel, Sreesanth

Fall of wickets: 1–0 (Virender Sehwag, 0.2 ov), 2–31 (Sachin Tendulkar, 6.1 ov), 3–114 (Virat Kohli, 21.4 ov), 4–223 (Gautam Gambhir, 41.2 ov)

BOWLING	O	M	R	W	ECON	0s	4s	6s	WD	NB
Lasith Malinga	9	0	42	2	4.66	31	4	0	2	0
Nuwan Kulasekara	8.2	0	64	0	7.68	20	8	1	0	0
Thisara Perera	9	0	55	1	6.11	27	5	1	2	0
Suraj Randiv	9	0	43	0	4.77	24	3	0	0	0
Tillakaratne Dilshan	5	0	27	1	5.40	14	2	0	1	0
Muthiah Muralidaran	8	0	39	0	4.87	23	3	0	1	0

Result: India won by 6 wickets

The Formula Works, Again!
(Target: 270 runs from 50 overs)

INDIA		R	B	M	4s	6s	SR
Gautam Gambhir	lbw b McKay	92	111	140	7	0	82.88
Virender Sehwag	c Hussey b McKay	20	21	38	3	0	95.23
Virat Kohli	c Forrest b McKay	18	28	41	1	0	64.28
Rohit Sharma	c Starc b Harris	33	41	49	1	1	80.48
Suresh Raina	b Doherty	38	30	65	3	1	126.66
MS Dhoni (c)†	not out	44	58	76	0	1	75.86
Ravindra Jadeja	c Ponting b Doherty	12	8	11	0	0	150.00
Ravichandran Ashwin	not out	1	2	8	0	0	50.00
Extras	(lb 2, nb 1, w 9)	12					
TOTAL	49.4 Ov (RR: 5.43, 217 Mts)	270/6					

Did not bat: Vinay Kumar, Zaheer Khan, Umesh Yadav

Fall of wickets: 1–52 (Virender Sehwag, 9.1 ov), 2–90 (Virat Kohli, 18.1 ov), 3–166 (Rohit Sharma, 32.2 ov), 4–178 (Gautam Gambhir, 34.1 ov), 5–239 (Suresh Raina, 46.1 ov), 6–257 (Ravindra Jadeja, 48.4 ov)

BOWLING	O	M	R	W	ECON	0s	4s	6s	WD	NB
Ryan Harris	10	0	57	1	5.70	29	6	0	1	0
Mitchell Starc	8	0	49	0	6.12	21	4	1	1	0
Clint McKay	9.4	1	53	3	5.48	31	3	1	2	1
Dan Christian	10	0	45	0	4.50	25	2	0	0	0
David Hussey	3	0	13	0	4.33	5	0	0	0	0
Xavier Doherty	9	0	51	2	5.66	19	0	1	2	0

Result: India won by 4 wickets

Magician Mahi's Rescue Act

INDIA		R	B	M	4s	6s	SR
Gautam Gambhir	b Mohammad Irfan	8	17	25	1	0	47.05
Virender Sehwag	b Junaid Khan	4	11	20	1	0	36.36
Virat Kohli	b Junaid Khan	0	5	9	0	0	0.00
Yuvraj Singh	b Junaid Khan	2	3	6	0	0	66.66
Rohit Sharma	c Mohammad Hafeez b Junaid Khan	4	14	19	0	0	28.57
Suresh Raina	b Mohammad Hafeez	43	88	116	2	0	48.86
MS Dhoni (c)†	not out	113	125	177	7	3	90.40
Ravichandran Ashwin	not out	31	39	78	2	0	79.48
Extras	(lb 11, nb 2, w 9)	22					
TOTAL	50 Ov (RR: 4.54, 228 Mts)	227/6					

Did not bat: Bhuvneshwar Kumar, Ishant Sharma, Ashok Dinda

Fall of wickets: 1–17 (Virender Sehwag, 3.5 ov), 2–17 (Gautam Gambhir, 4.4 ov), 3–19 (Virat Kohli, 5.4 ov), 4–20 (Yuvraj Singh, 5.6 ov), 5–29 (Rohit Sharma, 9.4 ov), 6–102 (Suresh Raina, 33.2 ov)

BOWLING	O	M	R	W	ECON	0s	4s	6s	WD	NB
Mohammad Irfan	9	2	58	1	6.44	26	6	1	1	0
Junaid Khan	9	1	43	4	4.77	35	3	1	2	2
Umar Gul	8	0	38	0	4.75	27	2	0	1	0
Saeed Ajmal	10	1	42	0	4.20	33	2	1	0	0
Mohammad Hafeez	10	2	26	1	2.60	38	0	0	0	0
Shoaib Malik	4	0	9	0	2.25	16	0	0	1	0

Result: Pakistan won by 6 wickets

Thala Enthrals Chennai in Whites!

INDIA 1ST INNINGS		R	B	M	4s	6s	SR
Murali Vijay	b Pattinson	10	15	17	2	0	66.66
Virender Sehwag	b Pattinson	2	11	28	0	0	18.18
Cheteshwar Pujara	b Pattinson	44	74	116	6	0	59.45
Sachin Tendulkar	b Lyon	81	159	257	7	0	50.94
Virat Kohli	c Starc b Lyon	107	206	266	15	1	51.94
MS Dhoni (c)†	c †Wade b Pattinson	224	265	365	24	6	84.52
Ravindra Jadeja	b Pattinson	16	45	63	3	0	35.55
Ravichandran Ashwin	b Lyon	3	6	13	0	0	50.00
Harbhajan Singh	b Henriques	11	31	37	0	1	35.48
Bhuvneshwar Kumar	c Clarke b Siddle	38	97	167	4	0	39.17
Ishant Sharma	not out	4	18	32	0	0	22.22
Extras	(b 14, lb 14, w 4)	32					
TOTAL	154.3 Ov (RR: 3.70, 685 Mts)	572					

Fall of wickets: 1–11 (Murali Vijay, 3.2 ov), 2–12 (Virender Sehwag, 5.2 ov), 3–105 (Cheteshwar Pujara, 28.4 ov), 4–196 (Sachin Tendulkar, 63.1 ov), 5–324 (Virat Kohli, 89.2 ov), 6–365 (Ravindra Jadeja, 102.6 ov), 7–372 (Ravichandran Ashwin, 105.4 ov), 8–406 (Harbhajan Singh, 115.2 ov), 9–546 (MS Dhoni, 146.3 ov), 10–572 (Bhuvneshwar Kumar, 154.3 ov)

BOWLING	O	M	R	W	ECON	WD	NB
Mitchell Starc	25	3	75	0	3.00	2	0
James Pattinson	30	6	96	5	3.20	2	0
Peter Siddle	24.3	5	66	1	2.69	0	0
Nathan Lyon	47	1	215	3	4.57	0	0
Moises Henriques	17	4	48	1	2.82	0	0
Michael Clarke	8	2	25	0	3.12	0	0
David Warner	3	0	19	0	6.33	0	0

Result: India won by 8 wickets

The Caribbean Heist
(Target: 202 runs from 50 overs)

INDIA		R	B	M	4s	6s	SR
Rohit Sharma	b Herath	58	89	146	5	1	65.16
Shikhar Dhawan	c †Sangakkara b Eranga	16	35	38	2	0	45.71
Virat Kohli	c †Sangakkara b Eranga	2	5	8	0	0	40.00
Dinesh Karthik	c Jayawardene b Herath	23	37	58	3	0	62.16
Suresh Raina	c †Sangakkara b Lakmal	32	27	51	1	1	118.51
MS Dhoni (c)†	not out	45	52	98	5	2	86.53
Ravindra Jadeja	lbw b Herath	5	14	15	0	0	35.71
Ravichandran Ashwin	lbw b Herath	0	1	1	0	0	0.00
Bhuvneshwar Kumar	lbw b Malinga	0	15	21	0	0	0.00
Vinay Kumar	c sub (SMSM Senanayake) b Mathews	5	16	25	0	0	31.25
Ishant Sharma	not out	2	7	17	0	0	28.57
Extras	(b 2, lb 2, w 11)	15					
TOTAL	49.4 Ov (RR: 4.08)	203/9					

Fall of wickets: 1–23 (Shikhar Dhawan, 8.4 ov), 2–27 (Virat Kohli, 10.4 ov), 3–77 (Dinesh Karthik, 22.6 ov), 4–139 (Rohit Sharma, 31.1 ov), 5–145 (Suresh Raina, 34.1 ov), 6–152 (Ravindra Jadeja, 37.1 ov), 7–152 (Ravichandran Ashwin, 37.2 ov), 8–167 (Bhuvneshwar Kumar, 41.5 ov), 9–182 (Vinay Kumar, 46.2 ov)

BOWLING	O	M	R	W	ECON	0s	4s	6s	WD	NB
Shaminda Eranga	9.4	2	50	2	5.17	37	4	2	1	0
Suranga Lakmal	10	1	33	1	3.30	41	1	1	3	0
Angelo Mathews	10	1	38	1	3.80	38	3	0	0	0
Lasith Malinga	10	1	58	1	5.80	34	7	1	3	0
Rangana Herath	10	2	20	4	2.00	45	1	0	0	0

Result: India won by 1 wicket

Standing Tall amidst the Ruins
Fourth Test

INDIA 1ST INNINGS		R	B	M	4s	6s	SR
Murali Vijay	c Cook b Anderson	0	14	19	0	0	0.00
Gautam Gambhir	c Root b Broad	4	7	13	0	0	57.14
Cheteshwar Pujara	c Jordan b Broad	0	6	13	0	0	0.00
Virat Kohli	c Cook b Anderson	0	2	3	0	0	0.00
Ajinkya Rahane	c Bell b Jordan	24	52	90	3	0	46.15
MS Dhoni (c)†	c Jordan b Broad	71	133	200	15	0	53.38
Ravindra Jadeja	lbw b Anderson	0	7	13	0	0	0.00
Ravichandran Ashwin	c Robson b Broad	40	42	69	3	1	95.23
Bhuvneshwar Kumar	b Broad	0	6	9	0	0	0.00
Varun Aaron	not out	1	8	24	0	0	12.50
Pankaj Singh	b Broad	0	3	3	0	0	0.00
Extras	(b 10, lb 1, w 1)	12					
TOTAL	46.4 Ov (RR: 3.25, 232 Mts)	152					

Fall of wickets: 1–8 (Gautam Gambhir, 3.1 ov), 2–8 (Murali Vijay, 4.2 ov), 3–8 (Virat Kohli, 4.4 ov), 4–8 (Cheteshwar Pujara, 5.1 ov), 5–62 (Ajinkya Rahane, 23.2 ov), 6–63 (Ravindra Jadeja, 26.3 ov), 7–129 (Ravichandran Ashwin, 40.2 ov), 8–137 (Bhuvneshwar Kumar, 42.2 ov), 9–152 (MS Dhoni, 46.1 ov), 10–152 (Pankaj Singh, 46.4 ov)

BOWLING	O	M	R	W	ECON	WD	NB
James Anderson	14	3	46	3	3.28	0	0
Stuart Broad	13.4	6	25	6	1.82	0	0
Chris Woakes	10	1	43	0	4.30	1	0
Chris Jordan	9	4	27	1	3.00	0	0

Result: England won by an innings and 54 runs

Fifth Test

INDIA 1ST INNINGS		R	B	M	4s	6s	SR
Murali Vijay	c Root b Woakes	18	64	91	0	0	28.12
Gautam Gambhir	c †Buttler b Anderson	0	1	3	0	0	0.00
Cheteshwar Pujara	b Broad	4	19	24	0	0	21.05
Virat Kohli	lbw b Jordan	6	18	34	1	0	33.33
Ajinkya Rahane	c & b Jordan	0	8	13	0	0	0.00
MS Dhoni (c)†	c Woakes b Broad	82	140	212	15	1	58.57
Stuart Binny	c Cook b Anderson	5	30	51	0	0	16.66
Ravichandran Ashwin	c Root b Woakes	13	17	31	1	0	76.47
Bhuvneshwar Kumar	c †Buttler b Jordan	5	11	12	1	0	45.45
Varun Aaron	c & b Woakes	1	17	27	0	0	5.88
Ishant Sharma	not out	7	42	73	0	0	16.66
Extras	(b 6, lb 1)	7					
TOTAL	**61.1 Ov (RR: 2.41, 289 Mts)**	148					

Fall of wickets: 1–3 (Gautam Gambhir, 0.4 ov), 2–10 (Cheteshwar Pujara, 5.6 ov), 3–26 (Virat Kohli, 13.4 ov), 4–28 (Ajinkya Rahane, 15.6 ov), 5–36 (Murali Vijay, 18.5 ov), 6–44 (Stuart Binny, 30.3 ov), 7–68 (Ravichandran Ashwin, 36.4 ov), 8–79 (Bhuvneshwar Kumar, 39.1 ov), 9–90 (Varun Aaron, 44.5 ov), 10–148 (MS Dhoni, 61.1 ov)

BOWLING	O	M	R	W	ECON	WD	NB
James Anderson	17	4	51	2	3.00	0	0
Stuart Broad	15.1	4	27	2	1.78	0	0
Chris Jordan	14	7	32	3	2.28	0	0
Chris Woakes	14	7	30	3	2.14	0	0
Moeen Ali	1	0	1	0	1.00	0	0

Result: England won by an innings and 244 runs

The Second Lead to the Second Lead
(Target: 288 runs from 50 overs)

INDIA		R	B	M	4s	6s	SR
Rohit Sharma	c Sikandar Raza b Panyangara	16	21	24	2	0	76.19
Shikhar Dhawan	b Panyangara	4	20	27	1	0	20.00
Virat Kohli	b Sikandar Raza	38	48	71	4	0	79.16
Ajinkya Rahane	run out (Sikandar Raza/†Taylor)	19	24	40	3	0	79.16
Suresh Raina	not out	110	104	141	9	4	105.76
MS Dhoni (c)†	not out	85	76	113	8	2	111.84
Extras	(b 1, lb 2, nb 1, w 12)	16					
TOTAL	48.4 Ov (RR: 5.91, 210 Mts)	288/4					

Did not bat: Ravindra Jadeja, Ravichandran Ashwin, Mohit Sharma, Mohammed Shami, Umesh Yadav

Fall of wickets: 1–21 (Rohit Sharma, 6.1 ov), 2–21 (Shikhar Dhawan, 6.5 ov), 3–71 (Ajinkya Rahane, 16.3 ov), 4–92 (Virat Kohli, 22.4 ov)

BOWLING	O	M	R	W	ECON	0s	4s	6s	WD	NB
Tinashe Panyangara	8.4	1	53	2	6.11	30	5	2	2	0
Tendai Chatara	10	1	59	0	5.90	35	8	0	6	1
Tawanda Mupariwa	10	0	61	0	6.10	25	5	1	2	0
Solomon Mire	5	0	29	0	5.80	15	4	0	0	0
Sean Williams	5	0	31	0	6.20	16	2	2	0	0
Sikandar Raza	8	0	37	1	4.62	20	2	0	1	0
Hamilton Masakadza	2	0	15	0	7.50	6	1	1	1	0

Result: India won by 6 wickets

Tiger Abhi Zinda Hai!

INDIA		R	B	M	4s	6s	SR
Rohit Sharma	b Rabada	3	10	6	0	0	30.00
Shikhar Dhawan	c Duminy b Morkel	23	34	57	4	0	67.64
Ajinkya Rahane	b Imran Tahir	51	63	94	6	0	80.95
Virat Kohli	run out (Behardien/ Steyn/†de Kock)	12	18	24	0	0	66.66
MS Dhoni (c)†	not out	92	86	144	7	4	106.97
Suresh Raina	c †de Kock b Morkel	0	5	6	0	0	0.00
Axar Patel	lbw b Steyn	13	27	20	0	1	48.14
Bhuvneshwar Kumar	b Imran Tahir	14	32	42	1	0	43.75
Harbhajan Singh	c †de Kock b Steyn	22	22	33	2	1	100.00
Umesh Yadav	c †de Kock b Steyn	4	3	3	1	0	133.33
Mohit Sharma	not out	0	1	16	0	0	0.00
Extras	(lb 2, nb 1, w 10)	13					
TOTAL	50 Ov (RR: 4.94, 227 Mts)	247/9					

Fall of wickets: 1–3 (Rohit Sharma, 1.4 ov), 2–59 (Shikhar Dhawan, 12.3 ov), 3–82 (Virat Kohli, 17.6 ov),
4–102 (Ajinkya Rahane, 22.4 ov), 5–104 (Suresh Raina, 23.4 ov), 6–124 (Axar Patel, 29.3 ov), 7–165 (Bhuvneshwar Kumar, 39.3 ov), 8–221 (Harbhajan Singh, 46.3 ov), 9–225 (Umesh Yadav, 46.6 ov)

BOWLING	O	M	R	W	ECON	0s	4s	6s	WD	NB
Dale Steyn	10	0	49	3	4.90	38	7	0	2	0
Kagiso Rabada	10	1	49	1	4.90	43	7	1	3	1
Morne Morkel	10	0	42	2	4.20	32	3	0	3	0
Jean–Paul Duminy	9	0	59	0	6.55	26	3	4	1	0
Imran Tahir	10	1	42	2	4.20	28	1	1	1	0
Farhaan Behardien	1	0	4	0	4.00	3	0	0	0	0

Result: India won by 22 runs

Marvellous at the G!
(Target: 231 runs from 50 overs)

INDIA		R	B	4s	6s	SR
Rohit Sharma	c Marsh b Siddle	9	17	1	0	52.94
Shikhar Dhawan	c & b Stoinis	23	46	0	0	50.00
Virat Kohli (c)	c †Carey b Richardson	46	62	3	0	74.19
MS Dhoni †	not out	87	114	6	0	76.31
Kedar Jadhav	not out	61	57	7	0	107.01
Extras	(lb 1, w 7)	8				
TOTAL	49.2 Ov (RR: 4.74)	234/3				
Did not bat: Dinesh Karthik, Vijay Shankar, Ravindra Jadeja, Bhuvneshwar Kumar, Mohammed Shami, Yuzvendra Chahal						
Fall of wickets: 1–15 (Rohit Sharma, 5.6 ov), 2–59 (Shikhar Dhawan, 16.2 ov), 3–113 (Virat Kohli, 29.6 ov)						

BOWLING	O	M	R	W	ECON	0s	4s	6s	WD	NB
Jhye Richardson	10	1	27	1	2.70	41	0	0	2	0
Peter Siddle	9	1	56	1	6.22	28	6	0	3	0
Billy Stanlake	10	0	49	0	4.90	32	4	0	1	0
Glenn Maxwell	1	0	7	0	7.00	1	0	0	0	0
Adam Zampa	10	0	34	0	3.40	32	0	0	0	0
Marcus Stoinis	9.2	0	60	1	6.42	27	7	0	1	0

Result: India won by 7 wickets

2.0

(Target: 162 runs from 20 overs)

CHENNAI SUPER KINGS INNINGS		R	B	M	4s	6s	SR
Shane Watson	c Stoinis b Steyn	5	3	6	1	0	166.66
Faf du Plessis	c de Villiers b Yadav	5	15	25	0	0	33.33
Suresh Raina	b Steyn	0	1	1	0	0	0.00
Ambati Rayudu	b Chahal	29	29	66	2	1	100.00
Kedar Jadhav	c de Villiers b Yadav	9	9	10	2	0	100.00
MS Dhoni (c) †	not out	84	48	82	5	7	175.00
Ravindra Jadeja	run out (Saini)	11	12	19	0	0	91.66
Dwayne Bravo	C †Patel b Saini	5	4	16	0	0	125.00
Shardul Thakur	run out (†Patel)	0	0	8	0	0	–
Extras	(lb 9, nb 1, w 2)	12					
TOTAL	20 Ov (RR: 8.00, 116 Mts)	160/8					

Did not bat: Deepak Chahar, Imran Tahir

Fall of wickets: 1–6 (Shane Watson, 0.5 ov), 2–6 (Suresh Raina, 0.6 ov), 3–17 (Faf du Plessis, 3.6 ov), 4–28 (Kedar Jadhav, 5.5 ov), 5–83 (Ambati Rayudu, 13.1 ov), 6–108 (Ravindra Jadeja, 16.4 ov), 7–136 (Dwayne Bravo, 18.6 ov), 8–160 (Shardul Thakur, 19.6 ov)

BOWLING	O	M	R	W	ECON	0s	4s	6s	WD	NB
Dale Steyn	4	0	29	2	7.25	8	2	1	0	0
Navdeep Saini	4	0	24	1	6.00	15	2	1	0	1
Umesh Yadav	4	0	47	2	11.75	11	4	4	1	0
Pawan Negi	1	0	7	0	7.00	2	1	0	0	0
Marcus Stoinis	3	0	20	0	6.66	8	1	1	1	0
Yuzvendra Chahal	4	0	24	1	6.00	7	0	1	0	0

Result: Royal Challengers Bangalore won by 1 run

Photos by Kamal Sharma

MS Dhoni giving it all to start the penultimate over of the chase against New Zealand in the 2019 World Cup semi-final with a 6. The 6 proved to be his last in India colours as he would be run out by Martin Guptill one ball later.

The last walk back to the pavilion. Dhoni walks back after getting run out for 50 in the semi-final against New Zealand in the 2019 World Cup. India's final hope was gone with his departure.

Yuvraj Singh celebrates with his captain Mahendra Singh Dhoni, who has just finished the chase at the Wankhede against Sri Lanka in the 2011 World Cup Final with a 6.

MS Dhoni acknowledges the Wankhede crowd on his way to collecting the
World Cup trophy in the 2011 World Cup final against Sri Lanka.

There were two scores in excess of MS Dhoni's 91* in the 2011 World Cup final
but the Man of the Match went to the Indian captain, who had held forte till the
end and delivered the knockout punch.

MS Dhoni with the inaugural World T20 trophy won by India by beating
Pakistan in a nail-biting thriller at the Wanderers in Johannesburg.

A proud MS Dhoni with the World Cup medal around his neck walks hand in hand with wife Sakshi Dhoni at the end of the 2011 World Cup Final in Mumbai.

MS Dhoni's giving the final over of the 2007 World Cup final to unheralded medium pacer Joginder Sharma remains a masterstroke as Misbah-Ul-Haq got out to Sharma, allowing India to win the final by 5 runs.

MS Dhoni played crucial knocks when the team required runs from him. His 45 against South Africa on a difficult pitch and 36 against Australia in the semi-final were invaluable contributions.

MS Dhoni appeals from behind the stumps against New Zealand in the 2019 World Cup semi-final, which was also the 350th ODI played by him.

MS Dhoni takes off his helmet to celebrate his century against Sri Lanka in Jaipur. He would go on to take the century to his highest score of 183*.

The captain of the 2007 World T20 winning team enjoys the attention as he holds a placard that reads 'MS Dhoni for President'. Teammate Robin Uthappa is also amused.

MS Dhoni walks off with Yuvraj Singh and Zaheer Khan in India's Test series against Pakistan in 2006.

Over the years, MS Dhoni has chosen to don many hairstyles. Post the 2011 World Cup win, he took everyone by surprise by shaving off his head.

Lalit Modi handing over the Man of the Match cheque after MS Dhoni hit 183* at Jaipur against Sri Lanka to help India chase down 299 with ease.

Virender Sehwag hugs MS Dhoni after India's win in the 2007 World T20 final. Sehwag missed out the final due to an injury leading to MS Dhoni opening India's innings with Yusuf Pathan.

Completely focussed on his job in the 2005 bilateral series against Sri Lanka. The discussions around his captaincy and batting often obscured the man's efficiency behind the stumps.

Captain MS Dhoni with two men who took care of the top order for India for much of the initial years of Dhoni's captaincy career.

MS Dhoni drives one against Pakistan in the home series in 2007. He relished batting against Pakistan and averaged 64 against the arch-rivals in Tests and 53.52 in ODIs.

A young MS Dhoni signals thumbs up to the photographers after his whirlwind knock of 148 against Pakistan in the Faisalabad Test.

Captain MS Dhoni celebrates the 2007 World T20 triumph with his team after they successfully defended 157 in the final against Pakistan at the Wanderers.

The Indian team celebrating the 2007 World T20 win.

The Indian team celebrating the 2011 World Cup win.

MS Dhoni played under the captaincy of Sourav Ganguly and Rahul Dravid and
went on to captain them as well.

PART II

Dhoni through the Eyes of . . .

1

A Media Personality

Joy Bhattacharjya

It was May 2011 and midseason in the IPL, the night before CSK played KKR at Eden Gardens. The two teams had clashed on the opening day of the tournament and Chennai had prevailed right at the end, putting the squeeze on the KKR batting after Jacques Kallis and later Manoj Tiwary had put KKR in the pole position to win. However, as seemed inevitable in those days, Eoin Morgan was stumped by Dhoni, Gautam Gambhir was run out and CSK somehow contrived another unlikely win—yet another from a position that scarcely seemed possible.

Now, almost exactly a month later, KKR was again playing CSK at Eden Gardens. At dinner that evening in the KKR camp, the entire conversation was about the tactics we needed to deploy against CSK: how to restrict their run machines, David Hussey and Suresh Raina; how to counter the wiles of Ravichandran Ashwin, who was just making a mark; opening the bowling with Morkel; and as always, how to beat Dhoni.

Somebody then wondered what Dhoni would be worrying about at the time, and we all laughed aloud at the absurdity of it.

Dhoni worrying? He would be chatting away with his teammates in his hotel room with room service being ordered every half hour, or happily playing FIFA on his PlayStation! After all, worrying was for regular players and mortals; in 2011, Dhoni clearly didn't seem to belong to either category.

The next day CSK won the toss and chose to bat and then crawled to 114 in their 20 overs. Albie Morkel had been promoted in the order ahead of Dhoni and simply couldn't buy a run, ending with exactly 30 from his 30 balls, as Iqbal Abdullah and Rajat Bhatia gave him no pace to play with. Halfway through KKR's chase it started raining, and KKR finally won the match with Duckworth Lewis in the tenth over. Even though we got the points, it still felt like we had been cheated; the rain-affected result simply did not give the pleasure of a thumping win. The flip side? Even with Chennai's small total, there was always the feeling that had the match continued to 20 overs, Dhoni might have pulled off another sleight-of-hand win.

These were seasoned pros—not rabid fans or fresh-faced rookies—who felt that way about Dhoni. In those four years since he had first captained India in South Africa, Dhoni had already created an aura around him, which no one had ever had before in Indian cricket. While he didn't win every big game, it just seemed to everyone else that he did.

* * *

I first heard about Mahendra Singh Dhoni from Sourav Ganguly, the then Indian captain, on a tour of Bangladesh in 2004. A small aircraft was ferrying the team and some of the broadcast crew from Dhaka to Chittagong. Sourav was chatting affably about the travails of a Bangladesh tour. He excitedly mentioned a young cricketer from Jharkhand, who hit the ball harder than anyone he'd seen, calling him a 'chabuk player', a term literally meaning 'whiplike', often used in the Calcutta maidan to describe an exciting talent. As it turned out, Dhoni did little of note on that tour, but in the next series against Pakistan, he ensured he would be a fixture in the Indian team for time to come.

I've had the opportunity to watch Dhoni from three very different angles: as a television producer looking for good interviews and drama to put on screen; as the team director of an opposing IPL franchise, wondering which new way he'd find to put it across us; and finally as an analyst, that too at a time when his fabled reflexes and finishing skills seemed to be rapidly eroding.

For all his amazing feats before 2017, it's Dhoni's journey in the last few years that has been the most interesting. From his uncharacteristic 13 runs from 10 balls in the 2017 IPL final for the Rising Pune Supergiants that saw them lose to the Mumbai Indians, to that heartbreakingly close run-out in the 2019 World Cup semi-final, Dhoni was actually ending up marginally on the wrong side of close decisions. A year later, he led a CSK team that shockingly failed to qualify—for the first time—for the IPL play-offs, losing 8 of their first 11 games after losing Suresh Raina even before the tournament started, while looking old and out of practice in the field. Dhoni himself looked so woefully out of touch that many questioned whether he would want to play out another season.

Yet, the next year, Dhoni returned; still not the middle-order destroyer with the bat, but just as capable as a captain. With his top order, Rituraj Gaikwad, Faf du Plessis and Moeen Ali, firing and Ravindra Jadeja and Shardul Thakur giving him versatility with the ball and bat, CSK ascended to its more customary position at the top of the IPL heap. Although Dhoni finished with just 114 runs at a strike rate of 106, his team more than compensated for the slack.

Everyone wondered if Dhoni would be retained for the next series; after all, retaining a 40+ captain in a large auction that sets teams up for three years was a huge call, no matter how successful the captain is. But CSK always said they'd pick Dhoni, as long as he wanted to get picked, and they kept their word. It was in keeping with his desire to get the best deal for his top players that Dhoni requested that Jadeja be retained as the top pick, given his contribution to the side. That signals that he is comfortable with the idea of leading more talented and able players without feeling threatened.

It's fascinating to see how Dhoni has adjusted to the role of being a top captain, wicketkeeper and strategist without that fearsome finishing ability at the end. Even when he's not the batsman he was, it is instructive to hear from opposing players about how they still fear his abilities.

Dhoni has always had that unique ability of telling you everything and yet not revealing a single thing of significance. While he navigates what should be the last few years of a storied career, it will be fascinating to see how he plays his cards. As always, he'll keep us all guessing!

2

A Contemporary
Wicketkeeper-Batsman

Deep Dasgupta

Mavericks have always been products despite the system, and Mahendra Singh Dhoni is one such outlier who made unorthodox the 'new normal' in Indian cricket.

Indian cricket is almost certain to have a 'Pre-Dhoni Era' and a 'Post-Dhoni Era' with countless analyses and number crunchers trying to figure out what worked for him. However, to quantify his impact just with numbers would be criminal.

I did not exactly belong to MS Dhoni's inner circle of friends, but I did play a decent amount of first-class cricket with and against him between 2000 and 2005. So, I have some idea about the player he was back then.

Working as a broadcaster for over a decade after also helped me see his evolution into a world-class competitor and a fine captain, and arguably also the safest gloveman India has ever produced. Distance, they say, gives perspective and it probably helped me watch and analyse his game unbiasedly.

Where do I start? Well, why not the first time I saw him back in 2000 when Bihar was still playing the Ranji Trophy and we had a match at Eden Gardens?

If I recall correctly, a 19-year-old Dhoni had smashed Laxmi Ratan Shukla for 4 consecutive boundaries. Not much in terms of aesthetics but very high on brute power quotient.

Keepers, just like fast bowlers, have their own little competitions and I was a little agitated with Laxmi because of how he was being bludgeoned. What came next though was not something I was expecting. Laxmi was still a very skiddy bowler in those days and was in the standbys for the 1999 World Cup squad. He was livid and bowled a beamer, and yet Dhoni was totally unfazed. Standing behind, I could sense that this man's temperament was a bit different from the average first-class player. The next year, I was in the Indian team and I was busy with international commitments, but I would keep hearing the name MS Dhoni—the man who hit really big 6s.

The next time I met him was during a Deodhar Trophy game against South Zone. It was a target in excess of 300 and in those days in domestic cricket, it was above par. In came this guy who just massacred the South attack. Rohan Gavaskar and Devang Gandhi also got runs and I didn't need to bat.

Dhoni's leaps from the Ranji Trophy to the international scene happened in a space of two years, and it was a quantum leap! Even at that age, he was his own man, not at all bothered about general convention.

To give an example, during the Duleep Trophy in 2004, where the England Lions were supposed to play East Zone, I asked him if we could do the pre-match drills together, as was usually the norm. He politely said: 'Chaliye, aapko karwa deta hoon pahle' (Let me help you first).

So he helped me with my drills and after I was done, I said, 'Chalo, ab tumhara kara dete hain.' He smiled and said, 'Nahi, main theek hoon.'

Then to my amazement, I saw that instead of doing his keeping drills, he bowled seam-up in the nets and then went to play football. It was unusual, but that was typical Dhoni.

Those days, our dearness allowance in domestic zonal games was Rs 250–300 and five or six of us would have dinner together.

I remember one evening when we all gathered in the lobby and I asked Mihir Diwakar (Jharkhand pacer, who is now Dhoni's business manager), 'Where is Dhoni?' It was 8.30 p.m. Mihir's answer stunned me: 'It's 8.30; he must have had a glass of milk and is off to sleep.'

This story is for those who feel that Dhoni had become a recluse after becoming the Team India captain. He was, in fact, a recluse even then when he was an unheralded junior cricketer.

The Deodhar Trophy in 2004, just after the Australian tour (where I was a part of the Indian team), was significant for me, probably because there, I started realizing that Dhoni was also on the radar of the senior team.

It was before the start of a match against the North Zone in Chandigarh when I fell out with the East national selector Pranab Roy about who should be keeping wickets. I was annoyed because Pranab told me to play as a pure batsman and let Dhoni keep wickets. I was so angry that I excused myself from the game with the excuse of back pain, and Dhoni scored some 60-odd runs. The next thing that happened was that he went to Nairobi with the A team and put in a few excellent performances to get himself into national contention.

I remember another funny incident I can recall during one of the domestic tours. Dhoni used to have a red Manchester United cap those days as he was a big United fan. It was his prized possession and he would wear it often during training sessions. During a particular game, as the East Zone opted to field, one senior player saw Dhoni wearing the Manchester United cap and said: 'This is a serious first-class game, please wear your state team cap if you don't have a cricket cap.' Dhoni was respectful and immediately got a white cap. He was always very respectful towards seniors and what they said. You got to know one more aspect about him: while he liked doing things his own way, he was also open to other views. He was an introvert—warm and polite to a fault during conversations—but he would always keep his distance.

We were competing for the same national team slot till 2005, but by then, in my mind, I knew he was special. My father, Biplab Dasgupta, always narrated the following incident.

'I remember that morning, fifteen years ago, when I went to drop my son, Deep, to the New Delhi airport as he was leaving for his Duleep Trophy match. He was representing the East Zone cricket team. When I parked my car in the parking lot and went in, my son dragged me to one corner of the airport. We found a young boy loitering alone and doing a bit of shadow practice. My son called out to him and introduced me, saying, "He is Mahendra Singh Dhoni, the brightest star, the future of Indian cricket. You may not be lucky enough again to come so close to him. This is my prediction." I shook hands with him. He had a very shy look. He addressed me with folded hands at first and then shook my hand. I kept standing there, gazing at him.'

What was it that made Dhoni put everyone so far behind that suddenly we were all fighting for the second keeper's slot rather than the first? It was his tremendous belief in his own game and his ability to simplify. As they say, cut the clutter.

I was old-school, having learnt my cricket in Delhi in the early 1990s and then in Bengal where we developed a very orthodox brand of cricket. Dhoni was the complete opposite of how most from our school played the game: brilliant hand-eye coordination, but very unorthodox while batting or keeping wickets. Mind you, his keeping wasn't the greatest back then.

Most of us were too concerned about doing it right and had the tendency to be over-analytical; he was the exact opposite. He understood the bottom line, and his attitude was: 'At the end of the day, I have to get runs, catch a cricket ball; how I do it is my business.'

He always had some amazing abilities like brute power, exceptional game awareness, calmness and the ability to simplify complex situations; these more than compensated for his lack of orthodox technique.

Did I foresee him getting where he is? I thought he would be a big thing in white-ball cricket, but I never thought he would go on to play 90 Tests. It is also useful to remember that he chose to leave the format on his own terms, walking away from the lure of the milestone of 100 Tests.

Dhoni always had two things: natural talent and, more importantly, faith in that natural talent.

The best part was that while his batting prowess was at its peak, he quietly worked on his keeping. That's what cricketing smarts are all about. He knew that he would not have a great run with the bat all the time, so he made sure his keeping would keep him indispensable. It was a lesson I learnt the hard way. I played eight Test matches, and I scored runs in the first four Tests: a 100, a couple of 50s and everything was fine. Then I had a couple of bad outings with the bat and suddenly, my keeping came under the microscope. That pressure really got to me.

As a fellow keeper, his glovework fascinated me. Dhoni is to keeping as what Lasith Malinga or Jasprit Bumrah is to pace bowling. He disintegrated that conventional process and showed us that there is no one way to do things correctly. Dhoni didn't change his unorthodox style but worked on it to make it cleaner and more functional.

One thing he was blessed with was a keen sense of awareness: he almost always knew where the ball would go, and that was his strength. That and his ability to read the bowler and assess the pitch and bounce.

His keeping was built on that simple foundation—watch the ball and be there. He didn't try to be someone else. He figured out what his strengths were and worked on them.

If you look at other Indian keepers over the years, you will find that unlike them Dhoni doesn't move a lot. He found his own way and made us realize that there are two parts to every technique: parts that are negotiable, and parts that are non-negotiable. He understood the non-negotiables and respected them and then worked around the negotiables. If you follow the ball and keep your eyes on it for as long as possible, chances are that you will get there. Finally, it's also about catching the ball. He was efficient in his own way without changing his basic nature.

In core keeping parlance, Dhoni never believed in the concept of 'giving'. 'Giving' is when your hands work as shock absorbers to cushion the impact, like how a car bumper absorbs the shock when a car hits a bump. That was the foundation of wicketkeeping before Dhoni showed the next generation of keepers an alternate and equally effective way to do. Now, everyone wants to just grab the ball and take the bails off without giving. The player who had the closest style to that before Dhoni was Karnataka's Sadanand Viswanath. His stumping of Javed Miandad in the finals of the Benson & Hedges Championship of Cricket was a textbook 'Dhoni dismissal' two decades before Dhoni. No 'give', just soft hands which act as shock absorbers.

Dhoni wasn't a natural on turning tracks at the start of his career, but by the time he ended, he was probably the best in the business. The testimony to that was how he kept to Ravindra Jadeja on rank turners. Most keepers will tell you that keeping up with Jadeja is extremely tough, as you don't know which ball will turn and which one will go straight. Ashwin still gives you a split second extra in terms of pace and there is a little bit of predictability in terms of when he will turn the ball, but not so for Jaddu. Dhoni has a wide stance, which means less movement, but an extremely stable base. A stable base means that his eyes are stable, and he can watch the ball longer, helping his near-perfect estimation of where the ball would finish. He used the same logic when he kept for the faster bowlers.

People often ask me why Dhoni is such a good DRS (Decision Review System) caller, and my answer always has been simple: it's the same reason that makes him such a good keeper: his assessment of the conditions and estimation of where the ball would finish was immaculate. Which brings us back to that stable base and the exceptional anticipation.

I also have to credit him for successfully customizing and 'internationalizing mohalla cricket smartness' like lifting his leg to stop a late cut, or diverting a wayward throw without bothering to waste precious extra seconds to gather the ball, or stopping a half-volley by joining the pads together. We've all tried that at lower grades but never had the conviction or confidence to do it at the highest level.

That's what is special about MS Dhoni: speaking less, observing more, and quietly going about doing his work, his way.

You won't have another MS Dhoni but he will always be an inspiration for others to be themselves.

3

A Journalist

Sharda Ugra

Everyone remembers the first major Mahendra Singh Dhoni sighting. Vizag 2005 vs Pakistan. He turns up at the fall of Sachin Tendulkar's wicket, the switch in the order meant to make a statement. He is shoulder-rolling, swaggering to the crease, his thick brush of orange hair sticking out beneath his helmet, bat in hand—not quite a log, but an extension of what looked like powerful arms.

Off his very first ball, Dhoni's arrival at the crease became, in *filmi* terms, an 'entry' moment. In popular Indian cinema, the entry is an eagerly anticipated event, marking the first glimpse of the lead actor aka 'hero', on the screen. Dhoni's entry happened after Virender Sehwag had already creamed 21 runs off 12 balls.

It is the fourth over; Mohammad Sami is bowling and with the first ball, Dhoni sends an express delivery notice of his ability to the opposition and the world. In the video of the match, we see that he steps and Sami is reduced to dibbly-dobbly status; the scimitar of a bat arcs, the ball is lashed through extra cover on the up. The innings end in a first international 100 runs off 88 balls,

Dhoni punching the air, wide-grinned, helmet in hand, having scored 148 runs in 123 balls with four 6s and fifteen 4s. It was 5 April 2005 when India first met Mahi thus.

That's who he was at the time—Mahi, the boy from a mining backwater town with his own backstory. He was a schoolboy footballer and ticket collector, a big hitter with his eyes on the horizon. When he brought to an end his international career, in the midst of a global pandemic via an Instagram post, Mahi had been transformed by the fifteen years that passed in between, and he too had transformed them.

The public had grown hungry, always on the lookout for new deities in Indian cricket. But Dhoni was his private self, retreating behind several personas and brands. He was Captain Cool, 'EmEss', Mahibhai, Thala and in recent short snatches Territorial Army Combat Man.

On the field, Dhoni's cricket at his best was expressive, expansive, fluid and unpredictable. The eyeball to eyeball, my-pulse-rate-is-lower-than-yours finisher, the doer of deep damage, the streets-ahead white-ball captain, the one with lightning hands at the wicket and behind-the-back wrist-flick stumpings and run-outs, the seeker of opportunities, the finder of weaknesses, the planner of heists. As the years wore on, he stayed poker-faced and his expression remained stoic, treating Kipling's impostors as mere ships passing through the many days and nights of his career.

That persona was to make him a megabrand, successful social media handle, influencer, uber-celebrity, the self who was accessible only via a range of calibrated platforms: the press conferences filled with quotable remarks and mysterious analogies, the rationed Instagram posts, and the non-stop flood of advertising campaigns that changed with age as they grew in scale.

Contrary to common belief, Dhoni was not the breakout cricketer from a non-cricketing metro, nor was he its first captain. That was Kapil Dev from 1970s Chandigarh. Ranchi's distance from Delhi is far greater than Chandigarh's, but the Dhoni story reflected the age in which the spread of cricket through cable television found its leading man. He became both the cricketer and the captain when the game was fast-forwarding to its shortest, sharpest and most lucrative format. Which was to reinvent the rhythm and structures of the game itself for the first time in over a century.

Dhoni's India debut had taken place two months before the first Twenty20 International was played between Australia and India. When he led India to victory at the 2007 ICC World T20 Cup, we didn't know it then but cricket had walked into its future. Within a year came the IPL, the first successful model for club vs club franchise cricket. Twenty20, where unlike other longer forms wickets aren't precious, batsmen must necessarily attack and bowlers must defend. Here the loudest language is hitting 6s. The format that was to make Dhoni a megastar and shape his destiny.

* * *

The only time I met Dhoni outside of a press conference was in Rajkot in the very early days when he was essentially Mahi. By then, he had spent five years playing domestic cricket for Bihar, East Zone and Jharkhand before being picked for India A. With the Vizag century, stories of his 6-hitting came flooding in: a 6 into his Sanskrit teacher's house; one through a window where a selector was sitting after Dhoni was not picked for an under-19 camp; in a Ranji Trophy Plate semi-final, the ball changed six times because he kept hitting them out of the Sector 16 Stadium in Chandigarh.

Mahi was always proud of his 'smaller metro' origins, saying the province made its cricketers tougher, more inventive and improvisational. Ranchi had only one turf wicket, no famed coach, no fancy academy, no modern gym; it gave rise to a game founded on hand, eye and confidence. Many claim to be his formative coach, but Dhoni's shots came from a textbook written in his own hand. He was perhaps the first Indian to play the scoop/dilscoop/reverse lap/ramp, call it what you will. As for the Helicopter, it is argued that Gundappa Viswanath played versions of it,* but it was Dhoni who made it memorable. That afternoon in Rajkot, Mahi believed he could hit his signature 6s anywhere in the world. 'Out of the ground', he said cheekily. 'Easy.' No ground was big enough to contain Mahendra Singh Dhoni's ambitions.

His ascent to the Indian captaincy and India's victory in the 2007 ICC T20 World Cup was to change world cricket, Indian cricket and Dhoni the man himself. After the three senior-most players Rahul Dravid, Sourav Ganguly and Sachin Tendulkar decided to sit out the World T20, the decision to pick Dhoni was taken over a phone call between Indian selectors. He had not completed three years with India, had not even captained Jharkhand. The selectors could have picked anyone between the other senior players—Virender Sehwag, Yuvraj Singh, Harbhajan Singh or Gautam Gambhir. They chose Dhoni because of a general on-field composure, presence of mind and inventiveness. He was appointed captain for a tournament format the Board of Control for Cricket in India (BCCI) had no interest in, and two other ODI series against Australia and Pakistan.

It was called the fastest rise to the Indian captaincy since Tiger Pataudi, and Dhoni spent eleven uninterrupted and unchallenged years as India's white-ball captain. He stepped down after the 2018 Asia Cup to 'give the new captain a chance to prepare a team for the 2019 World Cup'. He had already stepped down from Tests in 2014 after leading India in 60 Tests, 200 ODIs and 72 T20Is, a total of 332 matches.

Dhoni's capabilities as an all-format player had been acknowledged, and at the World T20 his leadership sparkled. Who could forget his calm, reassuring hand around Joginder

---

* See https://www.youtube.com/watch?v=s4tOuig1feY.

Sharma's shoulder in the frenetic, heated last over of the final against Pakistan? India had expected nothing and was given what looked like everything in a superhero package—a quicksilver keeper behind the sticks, a nerveless finisher with the bat, and now, a leader of quiet decisiveness and underplayed charisma. We could be so lucky.

If we revisit the photographs just moments after the World T20 triumph, Dhoni is exultant. He is beaming, cheering, fist pumping, his long hair flying. What had communicated itself to brand managers and advertisers and television producers was the other Dhoni: the poker-faced field marshal, the guy who could stare down 15 runs to win in 6 balls without sweating. Clint Eastwood with a cricket bat: it was to become his brand USP. The year had begun with Dhoni's first ghastly World Cup experience following India's early exit from the Caribbean, and ended in an open-top bus parade in Mumbai.

* * *

Dhoni has always talked about the 2007 World Cup defeat as his coming of age. As if the defeat wasn't bad enough, the public response was a shock. In an interview to ESPN Cricinfo just before the release of his biopic in September 2016, Dhoni recalled his return from the Caribbean.* He travelled, he said, in a police van with Virender Sehwag, chased by the bright lights of the media cars. 'It felt as if we had committed a big crime, maybe like a murderer or terrorist or something. We were actually chased by them.' After a 20-minute wait in a police station, they finally left in separate vehicles. 'That actually had a big impact on me and I channelized the aggression to become a better cricketer and a better human being.' With no disrespect to Dhoni's maturity, it must be

---

* https://www.espncricinfo.com/story/2007-world-cup-reaction-had-big-impact-on-me-dhoni-1057316.

noted here that the 'better X and better human being' suffix has been formally included in the dictionary of Sportsjargon™.

Senior journalist Sunandan Lele, who has followed Dhoni's career closely, tells the story of when Dhoni's father advised him not to return to Ranchi after the 2007 World Cup defeat. People bearing lathis would land up at the door asking for Mahi. Less than six months after the 2007 ICC World Cup, Dhoni returned with the World T20 Trophy and found those very TV vans plus tens of thousands of fans lining the streets of Mumbai in welcome. The experience of both extremes of Indian cricket may have given Dhoni an innate understanding of how he needed to handle the world around him rather than have it handle him.

Lele also asks us to look closely at victory photographs that have followed Dhoni's enviable and worthy acquisition of captaincy silverware. At every major victory under his captaincy—the 2007 World T20, the 2011 ICC World Cup, the 2013 ICC Champions Trophy—once the trophy is in his hands, Dhoni hands it over to a teammate and steps aside, far away from the centre of the photograph; which unfortunately tends to get dominated by many over-eager, non-cricketing BCCI support staffers pushing themselves into the frame. By moving to the sidelines, Dhoni's message was, my work is done. The pictures were meant to say so much that they made the words around them immaterial. The secret sauce in the Dhoni persona was just that—elusive, secret.

Within a few years following the World T20 victory, every Indian celebrity, and that includes Dhoni, understood the impact of social media—the quickest, best and most powerful route to their fan base. He could tell his own stories when he wanted to. For the rest, the market would tell it in its own glib, (and for Dhoni) profitable way. His multipronged retirements—from the Test captaincy and cricket (2014) in the middle of a series, from white-ball captaincy (2017) ten days before an ODI series versus England and finally the international game—all came packaged via official media release or social media. Standing down from the white-ball captaincy was explained while giving a motivational talk to the Central Industrial Security Force a year later. The most reporters got from Dhoni was at press conferences, where he answered questions in great detail, often wrapped in analogies about life jackets, hybrid fuel in non-hybrid engines, Kishore Kumar and Sean Paul. Outside of that nothing. He chose not to give interviews unless on an official platform, during sponsor commitments or as part of a corporate speaking venture.

The Dhoni era was to mark the phase where the cricket media—growing exponentially—found that access to the Indian team was shrinking into carefully formalized exchanges controlled by the BCCI's media department. The preferred means of communication became through official broadcasters or personal social media accounts: the bigger the star, the more the written word was treated as pointless.

Media interactions under Dhoni could also be exercises in power; the revolving door of team managers loathe to put their foot down and insist that the captain fulfil media duties. Before the 2008 Asia Cup final, coach Gary Kirsten was halfway to the team hotel in Karachi before turning around on realizing that no one had addressed the reporters at the ground. On Dhoni's watch the Indian team began on a whim ignoring the end-of-play media briefings, despite having performers to choose from. In 2010, following a heavy ODI defeat to Sri Lanka, the team played football while reporters waited for 90 minutes after post-match ceremonies had concluded. After an Ahmedabad Test, the wait was two hours before Dhoni deigned.

At ICC events, the Indian team now only does the absolute bare minimum media, no more than what is mandated in the participating nations' agreement. Just like the BCCI has acquired bully status in world cricket, the Indian cricket team, driven by captains and a diva or two, has acquired the unfortunate tag of international prima donnas. On one occasion, after a narrow win over Bangladesh at the 2016 World T20, Dhoni accused reporters of being 'not happy that India won'. The reporter's 'awaz (voice), tone and sawaal (question)' had him arrive at that conclusion. (Coach Ravi Shastri has seconded the feeling in the Kohli era, strangely leaving out the words 'anti' and 'national' from his assessment.)

After India was knocked out of the 2016 World T20 by the West Indies, when Dhoni was asked whether he wanted to continue playing, he invited Australian reporter Samuel Ferris to sit alongside him and counter-questioned him in a mock press conference mode. Dhoni said he had hoped an Indian reporter would have asked him the question. 'Then I would have asked him if he had a son who was a wicketkeeper and ready to play. He would have said no, then I would have said maybe a brother who is a wicketkeeper and ready to play. You fired the right ammunition at the wrong time.' The Mahi way of treating media as somewhere between nuisance, disruptor and enemy has become the fallback response of the Kohli era as well.

For many young reporters, this gulf between captain and media means they needn't get caught up in the vortex of toxic gossip or manufactured leaks that they imagined had suffused Indian cricket in the past. While this is a fair argument, the hermetically sealed Dhoni era left us with gaps in the story, where Instagram is insight and Twitter is tribute. It can also lead to mind reading around those gaps; in Dhoni's case, his relationship with Test captaincy and his deep attachment to his IPL franchise Chennai Super Kings. Maybe, the two *are* connected?

Dhoni's Test captaincy had tended to be overly defensive, several decisions in major series based on wild gambles over cricketing logic. His response to a string of Test defeats in England was to say that India played maybe 70 per cent of its cricket at home: 'The away series are there to improve you as a cricketer. So, it is very important to not get very critical about the technical aspect, [but] to go out there and enjoy cricket.' Dhoni was to lose 15 of his 30 overseas Tests as captain, winning 6 and drawing

9. When he led India to two successive 0–4 defeats in England and Australia, he was retained as India captain because of BCCI president N. Srinivasan's veto over the selectors' decisions. The equation between Dhoni and Srinivasan runs far deeper than an exercise in administrative power.

* * *

At the first IPL auction in 2008, Dhoni became the most valuable cricketer in the world, over and above the chosen marquee names of Sachin Tendulkar, Sourav Ganguly, Rahul Dravid, Yuvraj Singh and Virender Sehwag. He was bought for USD 1.5m by the CSK franchise, which was owned by Srinivasan's India Cements. Over 13 seasons, in which CSK has won three titles from eight finals, Dhoni has become the team's North Star and an object of the CSK fans' undying love. When CSK was banned for two years following the 2013 IPL corruption scandal in which an owner was accused of colluding with the illegal betting industry, Dhoni's response to a question about the same was silence and a smile.

In CSK yellow, it is as if Dhoni feels free to shed his India blue persona and perhaps be himself, like when he was openly upset after losing an IPL final to Mumbai Indians. On other occasions, he has done what he never does in India colours—angrily shout at a bowler for overstepping, and vehemently contest umpires' decisions. In one case with CSK batting, he marched onto the field to argue over an overturned no-ball call in a close last-over finish. In the 2020 IPL, he was involved in a show of anger about an overturned decision. What makes him this way? We don't know because he won't say.

The last few years have involved several out-of-character Dhoni appearances. He has struggled to launch his slog overs endgame and finish matches, but obstinately refused to change his role and anchor innings. In one of his last international matches, at the 2019 World Cup, India lost by 32 runs with 5 wickets still left, Dhoni's being one of them.

Outside of cricket, his passion lies in motorbikes, dogs and sport guns. Nothing, however, is as visible as his devotion to the Indian military, born of a boyhood dream to join the army. He was appointed an honorary lieutenant of the Territorial Army, and he takes the role and stripes seriously. In 2019, he skipped a tour of the West Indies to spend time with his Territorial Army in Kashmir. Within a week of a much-publicized posting in Srinagar, Jammu & Kashmir lost its statehood, went into high-security lockdown and had its internet cut off. We do not know how long he served his two-month stint with his unit.

The military today forms part of the Dhoni persona: in March 2019, he handed out camouflage caps to the Indian team to show their support for the army at an ODI in Ranchi. At the World Cup later that year, he wore keeping gloves with the Balidan Badge insignia (meant for special ops para commandos) and caused a stir. The badge had been spotted, thanks to social media, on another pair of wicketkeeping gloves, his mobile phone case and his casual headgear during the IPL. He turned up to receive his Padma Bhushan, India's third highest civilian award, in his Territorial Army uniform complete with a march and a salute at the formal ceremony, even though the Padma Bhushan was being given to the cricketer, not the TA Combat Man. Unless in a climate of heightened jingoism, post retirement from international cricket, this is an avenue for another Dhoni persona to emerge. If it is, he will not let it go unnoticed on social media. Keep your eyes peeled.

Even in the midst of considering such a cultivated enigma, we must not forget that MS Dhoni is India's greatest-ever wicketkeeper, batsman and white-ball captain. The world will end before India produces another of his kind, because Dhoni was always an original. He made sure a Bollywood biopic with due embellishments told us some of the story he wanted us to hear. A more complete portrait of MS Dhoni, cricketer extraordinaire, can only emerge, however, if he tells us what he truthfully can in a medium he has shown little trust in—words, in long-form.

4

A Teammate

Lakshmipathy Balaji

The first time I came across Dhoni was in the 2003 Deodhar Trophy where he came in at no. 4. In those days, the East Zone was not traditionally regarded as a strong team and we used to recognize only a couple of cricketers like Rohan Gavaskar and Devang Gandhi. So, while Dhoni got runs against us, we didn't really see him then as a player with potential for the Indian team.

The second brush was in 2005, when I was making my comeback to the team after an injury, in a match against Pakistan in a home series. It was a big occasion as the Pakistan team was returning to India after a long time; this was only the first bilateral series after we had defeated them in both the ODI and Test series in Pakistan a year before that. We had the Test series first and the one-day series followed it. Before the Test series, though, there was the NKP Salve Challenger Trophy. Sourav Ganguly was the captain of the India senior side in which I played alongside Dhoni for the first time.

Although Dhoni had played in the Bangladesh series, we hadn't really seen much of him. So this was the first time I was seeing him from close quarters. I soon realized that this man had an aura. In our team, we had Yuvraj Singh, Anil Kumble and quite a few other established cricketers, but there was something about Dhoni that made him stand out even in the presence of superstars.

In the tournament, apart from keeping wickets, he also opened the innings with Shikhar Dhawan. In the second match, we saw how explosive he could be. Not only did he smash bowlers like Ashish Nehra and Ramesh Powar all around the park, but one of his shots also resulted in Sridharan Sriram getting his webbing split and taken out of the attack after bowling just one ball. As the match was heading to a tame end, V.V.S. Laxman decided to turn his arm over and bowl some off-spinners. Dhoni again hit one straight back at him and Laxman quickly pulled his hand away just to avoid getting injured. Dhoni scored 102 runs in the match while Dhawan also scored 126 runs to make short work of the target. Those innings definitely left an impression on everyone who saw it.

In the final match, we lost to India A, which was led by Rahul Dravid. Despite it not being a memorable match for us, I distinctly remember two catches Dhoni took off my bowling in India A's chase. One was to dismiss Satyajit Parab and the other catch was to dismiss Dinesh Karthik. The Karthik dismissal was spectacular: Dhoni literally flew in the air and took it in front of the second slip. Although he's a natural athlete and a former goalkeeper, I have not seen him take another catch like that.

Interestingly, there was a catch dropped of Karthik in the slips in the same over. When I look back at that catch, I just think of how Dhoni possibly had looked at it as an opportunity that he just *had* to take. Karthik, another keeper-batsman, had already made his debut and travelled with the team to an ICC event. So, for Dhoni, that flying catch seemed to be a statement: one that showed his intent to not let go of an opportunity when it presented itself. With Dada (Sourav Ganguly) leading and the match being attended by all the bigwigs of Indian cricket since it was being held in Mumbai, it was definitely an opportunity for Dhoni to get noticed. I don't know whether Dhoni's statement came in those circumstances as a coincidence or that he raised his game knowing who was watching, but the one thing I can definitely vouch for is that nobody could take their eyes off of him that day.

From that day onward, everyone who saw him knew he was different. His stroke making and his ability to do things differently on the field made him stand out like Rajinikanth. For those of us who grew up in Chennai in the 1990s, there were two kinds of actors—Rajinikanth and others. This was because Rajinikanth did things differently and whatever he did, people followed. Dhoni too had that spark in him. I guess that's why the management went ahead with his selection for the ODIs against Pakistan despite Karthik having made his debut earlier in England and scoring 93 runs against Pakistan in the Test series. The Challenger Trophy was Dhoni's only chance to cement his place after a very subdued performance in the series in Bangladesh; look how he grabbed the opportunity!

When the second ODI of the India–Pakistan series began in Visakhapatnam, I was surprised to see this boy with coloured hair sitting padded up in the dressing room. He didn't look the most convincing in the first match at Kochi, which we had won, so we had no idea that he would get promoted in the batting order. After all, it's not too often that experiments are made in matches against Pakistan. But soon, he was on the ground and was hitting the likes of Shahid Afridi, Mohammad Sami and Naved-ul-Hasan as if it was his tenth year of international cricket. Not once did he look like he was under pressure in those innings. The entire team was on the balcony to watch him bat.

Such was the impact of that knock that at the end of the match, everyone who called me just enquired about the new boy; everyone was intrigued about him. This again was just one instance where I realized how Dhoni knew how to pick his game up on big occasions.

The biggest opportunity for any Indian cricketer to influence an Indian audience is an India–Pakistan encounter. Notwithstanding anything else I did in my career, the only incident people still talk about is the broken bat while hitting Akhtar for a 6 in Lahore. Dhoni had chosen the India–Pakistan stage to score a mammoth century. He knew it was an opportunity and went all out to score a match-winning 148 runs. Both these experiences of mine shaped my understanding of Dhoni as a cricketer.

As far as captaincy is concerned, it happened to MS Dhoni by accident. When the format was in its nascent stage, India's stance on T20 was a big no. People were afraid that it would harm Indian cricket's popularity. Four hours of cricket was seen as too little for Indian audiences. When all the seniors decided to give the inaugural World T20 a miss, Dhoni found himself at the helm of a young team, alongside limited resources. Not only was the team young, but the young leader also looked inexperienced amongst the likes of Graeme Smith, Ricky Ponting and Chris Gayle. The difference between India and Australia was stark because the Australian board had pretty much sent the same team that had just won the 50-over World Cup in the Caribbean.

And then, out of nowhere, Dhoni led India to the title by beating Pakistan in the final. Once again, we realized how when everyone saw obstacles and opposition, Dhoni saw an opportunity and made the most of it. If the win wasn't enough, his employment of the strangest of strategies that paid off captured everyone's imagination, just like Rajinikanth would get people glued to the television screen with his antics. But behind all those unconventional strategies were processes that had been set in motion when the team landed in South Africa. The major effect of all those processes working out to give India the trophy was that it made Dhoni actually see how things should be if he was in charge of the team for the 2011 World Cup. The processes towards conquering the 50-over World Cup four years later began there.

As a captain, he had his own plans for different tournaments that he started making from the day he selected his team. For him, winning a tournament is a culmination of all those plans and processes working when they mattered, and that's all where it ends. Once he commits to those processes, he just makes sure that they are executed as well as possible. The final result isn't as important for him as the success of the processes.

On field, Dhoni is a leader who doesn't interfere. If he has taken the decision to throw the ball at you, then it has been taken after a lot of thought post which he is happy to let you do what you want to do. That is a statement of trust which says, 'If I have chosen you out of the rest of the options, there's a reason which I have arrived at after considering the situation. So, now I am not going to interfere in your natural way of doing things.' For any cricketer, to have that faith from a captain is a major boost of confidence.

Dhoni can give you that faith and let go, because he has control, which as a captain is one of the greatest qualities to have. I still remember the last over that I bowled in the final against Rajasthan in the 2008 IPL. At that point in my career, I was getting wickets with my slower balls. For me, it didn't matter whether it was the final over, a final or a league game. Since my instinct told me to go for a slower ball, I wanted to go for it again. While I was on my way back to bowl the delivery, Albie Morkel asked me what I was going to bowl. When I told him that I was going for a slower ball, he emphatically said no. His rationale was that since only 8 runs were required from 6 balls, one hit would finish the match if the batsman could judge the pace of the ball. In the middle of that over, Dhoni, who was standing at covers, came up to me and said, 'Do whatever you feel right.' He didn't tell me what to bowl. What I found amazing was that even as a man who, less than a year ago, led the team to an ICC World T20 win as well as a tri-series win in Australia, he didn't impose his views in such a high-pressure situation.

In the Champions League 2010, we were playing the Western Warriors in the final, where we put up a good bowling effort. I had bowled 3 good overs up in the front but in my final over, I gave away runs including two 4s and a 6 in the last 3 balls of my spell. I was a little disappointed and while going back to the dressing room, I told Dhoni that I shouldn't have bowled that off-cutter. Dhoni quickly replied, 'No, Bala. It's not that. It was actually the ball before that where Bollinger came late and gave away 2 runs instead of 1. If that had not happened, the batsman [Craig Thyssen] who is a better hitter wouldn't have gotten the strike.' That moment made me understand another aspect of his leadership: understanding the root cause of whatever happened, which possibly helped him to make peace with any final result.

It is well known that he doesn't speak a lot as a captain. However, he does pick his moment to pass the message on to his troops. It doesn't need to be the lowest moment or the highest moment; he will just address what he thinks is going wrong. Normally, he doesn't say anything in the first phase of a tournament where he's calculating his moves and observing his troops, almost like an army general. It's generally in the second phase that he makes decisions to ensure that the momentum going into the knockout stages is maintained. In the first phase, he allows everybody to get into the zone and assesses his picks as to who will be his main soldiers in the battles ahead. In the second phase, his influence on the game increases drastically through his decisions. But even when he does speak to his teammates, it is always to the point.

Even in 2019, when we saw an agitated Dhoni charge down the ground over some umpiring confusion in the Rajasthan Royals vs Chennai Super Kings match, he gathered everyone for a team meeting at the end of the encounter. While everyone wondered what was on his mind and whether he would say anything on what just transpired, he decided to speak on the need of the middle order to fire. And that was it.

That's MSD for you.

5

A Brand Manager

Jeet Banerjee

I first met Mahendra Singh Dhoni in late 2004, a year after he was done with working at the Kharagpur Railway Station. He was playing with some success in the India A circuit and was gradually getting noticed as a big-hitting lad. Mahi, as I now know him, was in Kolkata with the Jharkhand team for a few matches and I wanted to meet him to discuss the possibility of my company Gameplan representing him.

The meeting was arranged by a Jharkhand Cricket Association official, and an ever-smiling, polite, shy youngster with shoulder-length orange hair greeted me in a small room at the Broadway Hotel in central Kolkata. Mahi was ready to sign up with Gameplan to manage his endorsements. Eager to get out of the hotel, he said he would come to my office the next day to complete the formalities.

I have often been asked what made me sign up this youngster even before his international debut. It is hard to explain this because what Mahi possessed then were qualities hitherto unseen in cricket. A cricketer from Jharkhand, a cricketer with orange hair, a cricketer who was undeniably photogenic, a cricketer who loved milk—not one of these a clinching quality—yet the sum of the parts topped up with a winsome smile made me believe in Mahi's dreams and potential.

Mahi got the call for national duty a few weeks later and made a very forgettable debut in three ODIs in Bangladesh (starting with a run-out without facing a ball). This was only the second player that Gameplan had signed up, and I was anxious about the Jharkhand youngster's future. To make matters worse, there was a long break from one-day cricket since India was taking on Pakistan in a Test series in early 2005. Mahi went back to Jharkhand duty while Dinesh Karthik played the Test series. The latter bolstered his claims with a score of 90-odd runs in one of the Tests, and it seemed very possible that the Tamil Nadu teenager would be considered for the ODIs as well.

The selection meeting for the ODI team against Pakistan was a fraught one for those in Mahi's corner, and there weren't many of us in that corner. After all, back then, Mahi was a young unheralded cricketer from Ranchi, a town that barely registered itself on India's cricket map. The selection meeting was conducted without BCCI secretary S.K. Nair, and joint secretary Gautam Dasgupta and president Jagmohan Dalmiya might have felt that this youngster from the east deserved a couple more chances to prove himself. I was relieved at the outcome of the meeting. Though the squad was announced for just two matches, I hoped that Mahi would acquit himself well. The guy who seemed most poised amid all this anxiety was Mahi himself. Still shy and retiring, he preferred to stay in his room with a video game and a milkshake. If he was aware of Karthik closing in, the clock counting down on his career and the possibility of losing his India cap, he did not show it as he shot enemies down with impunity on his video game console.

The first ODI in Kochi ended in a shock loss for India, and the result was even worse for Mahi—he did not get to bat, and there were a few fumbles behind the wickets.

As the teams squared off in Vizag, the equation was clear: one innings left and a blue jersey, national cap and career at stake for Mahi. The celebrated innings of 148 runs is now seen as the announcement of a new star on India's cricket firmament. For me, who had been watching that match nervously from the stands, it was the birth of Dhoni the finisher. With just one game left to prove himself, Mahi showed calm, aggression and in the end, grace. It was clear that he could remain focused, unflappable and nerveless in precipitous situations. It provided the first glimpse of the equanimity that taught a whole generation the virtues of not panicking when all seemed lost. The finisher had begun his memorable journey.

I went to Mahi's room after his Vizag knock and while he was exceedingly pleased, there was no over-the-top exuberance. My job was to manage expectations and help him keep focus as best I could (being elated and euphoric myself!), so I told him that the Vizag innings bought him eight to ten more games and that he needed to do more of the same. Mahi nodded thoughtfully between sips of his milkshake. Looking back at his innocence and sincerity that evening, rather unreasonably, I miss the young Mahi who was just embarking on a two-year honeymoon period.

Though his star was in the ascendant, he still came and stayed at Akash Ganga Hotel in Kolkata and played in the Cricket Association of Bengal's P. Sen tournament for Gautam Dasgupta's Shyambazar Club, scoring a double 100 which consisted of a couple of 6s that sailed out of Eden Gardens into the neighbouring Akashvaani Bhavan. The faith the joint secretary had shown in him was repaid in full measure.

Between 2005 and 2007, Mahendra Singh Dhoni was the man who could do no wrong. The Cinderella kid was a darling of the media, his teammates, marketing heads and spectators wherever he went. It was now my job to market this emerging icon in a manner that would grow his image and not infringe on his inner core and unwavering focus on the game.

* * *

What made Mahendra Singh Dhoni such a talismanic brand back then? His game was the biggest magnet as it reflected a fearless, audacious and irreverent brand of cricket that resonated with a young and confident India. To add to the charm, the man himself was polite and serious—quiet behind the stumps, smiling cheerfully after hooking Shoaib Akhtar; never getting into any verbal argument with opponents; never swearing and never frowning; always preferring a milkshake to a beer. Yet, there was also the hint of swag in Mahi's love for motorbikes and his long coloured/streaked hair. There was also the story: humble beginnings, small-town background and the meteoric rise. However, beyond all this, I personally saw Mahi as someone who made us believe in miracles. He was no child prodigy like Sachin Tendulkar, no big-city boy like Rahul Dravid or Sourav Ganguly, and no under-19 star like Virat Kohli, who came after him. He was a player who went to the edge of the ordinary, even succumbing to the system by taking up that government job. He had worn the black jacket of a railway employee and only played 'khap' cricket on weekends, reducing his dream to a pastime. Even the Railways did not consider him good enough to play for their Ranji team. Just when he was on the edge of the abyss of anonymity, Mahi rewound a few steps and chased his dream once more. Much is made of his small-town background, but the fact that Mahi did not give up hope and made it when he was 23 to24, not 18 to 20, is what makes him so special, not merely his location settings. Put in this perspective, it is natural that Mahi blossomed into the player who could turn things around when the margin of error was no margin at all.

Creating Brand Dhoni might have been a lazy and easy job if we charted the predictable course. The easiest thing would have been to reach out to one of the colas, a motorbike brand and sports apparel among other usual suspects in the cricket-corporate circuit. Mahi was not particularly interested in what offers were coming his/our way, and to his credit, he did not show undue interest in how many brands were signing him on. He was particular about the paperwork and the deal, but never at the expense of his cricket and practice. He was still that guy who did not want to meet corporate honchos, preferring to stay in his hotel room with his video games. The only thing that could tempt him away from a game console was the possibility of a bike ride!

I remember Vipul Prakash, a member of Pepsi's marketing team, asking why we had not reached out to him even after his amazing maiden century. I said: 'He needs more time, and to do more.' When Pepsi signed up Mahi eventually, he was the only cricketer they used in another brand, 7 Up, alongside Pepsi. It was the 7 Up ad that created the popular line *Anhonee ho gaya honi, aur main ban gaya Dhoni*. Apart from 7 Up and Pepsi, Mahi also endorsed Lays from the PepsiCo stable.

There were unusual brands as well, and Mahi helped break the silos in which cricket endorsement existed back then. Soaps were for screen divas, but Mahi was signed up by the heritage brand Mysore Sandal Soap. I told Orient Fans that there is an interesting ad that could be made with their fans and Mahi's hair flying around. We got a cement company, Lafarge, to back a cricketer and we signed up with a news channel, NDTV, which helped us in helping Mahi show sides to his personality that were hidden in those pre-social media times. Exide, a common brand across India, used Mahi as an image for their long-lasting battery power. These were established brands that had hitherto shied away from cricketers, but such was the Mahi tsunami that he broke through all preconceived ideas of what a cricketer could represent.

Being a young man in the metrosexual age, his hair was a big deal for Mahi. He wanted to find someone who would do a good job of his famed hairstyle, and since nothing had prepared me for such a project, I enlisted the help of my sister, who was based in Mumbai. Sapna Bhavnani was the hairstylist she reached out to, and the celebrity stylist has worked on Mahi's famed hairstyles ever since. She advised Mahi against the orange colour and streaks, and an understated version of the earlier technicolour mop was all the rage in 2006–7. It's significant that Mahi cut his long mane after the 2007 T20 World Cup win and sported a buzz cut after the 2011 World Cup. Every big moment needed to be celebrated with a new haircut—this was perhaps the only quirk in the otherwise Zen superstar.

When the NDTV deal was inked, I remember Mahi's first interview was with the chief of the channel, Prannoy Roy. When asked to end with a song, the young star did not need to be persuaded as he immediately belted out 'Kabhi Kabhie Mere Dil Mein' from the film *Kabhi Kabhie* (interestingly, he chose to sign off in August 2020 with another song by Mukesh from the same movie).

One of his favourite appearances for the channel was for the programme *Jai Jawan*, where a celebrity is taken to meet defence personnel on duty. Mahi was like a happy kid with the soldiers, racing with them, exercising with them and generally having a blast.

Several advertisements followed, and at one point, there were close to 20 endorsements for Mahi. Each of the brands was a reputed one: Pepsi, GE Money, Reebok, Boost, Pernod Ricard, Videocon and Parle amongst others. There was also the predictable motorcycle endorsement with TVS, the one that perhaps gave Mahi the greatest joy.

During the 18 months following his Vizag knock, the strides made by Brand Dhoni would create enough goodwill to last his entire career. Things happening at the time added to the swashbuckling image, like when the then Pakistan President Pervez Musharraf told Mahi to keep his hair long. I was at the stadium and remember the roar in the stands—Mahi had won the hearts of India's arch-rivals with his batting and the mix of swagger and goodwill that always made Mahi such a special ambassador for the game. In 2007, as India geared up for the World Cup in the West Indies, Mahi was clearly the player of the moment, blissfully unmindful of how easily it could all change.

* * *

The aftermath of India's exit from the 2007 World Cup was a disaster for all the cricketers in that squad. The media witch-hunt targeted Mahi, who had the misfortune of scoring a duck in the decisive match against Sri Lanka. His home in Ranchi was stoned, the newspapers scrutinized his ad deals, and even I was called by news channels to explain myself for having 'misled' a player from the straight and narrow into the world of endorsements. On his return to India from the West Indies, Mahi was not sure of what awaited him in Ranchi, so he decided to stay on in Kolkata for a few days. Tollygunge Club seemed a perfect haven for him to keep away from the limelight. I remember going to meet him one evening, and as he went back to his room, I heard a club member comment: 'Lojja kore na, dekho hashchchey (Shameless fellow, look at him laughing)!' This in a line encapsulates the crashing lows that Indian fans can take a player to when things do not go well. Mahi would spend the whole day in his room, coming out for a drive and kathi rolls at Kusums at Park Street after sunset. This was April 2007, exactly two years after Vizag, and Mahi had now seen the whole ride that was on offer when you sign up for the roller coaster called Indian cricket.

Redemption came soon after, as Mahi saved a Test match at Lord's and played well in the England tour. But Mahi never forgot the dark days that followed the 2007 World Cup; it was perhaps the phase that made him build walls between himself and the media. Mahi's interactions with the press never went back to pre-2007 bonhomie; he remained unfailingly polite but unshakeably aloof as well.

Indian cricket quickly moved on from the World Cup loss, more so because change was in the air. A new form of cricket was gaining currency—an abbreviated form called Twenty20 which the BCCI was not particularly excited about. The Indian Cricket League was a rebel circuit that played in this format with a few players who had left their Ranji teams to be part of the new league. When a T20 World Cup was announced, India had played just one T20 game, and the mandarins of cricket looked at the tournament with polite indifference. A new team comprising fresh faces minus the triumvirate of Sachin Tendulkar, Sourav Ganguly and Rahul Dravid was announced. Mahi was made captain, and a team that was raw and untried congregated in South Africa—the weight of expectations could not have been lower than it was for this young squad.

The first match was against Pakistan and ended in a tie. While the Pakistanis went with their pacers in the bowl-out (a precursor to the current super over), Mahi used bowlers like Robin Uthappa and Virender Sehwag to hit the stumps, to win an incredible game. This was the first hint that we had a captain who was innovative, quick-thinking and unafraid. The Indian team went from strength to strength after that, and when the finals saw India and Pakistan face off once again, it was clear that T20 had converted Indian fans. The last over by Joginder Sharma (who incidentally debuted in the same match as Mahi did in Bangladesh) is now the stuff of legend, and possibly marks the most epochal moment in cricket this century. A new format was born, and it reimagined the game in a way that ignited the imagination of youngsters, even as another generation worried about the future of Tests and ODIs.

The Indian team's victorious bus ride from the Mumbai Airport to the Wankhede Stadium took half a day, and it was a journey that changed Mahi and cricket in India. A tectonic shift had taken place in Indian cricket, and Mahi was at the dead centre of it. Here was a player who had found a format that was made to highlight his qualities of big hitting, presence of mind and keeping cool in a chase. Mahi and T20 were made for each other, and the IPL that was to follow in a few months grew on the wings of this wonderful jugalbandi.

At the now famous auction that preceded the first IPL, I watched Mahi being bought by Chennai Super Kings as I bid on Kolkata Knight Riders' behalf. Chennai did not have an icon player, so Mahi walked into the role with ease.

At the end of the 2008 IPL, Mahi and Gameplan parted ways on less than amicable terms. Fortunately, the personal bonds we shared helped us both get past the acrimony and look ahead, albeit separately. Mahi's legend grew in giant strides, peaking with the 2011 World Cup. I met Mahi after the presentation ceremony as he was headed for the victory lap. He took off his India cap and handed it to me. I already had his 2007 T20 World Cup jersey.

Gameplan continues to work with the IPL and with KKR besides being present in diverse aspects of sports marketing. However, we never signed on another player after 2008.

6

An Academic

Jaideep Mukherjee

Our perceptions of Mahendra Singh Dhoni are shared and kaleidoscopic. Take your pick from his long-haired look; *that* helicopter shot; his bat, both stiletto and sledgehammer; lightning-fast hands in camo gloves; talking to his bowlers, always in Hindi; a serial winner for India and Chennai; his admiration of the armed forces; his smile changing wattage from shy to dazzling; and his ubiquity in adverts. Decoding these images is tough, as cricket and India had not seen anything like Dhoni before. An outlier once, he is everywhere now.

Dhoni is among India's greatest and the world's best of his era. While much is known of Dhoni, little is understood. He rarely opens up to the media or shares on social media. Yet, he is seen as a 'revolutionary' figure in sport and society. Were there many mutinies that made him? What were his acts of resistance and reorganization? Where does he fit in the evolving narrative of sport, society and nation? Trying to answer these questions will take us beyond the binary that Ranchi is Dhoni and Dhoni is Ranchi—a simplistic and shared frame of reference. Instead, if we take the approach that to decipher Dhoni, one must first understand Ranchi, we could start to see how Ranchi made, and nearly unmade, the person, performer and paradox that is Dhoni.

Where Revolutionary Roads Meet

Ranchi can be rich in meaning depending on how, when and where you see it from. At least three claims contest the origin of the name. Any one of these—the mispronounced name of *archi* (meaning bamboo grove) village, or the word *aranchi* (a short stick used to drive cattle, in Mundari, the language of the Munda people), or another Mundari word, *richi* (meaning black kite) and a hillock known locally as *Richi-buru* (the hill of kites)— may have given Ranchi its name. Despite being a modern city, a former summer capital and the present state capital, 'Ranchi' is shorthand for insanity in India. In 1918, the Ranchi European Lunatic Asylum was established in Kanke, a locality of Ranchi. It was India's first psychiatric institute that still treats patients with mental health problems and offers medical courses. Infuriatingly, this is an unfortunate tag that Ranchi has never shaken off.

The region was once part of the Magadha territory under the Nanda, Maurya and Gupta empires, where a dynasty of Nagvanshi Rajputs was granted tributary control that ran from 83 AD to 1952, when zamindari was formally abolished in India. The name Chhotanagpur is owed to the Nagvanshis, who were reduced to zamindars after the East India Company's victory at the Battle of Buxar. The Company established direct control (1817) over Chhotanagpur, and set up the South West Frontier Agency (1831) to formalize taxation and trade. The Nagvanshi zamindars and other local chieftains unsuccessfully rebelled against the Company in 1857.

Several defiant but doomed Adivasi uprisings across Chhotanagpur rocked the zamindars, the Company, the Raj and later, the Indian state. Most impactful in raising consciousness and celebrated in folklore were the 1855 Santhal Hool (rebellion) led by the brothers Sidhu, Kanhu, Chand and Bhairav; and, Birsa Munda's millenarian movement, the Ulgulaan (1894–1900). A sporadic Maoist Naxalite insurgency continues till the present day. A very different Nehruvian industrial revolution would 'steel' the region after 1947.

Paschim—Bengali Migration and Cricket in Exile

Chhotanagpur's wealth of natural resources starkly contrasted its sparse population and poverty of skills. Except for basic education provided by Christian missions, the region that once hosted ancient centres of learning like Mithila, Nalanda and Vikramashila had few higher institutions to supply the area's industry and administration. While the Company and the Raj could extract lumber and ore with local labour, it needed educated migrants to collect tax, practise law and medicine, teach, keep order and run the railway. Jobs in policing, soldiery and the railway were only open to specific Indian 'martial races' or Anglo-Indians—those trusted not to disrupt.

Since the mid-nineteenth century, this void was filled by enterprising young Bengali men (it was only men at the time, and their families would follow later). First Company clerks, then the professional and mercantile classes arrived in droves into Chhotanagpur, particularly Ranchi. Bihar and Jharkhand, as they are today, were a part of the Bengal Province, and to the Bengali mind this was Paschim, where fortunes could be made. It was also an early destination for Bengali tourism. Most of these families would find brides and grooms in the migrant community and put down permanent family roots outside Bengal. A few could even afford large estates like Ranchi's Tagore Hill, once home to Rabindranath's eldest brother Jyotirindranath (1849–1925), that still bear their names.

Many educated upper-class men of urban Bengal had embraced organized sport, and upon migrating, they took this with them to the new clubs they formed. Cricket in Bihar, or Assam, Odisha and Tripura for that matter, would be dominated by Bengali-origin players for decades to come. Bihar's first Ranji Trophy match was against Bengal at Kolkata in December 1936, and the two XI-s together had nine cricketers of Bengali origin, four for Bihar and five for Bengal. Between 1941 and 1964, three Bengali brothers—Bimal, Bikash and Biraj Bose—played 54 first-class matches for Bihar. Incidentally, the oldest Bose brother was the revolutionary Benoy Krishna Bose of Benoy–Badal–Dinesh fame.

Sujit Mukherjee (1930–2003) followed the Brothers Bose, making five appearances for Bihar with little success, but is better remembered as one of India's first and finest cricket writers, a publisher and scholar of comparative literature. Of Mukherjee, Suresh Menon wrote: 'There were, and will be, better cricketers than him, but few better writers on the game he described with a mixture of schoolboy enthusiasm and professorial precision.'

In an essay written in the 1980s, Mukherjee felt: 'I think I write mainly in order to rediscover Indian cricket. In the act of writing, our cricket past becomes clear and real to me. Born to a race of idol-worshippers I am very conscious of the fact that it is the worshipper who lends life to the idol, which would cease to exist if he ceased to worship.' Regrettably, Mukherjee passed away before Dhoni's pomp, and could never cast his gimlet eye on Bihar's beloved idol.

Historian Ramachandra Guha, an admirer of Mukherjee, mentioned that: 'Sujit Mukherjee was the only Bengali I knew who could laugh at other Bengalis.' A more serious reason for these paragraphs of parochial detour, is to signpost the presence of many Bengali women and men on Dhoni's journey from small town to superstardom.

Steeling Ranchi—a Nehruvian Reorganization

Starting in the 1950s, a series of steel plants were commissioned in the region with World Bank aid and partnerships with the most advanced steelmaking nations. There were two private sector steel plants running in the area: the Tata Iron and Steel Company at Jamshedpur, and the Indian Iron and Steel Company at Burnpur. Between 1955 and 1964, public sector steel plants started production at Bhilai, Rourkela, Durgapur and Bokaro. The sites were supposedly near iron ore and coal mines, and rail networks to connect them to the rest of India. Actually, the influence of senior Congress leaders Rajendra Prasad, Dr Bidhan Chandra Roy and Biju Patnaik prevailed in the allocation of these units to their states.

Hindustan Steel Limited (HSL, precursor to the Steel Authority of India), set up in Rourkela in 1954 to manage the plant there, later took over the Bhilai and Durgapur plants. In 1959, HSL's HQ was shifted from Rourkela to Ranchi—in effect, a *gift* from Nehru to Rajendra Prasad. This was also how Ranchi 'got' the Heavy Engineering Corporation Limited (HEC or HECL), then India's largest integrated engineering complex, in 1958. The ambition was for HEC to indigenously manufacture the entire panoply of steel plant equipment and supply engineered products to the core sectors of mining, defence, transport and energy using Indian steel.

In 1959, HSL created the Central Engineering and Design Bureau (CEDB) as India's frontline engineering, consultancy and contracting firm to build future steel plants. With HSL reconstituted as Steel Authority of India Limited (SAIL) in 1973, CEDB was spun out as a subsidiary called Metallurgical and Engineering Consultants (India) Limited (MECON) and headquartered in Ranchi. Making steel needed expertise from every engineering stream, and HSL recruited India's best young engineers by funding their master's degrees and apprenticeships in the US, Germany and the UK. These engineers were selected in open, competitive examinations and sent abroad for training on five- or ten-year bonds to work for HSL on their return. Homes and infrastructure needed to house steelworkers and management were built from scratch in Rourkela, Bhilai, Durgapur and the newer part of Ranchi as planned, creating India's Steel Towns.

Located on prime greenfield land acquired by HSL in Ranchi's Doranda area, the Shyamali housing complex had the Subarnarekha river running to the south and good schools nearby, making it an attractive proposition for young families moving there. Infused with pride and responsibility for building their new India, CEDB's management poured their expertise into Shyamali's development. In 1973, with the transformation of HSL into SAIL, and CEDB into MECON, HSL's assets in Ranchi were transferred to MECON by an Act of Parliament.

CEDB did engineering design and consultancy and had no factory or plant as such, but needed infrastructure for housing, healthcare, schooling, leisure and sport. HSL spared no expense in funding these, which later grew into top institutions of Ranchi. The Happy Nursery, started as a creche for CEDB children, was merged into the Dayanand Arya Vidyamandir organization, at the initiative of two stalwart wives of HSL engineers, the late Manjula Banerjee and Meera Krishnaswami, who has retired to Bangalore. This is Jawahar Vidya Mandir (JVM) today, where the wives of many MECON engineers are teachers and every child of a MECON employee can study.

The Loreto (girls) and St Xavier's (boys) schools were older and better reputed but they offered classes only till Year 10, while JVM had the sought-after plus two provision. Ranchi's Ispat Co-op Hospital, started in 1961 as a medical inspection room for 500 CEDB families, is today a specialist government hospital treating 125,000 outpatients. Extensive sports facilities, including the MECON Stadium (a ground that's hosted Ranji Trophy games), new football and hockey pitches, badminton, tennis and basketball courts were laid out. MECON even had a top hockey side, drawing upon Ranchi's tradition of producing players.

MECON and Shyamali brought together a diverse range of families from many corners of India, each following their dreams and destinies. It was here that the paths of Salil Kumar Sanyal and Pan Singh Dhoni first crossed. Salil Kumar Sanyal (b. 1930), a civil engineer from Bengal Engineering College, Shibpur, recently returned with an engineering diploma from the Imperial College and work experience with Guest, Keen and Nettlefolds in London, joined CEDB in 1959. His first posting was at Rourkela, where he lived with his new bride Meera and they moved to Ranchi in 1964 with their newborn son, Debashis.

The Sanyal family had quarters at the newly built Shyamali, where their daughter Paromita was born in 1967. Both Debashis and Paromita, once toddlers at Happy Nursery, returned from St Xavier's and Loreto respectively to JVM for their plus two, and went on to careers in management and engineering. S.K. Sanyal retired from MECON in 1988 and settled in Salt Lake, Kolkata. He would soon lose Meera to diabetes and perhaps the added heartbreak of leaving Ranchi. Debashis would start his own family with childhood sweetheart and schoolmate, Lata Venugopal, daughter of another MECON engineer. Their innings played, and now dispersed in Kolkata, Goa and Singapore, the Sanyal clan maintain that their happiest years as a family were spent at Shyamali.

Pan Singh Dhoni, a Rajput from Lawli village in the Almora district of present-day Uttarakhand, applied for a Class IV 'fitter' position at the colony's newly commissioned waterworks, and was appointed by a board chaired by S.K. Sanyal. Pan Singh, his wife Devaki Devi and son Narendra (b. 1971) moved to Ranchi in 1973 and were allocated quarter E25 in Shyamali. Pan Singh supervised the colony's water supply and helped build the water tank that stands beside the MECON stadium. Devaki Devi and Pan Singh had two more children, Jayanti and Mahendra, both born in Ispat Hospital, and all three attended JVM, which today calls itself MS Dhoni's school. Dhoni, who now lives in a 7-acre farmhouse 7 miles due west of Shyamali, remembers the two-bed apartment being so tiny that his cricket kit had to be kept at a friend's shop.

Pan Singh used to water the field Dhoni played on, though he actually supervised the entire colony's waterworks. It's not unusual for groundsmen's sons to take up cricket. Eknath Solkar's (1948–2005) father was a groundsman at Mumbai's Hindu Gymkhana as was England's Dan Lawrence's dad at Chingford CC. Not every father, however, gets to see a ground he once nurtured be named for his son, as the MECON MSD Stadium was in 2015.

Gouri Majumder (b. 1940), who arrived in Ranchi from Bangalore in 1962 as the wife of HEC scientist Suprakash Majumder, recalls Ranchi being like 'a miniature, new India that we were all building'. Once her three daughters were in school, she started teaching science, first at Vivekananda Vidya Mandir, then JVM. Gouri Madam retired in 2000 to a small house the family had built nearby. Unlike their generation, who flocked to jobs in Ranchi, Mrs Majumder's daughters and most of her students pursued careers elsewhere.

After leaving JVM in 1999, Dhoni returned in May 2005 a few months after making his ODI debut for India. Photos in newspaper reports of that visit show a lady sitting next to him as he tucks into lunch. She was one of the teachers that Dhoni remembered by name that afternoon, a memory that still elates the now-retired Swapna Mukherjee. Swapna Madam taught science to several generations of JVM students between 1979 and 2016. She recalled 'Mahi' as 'a gentle, well-behaved student, who was diligent with his work'. When asked what Dhoni might have done if cricket didn't work out, she said, 'You can't keep kids like Mahi down. It's a little spark they have, and they just don't give up. Even if one door closes for them, they'll keep knocking till other doors open.'

The teenage Dhoni's switch from a promising football goalkeeper to budding wicketkeeper was engineered by Kesav Ranjan Banerjee, his school football coach, and Chanchal Bhattacharya, then a journalist with *The Ranchi Express* and administrator of the Commando Cricket Club where Dhoni learnt to play. In January 2015, an Indian TV channel took the World Cup that Dhoni had won for India in 2011 back to his school. Dhoni wasn't there that day, but JVM's students and teachers—especially, Kesav Banerjee—took great pride in his success.

Ranchi's progress seen in the light of the rest of Bihar, or the MECON Shyamali enclave seen in the context of other parts of Ranchi, clearly demonstrates a trajectory of being ahead of the curve. That is not to say that growing up in Ranchi's Shyamali colony would have been a bed of roses, but it could be far worse. His family and he had led a decent, relatively sheltered, trouble-free life in cramped but low-rent, public-sector housing. By all accounts, Shyamali was a haven of tranquillity, amidst the maelstrom that was Bihar. While their parents had not finished school, the Dhoni siblings got a solid education, with quality healthcare and sports facilities at their doorstep, and his wasn't a solitary success story.

Fellow JVM alumnus and six years senior to Dhoni is Rohit Prasad, whose father worked for MECON and grandfather for HEC in Ranchi. Prasad, who has an MS from Illinois and an MBA from MIT, is presently VP and head scientist of Amazon's Alexa division. Prasad, Dhoni and many others were the fruits of seeds planted in Nehruvian India, only that Dhoni's path was not the norm for a steel-town boy. While most in his generation surfed to success on waves of global opportunity unleashed by India's economic liberalization, his own choice of career took Dhoni into choppy waters.

Against the Tide in Cricket's Backwaters

It is claimed that anyone from anywhere can achieve eminence in Indian politics and cinema, perhaps now cricket too. Politics allows a person to organically develop a local following through campaigns and movements, then catapult themselves to regional or national prominence. Individuals also leverage their stature in one field of public life to transition into politics. Stars of screen and sport take advantage of the public construction of identity that these fields allow and use that to springboard into the political arena.

The search for stardom in film took Ashok and Kishore Kumar (Khandwa), Dev Anand and Vinod Khanna (Gurdaspur), Amitabh Bachchan (Allahabad), Rakhee (Ranaghat) and hundreds of hopefuls, baggage brimming with charisma, sex appeal and talent, on journeys from small town to Tinseltown. Since the arrival of satellite television, the path into cinema is often via TV contests and programmes, alongside training in theatre. But the reality of Indian cricket, while being as dramatic and keenly followed as India's cinemas and politics, was that it didn't offer clear pathways for entry and assimilation. But that too would change.

Just as realism replacing escapism in Indian cinema has helped deepen its already global appeal, inspiration for today's gritty narratives is increasingly drawn from India's hinterland. Realistic portrayals, authentically essayed on-screen by auteurs and performers with lived experience of these regions, are edging out stereotyped turns by big stars. An apt pair of films that exemplify this are Yash Chopra's *Kaala Patthar* (1979), loosely based on the 1975 Chasnala mining disaster at a Dhanbad colliery where flooding killed 380 miners, and Anurag Kashyap's epic diptych *Gangs of Wasseypur* (2012), which shows the same area's coal mafia at work and play.

A common trend in Indian politics, cinema and cricket is the number of dynasties they have spawned. This is at once a global and an Indian phenomenon, where children are primed and 'launched' to succeed parents in their fields. In India 15 families have produced just over 11 per cent (33 of 302 till date) of men's Test cricketers. On average, one in every Test XI has been from a cricketing family. That doesn't include ODI and T20 players, those marrying into other cricketers' families or sons of domestic cricketers. Also, each cricketer from such a 'family' has played 22.6 Tests on average, which is higher than the overall average of

19.9 Tests per capped player. Remarkably, 32 of the 33 'related' cricketers made their debuts before Dhoni (Test cap #251, debut 2005) and one, Stuart Binny (b. 1984, Test cap #281, debut 2014), since.

Even more important than lineage was location. Where you were from, and where you played your cricket mattered massively. Almost 4 in 10 of Indian Test cricketers (1932–2021) were born in the seven most affluent cities of Mumbai, Chennai, Delhi, Bengaluru, Kolkata, Hyderabad and Pune. Sporting cultures of specific regions played a part too. Bengal, Goa, Kerala and India's north-eastern states produce more footballers, Haryana more wrestlers, Punjab and central India's Adivasi communities more hockey players than cricketers.

If you overcame location, you'd still face selectorial bias. For the first 70-odd years of India's domestic cricket, amateur or poorly paid selectors at all levels would only watch elite matches and naturally select from a smaller talent pool. They'd use undue influence to pick players on reputation, or at the say-so of club or state officials, rather than promise or performance. Corruption was rife among these 'gatekeepers', with bribes openly demanded for selection.

Similarly, coverage was limited to local or regional media, while the vernacular press naturally focused on players from their regions. Unless a player achieved an incredible feat, there was no national coverage of it. Seamer Pradeep Sundaram (b. 1960) taking 10 runs out of 76 in an innings for Rajasthan against Vidarbha in 1985/86 made national news for a day. Pradeep's father, Gundibail Sundaram, a seamer of Kannadiga origin, played for Bombay and Rajasthan, and bowled for India in two Tests. Both Sundarams bowled themselves into domestic oblivion.

Bihar's Ranji sides started with British, Anglo-Indian and Bengali cricketers, marginalizing local talent. Bihar played the Ranji Trophy between 1936 and the present day, except between 2004 and 2018, with a largely dismal record. Within the East

Zone, it had always played second fiddle to Bengal and frequently trailed Odisha and Assam too. Their high point was in 1975–76, when they made the Ranji final at Jamshedpur only to lose to Bombay by 10 wickets.

The first Bihar-born cricketer to play for India was the Jamshedpur-born, Nirode Ranjan 'Putu' Chowdhury (1929–79), who appeared in two Tests in 1949 and 1951. An off-spinner, Chowdhury represented Bengal earlier but was picked for India on the strength of his performances for Bihar. To follow him were Saradindu Nath 'Shute' Banerjee (1 Test, 1949), Ramesh Saxena (1 Test, 1967), Randhir Singh (2 ODIs, 1981–83), Subroto Banerjee (1 Test and 6 ODIs, 1992) and the unlucky Syed Saba Karim (34 ODIs, 1997–2000; 1 Test, 2000), whose career as a keeper-batsman ended after being struck in the eye standing up to Anil Kumble.

There were other Bihar-born cricketers who represented India. Kirti Azad (b. Darbhanga, 1959) played 7 Tests and 25 ODIs, and in the victorious 1983 World Cup side, but played domestic cricket for Delhi and the North Zone. Kirti's father, Bhagwat Jha Azad, was a six-term Member of Parliament and Chief Minister of Bihar. Prithvi Shaw (b. Gaya, 1999), who has till date played 5 Tests and 3 ODIs for India, left Bihar for Mumbai as a 10-year-old when Bihar was disqualified from the Ranji Trophy. Shaw led the India Under-19 team to the 2018 World Cup and is presently skipper of Mumbai.

Before Dhoni, six cricketers from Bihar had played a cumulative 6 Tests and 42 ODIs. Dhoni's tally of 90 Tests, 350 ODIs and 98 T20 internationals for India is not just a statistical anomaly, it is almost an impossibility. Only five men in the history of the game have topped Dhoni's 538 international caps. Since Dhoni, Varun Aaron (b. Jamshedpur, 1989) and Shahbaz Nadeem (b. Muzaffarpur, 1989) have played Tests, Saurabh Tiwary (b. Jamshedpur, 1989) has played ODIs and Ishan Kishan (b. Patna, 1998) T20s. Ishank Jaggi (b. Bacheli, 1989) and Utkarsh Singh (b. Ranchi, 1998) have made their marks in the IPL.

Ranchi's favourite son wasn't even the first Ranchi-born player to be capped for India. That honour belongs to the off-spinner Rajesh Chauhan (b. 1966), who played 21 Tests and 35 ODIs between 1993 and 1998. His father, Govind Chauhan's job at a public sector unit took him to Ranchi, where Rajesh was born. They moved to Bhilai, and Rajesh followed Govind in playing for Madhya Pradesh and Central Zone.

If you were a budding Bihar cricketer in the late 1990s, having made it through district and state selection hurdles, your performances would get zero attention from selectors or the media. Dhoni remained unknown and perhaps in desperation or under parental pressure, briefly took the route where sporting ability brings employment opportunity. India's public sector, and some private sector firms, are generous employers of sportspersons. Dhoni was keen to continue working for Central Coalfields, which would keep him in Ranchi, but instead landed a dead-end job as a train ticket examiner with the South Eastern Railways based in Kharagpur, six hours away, all because it might give him a shot at a berth in the Railways' Ranji side. Dhoni was championed by the cricket-obsessed Animesh Kumar Ganguly, then divisional railway manager at Kharagpur. Even that didn't work; as at the Railways team trials, he wasn't given a decent hit in the nets. He quit Indian Railways soon after, as it just wasn't the ticket for him.

For Dhoni, the closing of one door meant knocking on others, and this time Lady Luck smiled on him. Buoyed by income from TV rights, the BCCI under Jagmohan Dalmiya, launched two parallel and far-sighted initiatives that radically changed how players were picked for higher representative honours—first, the National Cricket Academy (NCA) set up in 2000 at Bangalore with Sunil Gavaskar as chair, and then the Talent Resource Development Wing (TRDW), sometimes referred to as the Talent Development Resource Scheme (TRDS), under Dilip

Vengsarkar, were set up to scout and create pathways for talent from beyond traditional cricket centres.

The TRDS intended for talent to be spotted directly by the BCCI's network of full-time, Talent Resource Development Officers (TRDOs), rated on agreed, objective criteria and fast-tracked through zonal academies or the NCA, ready for India colours. Prakash Chandra Poddar (b. 1940), a former Bengal and Rajasthan cricketer, was TRDO on duty at a match in Jamshedpur when he spotted a stocky kid who kept wickets and hit the ball very hard. The form he filled had a box marked 'Recommendations', and what Poddar wrote in it that day changed Dhoni's life. 'Good striker of the ball, has a lot of power, but needs to work on his wicketkeeping. Technically not orthodox. Is very good at running between wickets.'

By August 2004 Dhoni was in the India A side on a tour of Zimbabwe and Kenya, excelling more as a batter than a keeper. He made his full India debut in an ODI against Bangladesh in December 2004. Poddar served as a TRDO for just over a year, and the BCCI abandoned the TRDS/TRDW after Dalmiya left office. The system was far more effectively deployed later in the IPL where every franchise runs a network of scouts to spot talent. The NCA, with Rahul Dravid in charge, is now focused on the Under-19 and India A sides. Interestingly, almost every India A player on the 2004 tour of Zimbabwe and Kenya, many scouted by TRDOs, went on to play for India. Three of them—Gautam Gambhir, MS Dhoni and Munaf Patel—would win World Cups in T20 and ODI cricket.

It was necessity more than opportunity that helped force Dhoni into India's XI. In ODIs, picking a batsman-keeper (as opposed to a keeper-batsman), that started with Alec Stewart and Andy Flower, made room for an extra bowler or batter in the side. Australia had set the standard very high with the free-scoring Adam Gilchrist. India had briefly given the gloves to Rahul Dravid with some success, and tried Nayan Mongia, Saba Karim,

Sameer Dighe, Vijay Dhaiya, Deep Dasgupta, Ajay Ratra, Parthiv Patel and Dinesh Karthik, before Dhoni. That the punt on Dhoni paid off was more relief than vindication for India's brains trust.

Dhoni's arrival was as spectacular and anarchic as that of Kapil Dev a quarter of a century before him. Though its cricketing implications had not quite been grasped. In 2007's *Men in White*, Mukul Kesavan rated Dhoni as 'a cheerful, *Afridiesque* brute, who made no claims to higher batsmanship'. In 2010 Kesavan added a new chapter on Dhoni to the book's revised edition, calling him 'India's first adult captain since Pataudi'. By 2015, Kesavan was comparing Dhoni to Srinivasa Ramanujan, 'as [a] *svayambhu*, not so much self-made as self-invented, created out of nothing but will alone. The great mathematician, self-taught and poorly schooled, shared with Dhoni the hero's ability to transcend context.'

Outlier—the Small-Town Superstar

In his book *Democracy's XI*, political journalist Rajdeep Sardesai wrote that, with Dhoni's emergence, 'there were no more dynasties in Indian cricket', and Indian 'cricket had become Indian democracy's alter ego'. He also argued, 'The cosy networks and elite privileges have been thwarted at the gates of a cricket ground. There is a democratic fervour, that makes cricket the authentic Indian dream, which is borne out by where Indian cricketers are emerging from.' But is the phenomenon of self-made stars surfacing from small towns new to Indian cricket?

The eighty-nine-year journey from Amar Singh (India's Test Cap # 1, b. 1910, Rajkot) to Axar Patel (Test Cap # 302, b. 1994, Anand) has seen many shine from obscurity, despite Indian cricket's predilection for talent from the metros. For every Vijay Merchant (b. 1911, Mumbai), Sunil Gavaskar (b. 1949, Mumbai), Mohammad Azharuddin (b. 1963, Hyderabad), Sourav Ganguly (b. 1972, Kolkata) and Sachin Tendulkar (b. 1973, Mumbai) there has been a Mohinder Amarnath (b. 1911, Gopipur), Vinoo

Mankad (b. 1917, Jamnagar), Polly Umrigar (b. 1926, Solapur), Kapil Dev (b. 1959, Chandigarh) and Virender Sehwag (b. 1978, Najafgarh).

While past journeys from humble origins to cricketing prominence took cricketers through the payroll of princely states, poorly paid public sector jobs, moving to more visible teams, while at the mercy of selectorial caprice, the IPL completely shattered that paradigm. From being scouted at a floodlit, dustbowl, tennis-ball tournament to playing in the IPL could happen in a matter of months. Where players were from or their previous experience in domestic cricket didn't matter; the skill they offered their side was everything.

Take India's pace attack since 2008, when the IPL launched. It's been spearheaded by bowlers born in Shrirampur (Zaheer Khan), Meerut (Bhuvneshwar Kumar, Mohammed Shami), Ikhar (Munaf Patel), Moyna village in Medinipur district (Ashoke Dinda), Ballabhgarh (Mohit Sharma), Palghar (Shardul Thakur), Karnal (Navdeep Saini) and Chinnappampatti village in Salem district (T. Natarajan), alongside those from Delhi (Ishant Sharma) and Ahmedabad (Jasprit Bumrah). While there were clear cricketing reasons for this, India's commerce, and those who write on it, gave this a completely different spin.

In 2007, author and business journalist Sandipan Deb—then editor of *The Financial Express*—despatched reporters to twelve Indian Tier II cities to report on the socio-economic impact of Dhoni being appointed India's captain, and ran the stories under *The Dhoni Effect* column header. Deb's rationale was:

> Something was happening in our country and no one had been paying attention. And . . . Dhoni was the pointer to that phenomenon: you could no longer shut your eyes and be in denial. Small-town India did not feel inferior to the metros any more. They wanted more, and they knew they could achieve as much as the people in the big cities, and

more than that. In a way, Dhoni became the symbol of this. Of course, Dhoni (also) revolutionised Indian cricket in socio-economic terms.

Deb identified two facets to this. In cricket, Dhoni's appointment as captain marked a shift of power from the dominance of cricketers from India's big cities to smaller towns. Chandu Borde (b. 1934, Pune), way before Poona was transformed to industrialized Pune, was cited as 'the last cricketer from a small town to captain India', and India's captains since 'were from Mumbai, Hyderabad, Chennai, Chandigarh, Kolkata and Bangalore'—which is debatable. In society, Dhoni's impact was much bigger, as a 'social and economic revolutionary' and 'every small town boy and girl can see him as an inspirational figure, whatever his or her aspirations . . . [Dhoni] has been an entrepreneur in every sense of the word, and a brand ambassador for the power of every young Indian who is willing to chase a dream till it is caught in the net and then fulfilled to its full potential'.

As the ultimate outlier, an Ekalavya of our time, the poster boy of small-town India rarely speaks of the sacrifice, the burning ambition, the years of rejection and disappointment before hitting the big time. One of the few times that he did, Dhoni's take was refreshingly blunt, 'I don't know if there is something special about playing cricket in a small town, but I guess we have fewer distractions.' Yet, in his endorsements, this was his badge of honour. In a STAR India promo, Dhoni said: 'I believe success isn't limited by how small your hometown is. It's as big as the world you take on. I believe chances are like heartbeats. You can't afford to miss a single one. I believe it's not the runs, but how you run the game that wins it. Believe, and the world is yours.'

In 2008, Ernst & Young published a report (also) titled *The Dhoni Effect*, which found significant changes in consumption with high aspiration levels beyond India's metros, that marketing men had not quite cottoned on to. Dhoni was not mentioned by name anywhere in the report, but his name had become, in socio-economic shorthand, a synonym for small-town India. At the time, research on the twenty-two towns and smaller cities highlighted their growing affluence levels, increased awareness due to media penetration and improved physical connectivity, all of which compelled marketeers to take notice. Marketing and advertising spends targeting these Dhoni Towns have increased dramatically since, for which Dhoni was perhaps inadvertently responsible, and reorienting the dreams and destinies of the children of small-town India. Long before Dhoni though, there was another Ranchi-born sportsman who tried to change the fate of his people.

Marang Gomke—a Great Leader

Long before cricket, India had hockey. And long before Mahendra Singh Dhoni, Ranchi had Jaipal Singh Munda.

He was born Pramod Pahan on 3 January 1903 to a Munda Adivasi family of cowherds in Takra-Hatudami village, near Ranchi. Spotted as a bright youngster, he was enrolled at St Paul's Church School by Anglican clergymen and baptised in November 1918. The Society for the Propagation of the Gospel in Foreign Parts (a Church of England mission) backed his academic promise and exceptional sporting ability with funds for travel and scholarship, first to finish his schooling at St Augustine's College, Canterbury, and then to study for the priesthood at St John's College, Oxford. Hockey, however, proved to be a higher calling.

Jaipal Singh studied Politics, Philosophy and Economics (PPE) at Oxford and was awarded his BSc in 1926. He was elected secretary (1924) then president (1925) of the college debating society. He excelled in both football and hockey, and represented Oxford in varsity matches from 1924 to 1926, winning him a hockey blue. He also started the Oxford Hermits—a sports society for 'Asiatics' in Oxford—who mainly played hockey, including 'friendlies' in Europe, and wrote on hockey for several London papers.

In 1928, he was selected in, and appointed captain of, India's hockey team for the Amsterdam Olympics. He led India to the first of six consecutive hockey golds, yet a dispute with the British team manager led to his being dropped for the final. India would wait 76 years for another Adivasi, Dilip Tirkey (b. 1977, in Odisha's Sundergarh), to lead the national team.

Jaipal Singh returned home an Olympic gold medallist, but to a completely different career. He had qualified for the Indian Civil Service while at Oxford, and when denied leave from training to play at the Olympics, he quit the qualification process. Instead, he found a role with Shell's Indian subsidiary, and after training in London was posted to Kolkata, as the first Indian in a covenanted mercantile assistant post.

Soon Jaipal Singh started the hockey side of Kolkata's Mohun Bagan Athletic Club, was elected to the Bengal Hockey Association and became a leading light of the sport-loving city. Here he married Tara Majumdar, the daughter of P.K. and Agnes Majumdar and granddaughter of W.C. Bonnerjee, one of the founders of the Indian National Congress. His marriage broke down shortly afterwards, and he later wed Jahanara Jeyratnam, the daughter of an ICS officer from Ceylon. As Jahanara Jaipal Singh, she later served two terms in the Rajya Sabha.

The Colonial Service took him from Kolkata to a teaching post at Achimota College (present-day Ghana) and then to Rajkumar College in Raipur, but he was soon drawn back to his roots. In 1939, he presided over the All-India Adivasi Mahasabha, an organization campaigning for tribal rights. At the 1940 Ramgarh Session of the Indian National Congress, he broached the possibility of an autonomous province of Jharkhand to Subhas Chandra Bose. Bose felt that such a demand would divert the course of the freedom movement, and as a result Jharkhand is not mentioned in the proceedings of the session.

Jaipal Singh represented the Adivasis of Bihar in the Constituent Assembly of India (1946–50), where Bihar's envoys included Rajendra Prasad, Jagjivan Ram and Sachchidananda Sinha. In a speech to the Assembly on 19 December 1946 he said:

> I rise to speak on behalf of millions of unknown hordes, yet very important-of unrecognised warriors of freedom, the original people of India who have variously been known as backward tribes, primitive tribes, criminal tribes and everything else, Sir, I am proud to be a *Jungli*, that is the name by which we are known in my part of the country, living as we do in the jungles . . . the whole history of my people is one of continuous exploitation and dispossession by the non-aboriginals of India punctuated by rebellions and disorder, and yet I take Pandit Nehru at his word. I take you all at your word that now we are going to start . . . a new chapter of independent India where there is equality of opportunity, where no one would be neglected.

Ramachandra Guha wrote, 'Jaipal Singh offered one prospective path for the tribals: autonomy within the Indian Union, safeguarded by laws protecting their land and customs and by the creation of a province where the tribals were a majority.' Singh's goodwill towards, and trust in the Indian state's benevolence has proven misguided, with Adivasi lands and resources ruthlessly and continuously exploited by state and private interests, with little or no fair recompense for the Adivasis themselves.

Following Independence, Jaipal Singh's Jharkhand Party (which the Adivasi Mahasabha had become) won 33 out of 352 seats in the 1952 Bihar Vidhan Sabha polls becoming a major opposition party. With only 20 seats by 1962 and dwindling support, he merged the party with the Congress in 1963. It was an unpopular decision, and several splinter groups continued the campaign for Jharkhand's statehood, finally achieving it in 2000.

Jaipal Singh, Marang Gomke (Mundari for 'the great leader') of the Adivasi people, a legend of his sport, a giant in his community and a serving MP, died of a cerebral haemorrhage on 20 March 1970. A small stadium in Ranchi, named in his honour, was built in 1978 and is in ruins today. In January 2013, Ranchi's Jharkhand State Cricket Association International Cricket Stadium was inaugurated nearby. It seats 50,000 and has till date hosted two Tests, five ODIs, two T20s and two 'home' games of the Chennai Super Kings. One of its air-conditioned pavilions is named after Mahendra Singh Dhoni.

Resist and Reorganize—from Mahi to Thala

Cricket teams, from club to country, have quirky traditions of nicknaming players. Usually, a cognomen coined by a teammate or coach sticks. Sometimes sobriquets created by fans or in media coverage gain traction. Anglicized short forms of names were commonest in Indian cricket: Gavaskar became Sunny; Vishwanath, Vishy; Kirmani; Kiri; Kapil, Kaps; and Sachin, Sach. The older Gavaskar was Sunny Bhai, while Kapil and Sachin had the honorific Paaji added by younger teammates. The early Yuvraj and Harbhajan Singh were Yuvi and Bhajji, before Yuvi-Pa and Bhajju-Pa (Paaji, shortened). Polly for Palhan Umrigar, and six decades on, Ché for Cheteshwar Pujara are pleasant anomalies.

Interestingly, Dhoni was and is Mahi, the nickname he took from home, through school and into the game. Few of serious stature in Indian cricket, like Tiger Pataudi and Jimmy Amarnath, went through cricket and life with childhood nicknames, and theirs was an entirely different era. In a recent advert for a mobile phone, a surprised schoolboy keeper whom Dhoni offers to mentor, mumbles 'Dhoni . . .? MS . . .?' till Dhoni says, 'Mahi is fine.' Mahi was his calling card, and the once-Ekalavya was a Dronacharya now.

Upon Dhoni's retirement from international cricket, Cricinfo's Siddharth Monga wrote an insightful essay that took as its starting point Dhoni's and his own origins in unfashionable outposts and their parallel cricketing journeys. In 2006, Dhoni had told Monga of:

> a mistrust of the media. He couldn't figure out why certain players were hyped in the press when better cricketers didn't get a mention. He didn't understand why he needed to do interviews with journalists who told him they were close to the India captain. Imagine being a young cricketer from a small town and being made to oblige journalists because they know the captain. Imagine how much worse it must get for the same young cricketer with club owners, administrators, selectors, sponsors, agents, commentators, umpires, scorers, employers' cousins, and a host of other people he thinks he can't afford to offend.

Refusing to toe the media line was unheard of at the time and was the first of many mini mutinies that Dhoni would lead as India's captain—which he became 'without resorting to any of the tactics he so abhorred'. Dhoni's tetchy relationship with, and his mistrust of the media was a recurrent theme in his career. Rajdeep Sardesai notes that 'no cricketer with the exception of Tendulkar has been so celebrated since the turn of the century, and yet no other player has so deliberately stayed away from the media whirl. No interviews, one-line staccato answers in press conferences, the odd witticism; Dhoni has managed to keep the prying media at bay'.

For Dhoni this was his 'satyagraha against the media. I don't want to speak when I do badly. I won't speak when I do well either, the media can write what they wish'. It was shaped by an incident following India's disastrous exit from the 2007 World Cup. 'Some people entered and just pushed a few bricks that we had laid out for the construction, that's all. But yes, it deeply affected my family. Now, you can visit my parents, they will give you chai, but won't speak to the press any longer', he told Sardesai.

After the World Cup T20 semi-final loss in 2016, when an Australian journalist asked him about retirement, Dhoni invited the journalist on to the podium and then cheekily told him, 'If you were an Indian, then maybe I would have asked you whether you have a son or a brother who is a wicketkeeper and can take my place.' Dhoni smiled, putting the bewildered and embarrassed journalist out of his misery, with the media corps in splits.

Since 2017, the actor and television presenter, Gaurav Kapur has hosted a web series called *Breakfast with Champions*, where he chats with cricketers, other sportspeople and sometimes their family members too. This is usually over a meal at home, a cafe or a restaurant. There's another series Kapur presents, called *22 Yarns*, specifically on cricket featuring personalities from the wider cricketing world. The rosters of the two series reads like a virtual who's who of contemporary cricket, yet Dhoni has never appeared on the shows. His teammates' titbits about him have shed more light on Dhoni than he ever has himself.

Dhoni's captains and coaches marvelled at the refreshing lack of put-on humility, and this continued through his captaincy. As one of many significant firsts, as captain he eliminated all external influences on the dressing room. Presciently, Siddharth Monga observed: 'Players' utility to the team was all that mattered now. Dhoni's rise from so far out of the system had given many boys like him a reason to dream; he was making sure their cricket mattered and not how worldly-wise they were.'

Captaincy wasn't something Dhoni craved, it arrived by default after the 2007 World Cup, when Dravid resigned and Kumble retired from ODIs. When it was announced he would be the ODI captain, he refused to speak to the media despite the BCCI's requests, and finally agreed to read out a statement. Once he took it on, he thrived, embracing the T20 format, which played a part in hastening the IPL revolution, which in turn opened the doors for a greater scale of employment for cricketers from India and elsewhere.

Dhoni had the unenviable task of leading legends of Indian cricket in Tests and ODIs, which didn't intimidate him. He made it known that the team would be run his way, and instead of taking matters to the media as previous skippers or even managers had done, which inevitably divided the dressing room, he told selectors that India's losses would be on them if they happened because India's fielding was too slow. When Ganguly, Dravid and Laxman were surplus to ODI requirements, he jettisoned them, but retained them for Tests, where they were still contributing. For Dhoni, fitness and at least 50 matches of experience going into a World Cup were non-negotiables, and he finally had his way in time for 2011.

Dhoni the captain empowered his players individually and as a unit. Trusting a complete unknown, Joginder Sharma, over more experienced bowlers in the side that day to bowl the last over against Pakistan in the 2007 T20 final with the words, 'Cricket won't let you down' is often cited. On the collective, he once said, 'I want a team that can stand before an advancing truck.' This was his captaincy mantra and where he led, the team followed—to the top in all formats, in rankings and titles. The look of his leadership was different—no grandstanding, jabbing fingers, stamping feet or knitted brows, and back in the shadows when the job was done.

Not only did Dhoni build teams in his own image, he got them to take public positions on issues he cared about, usually garnering great support but sometimes sharp criticism too. At Vizag on 29 October 2016, the India side wore their mothers' first names on their kits as part of STAR India's Nayi Soch campaign, which was widely lauded. At the toss, Dhoni mentioned that the contribution of mothers was as important as that of soldiers, and the country should remember that every day. At Ranchi on 8 March 2019, the India side played in camouflage caps in solidarity with the

40 Indian soldiers killed in the Pulwana terrorist attack. Though Kohli was India's captain, it was widely believed that it was Dhoni who suggested doing this. Dhoni is an ardent supporter of India's armed forces, holds the rank of an Honorary Lieutenant Colonel in the Territorial Army, and has trained and toured with his unit. A winged-dagger logo on Dhoni's keeping gloves during the 2019 World Cup led to a small war of words between the ICC and BCCI. Dhoni, of course, kept his counsel and the logo.

Like the way the India team was run, the role of India's coach/manager had been professionalized when Dhoni broke through, and with each of them he forged fruitful relationships. John Wright gave him his debut, but it was under Greg Chappell that Dhoni began to flower. Chappell noticed his rockstar looks, observed a strut that wasn't offensive and maintained that Dhoni's confidence never exceeded his belief. Chappell felt he read the game astutely, and during tight chases if he walked over to Dhoni in the pavilion for a chat, he found Dhoni had already worked out a plan of attack. A useful baseball player in his youth, Chappell noted and nurtured Dhoni's instinctive reading and calling 'plays', as a catcher in baseball would.

Dhoni won India the 2007 World T20 title with an interim manager (Lalchand Rajput) in charge, and the march to the 2011 World Cup crown under Gary Kirsten is well known. The days of Duncan Fletcher saw a string of poor Test results and Dhoni's retirement from red-ball cricket. Success in shorter formats continued under Fletcher, later Anil Kumble and Ravi Shastri, as Dhoni's career wound down, never to reach the heights of 2011.

Dhoni had a solid and successful axis with Stephen Fleming in the IPL, where they have been together for 12 seasons—10 at CSK and 2 at Pune, bagging 3 titles and 5 runner-up finishes. In an age of data-driven decisions, the Dhoni–Fleming mantra is not to over-rely on data, keep meetings short and trust players with responsibility to execute plans and processes. CSK has been the tightest of units with only 75 players over 12 seasons, and just two captains, Suresh Raina and Dhoni. Progression is usually from within, and former CSK teammates, Lakshmipathy Balaji and Mike Hussey, now coach the side's bowlers and batters.

Thala (Tamil for leader or boss and short for Thalaivar) is CSK fans' name for Dhoni. His popularity can be gauged from the iconic status of two other Thalaivars in the Tamil cultural universe: the actors, Rajinikanth and Ajithkumar. Let's also not forget that people from north of the Vindhyas are very rarely held in the esteem and affection that Dhoni is by the largely Tamilian fan base and, in that sense too, he is a genuine crossover icon. However, the Thala halo has sometimes cast a long shadow.

The Greying of Dhoni

Narayanswami Srinivasan, the chairman of India Cements and owner of CSK, acquired Dhoni's services for his franchise in 2008. Srinivasan also served as BCCI president (2011–13) and ICC chairman (2014–15). Dhoni's equation with him, while not unique in Indian cricket, illuminates another side to Dhoni. Srinivasan was alleged to have ensured that CSK retained Dhoni without an auction in 2010. As BCCI president he, legally, vetoed the removal of Dhoni from India's captaincy in 2012 following losses to England and Australia, and instead sacked the national selector soon after. Srinivasan has gone on record suggesting that he did veto 'the decision to drop Dhoni as captain. How can you drop someone as captain within a year of his lifting the World Cup?' Dismissing allegations that Indian cricket had entered an age where star players called the shots and Board officials were happy to pamper them, Srinivasan has said, 'What you call favouritism I say is my respect for a top-class cricketer's achievements.'

In 2013 it emerged that Rhiti Sports, a company in which Dhoni had a stake, was managing contracts of India and CSK players leading to allegations of conflict of interest. It was also revealed that CSK's marketing was run by Rhiti Sports, as was their kit-supply contract, suggesting that the company, and consequently Dhoni, was benefiting from CSK's off-field financial success too. Dhoni and Srinivasan's omertà when questioned on the matter reinforced the loyalty and respect they had for each other. Similarly, when it was alleged that Srinivasan's son-in-law, and at the time CSK team principal, Gurunath Meiyappan was alleged to be involved in spot-fixing of IPL matches, Dhoni told the probing Mudgal Committee that Meiyappan had nothing to do with the team's on-field cricketing decisions. Known for his innovative and unpredictable strokeplay, Dhoni had dead-batted this doosra straight back to the bowler. In 2015, CSK was suspended from the IPL for two years and Meiyappan banned for life from any involvement in cricket matches.

Dhoni has unapologetically defended his relationship with Srinivasan, suggesting that the former BCCI official 'was a true supporter of Indian cricket. I really don't care what people say, I found Srinivasan as someone who was always there to help cricketers'. Other than his complete mistrust in the media to put across his side of the story, it showed him to be a strong personality not swayed easily by criticism, and with a sense of unfathomable loyalty. It also confirmed that under that disarming image of the small-town cricketer and one-man brand, ticks a very sharp political mind. Siddharth Monga wrote masterfully, comparing the flecks of grey in Dhoni's hair and beard to the shades of grey in Dhoni's character that these incidents revealed.

The Road Ahead

When everyone in cricket thought Sir Don Bradman's *The Art of Cricket* and Mike Brearley's *The Art of Captaincy* had said it all, Dhoni pretty much rewrote the books for all to see without penning a word. But he does value the power of the written word, and it was apparent in how he signed off from international cricket. On 15 August 2020 he called it a day, not with a media release or press conference, but with an Instagram post featuring a montage of photos from his career, carefully cut to words of 'Main pal do pal ka shayar hoon'.

Written by Sahir Ludhianvi and sung by Mukesh, from the film *Kabhi Kabhie*, the lyrics ruminate on the transience of fame and success from a poet's perspective. The lyrics laud poets that came before, the mark they made, sang of better ones to follow and the new directions they'll take. The telling line is the one where the poet tells his audience that going forward, there will be better listeners than you; this is Dhoni gently admonishing his doubters. What Dhoni didn't do was cast any light on his future. He made everyone emotional without showing any emotion himself. These were in character for the cricketer who abhorred risk but took games deep and remained inscrutable in the glare of scrutiny. To his credit, Dhoni has successfully amalgamated his cricketing qualities—of leadership, unorthodoxy, determination, empathy, power and being the boy next door—into his image and accumulated a dizzyingly, lucrative portfolio of brand associations and endorsements. Those could quite easily be his launch pad for leadership in the public sphere.

Jaipal Singh Munda, the Oxford-educated hockey stalwart and Adivasi voice, is a forgotten saga of thwarted ambition, even a cautionary tale of a subaltern that spoke too loudly in incipient India. Post-Partition India hadn't yet healed itself and was unready for his brand of leadership, central to which was a better future for the dispossessed. The Government of Jharkhand has fully embraced the legacy of Jaipal Singh's clansman, Birsa Munda. There is already a stadium and an airport in Ranchi named after Birsa Munda, and there are plans for a 150-foot (45.7-m) statue on the Jamshedpur–Ranchi NH33. It won't soar as high as Sardar Patel's (182 m) or Chhatrapati Shivaji's (212 m, proposed) likenesses, but in India upward mobility of icons does matter.

Mahendra Singh Dhoni has had a hand in shaping the India he will live in for the next half of his life. Dhoni's rise is as much owed to the springboard of Steel Town India, as it was in spite of every tether of small-town India that held him back. His climb from cricket's boondocks to a sporting galactico, crossover icon and multimillionaire businessman has touched, energized and perhaps weaponized the ambitions of more Indians than Jaipal Singh ever could. For Dhoni, who loves his bikes and SUVs, the open road beckons for his life after cricket. He can choose to freewheel in any direction he wants, yet no one knows what he's planned. With his impeccable sense of timing and occasion, expect Dhoni's next move to be straightforward, but completely unexpected.

7

A Fan

Amit Sinha

During my college days, I became good friends with a soft-spoken, witty and cricket-loving Tamil Nadu boy named Rahul. We never belonged to the same friend circle, but Rahul was too nice a guy to not be friends with. It was in the third year of our college life that we discovered our deep love for cricket, and we hit it off. In fact, it was with Rahul that I watched my first IPL game in the stadium, just a week before our final semester exam. There was little doubt about his loyalties as far as the IPL was concerned. Chennai Super Kings, Dhoni, Whistle Podu: you mention one of the three in front of him, and you were guaranteed a long conversation. He loved them all.

Post college, Rahul moved to Germany for his master's. We continued to talk on WhatsApp for a while before the conversations began drying up as it generally happens. Suddenly, on the night of 23 March 2016, I got a WhatsApp call from Rahul. Calling from Berlin, Rahul was gasping for breath as the conversation began at around 11 in the night. There was little in terms of niceties being exchanged. Rahul just wanted to talk about the events that had panned out a few minutes ago—the events that had forced him to willingly invite punishment from his teacher so that he could come out of the class. The events that had left him breathless, when he decided to call a friend thousands of miles away in Delhi.

In the next 10 minutes, we just talked about the magic of MS Dhoni, his ability to turn things around when all hopes seemed lost and, of course, the alpha move of taking off his glove to run out Mustafizur to give India a win that had almost seemed impossible a few minutes before that. In those 10 minutes, it didn't seem for a single second that we were listening to each other's voices after a good eleven months. It just seemed like he was sitting on the parapet right across our classroom in college and discussing cricket with me as he used to with his usual exuberance. We were happy—madly happy—and in awe of MS Dhoni. All that came out in that brief conversation was pure and raw emotion. It goes without saying that the Thala fan was mighty proud too.

Sitting in a classroom full of people who didn't understand much about the game, my friend, a perennial CSK fan, had a tough time controlling his emotions, which ebbed and flowed with the wildly oscillating fortunes of the two teams playing in that 2016 T20 World Cup decisive match. When Dhoni ran with the ball in one hand to take down the stumps, he almost shrieked with excitement in the classroom.

Truth be told, a part of me wanted to reach out to him to discuss the manic events of the evening the moment the Chinnaswamy big screen flashed 'OUT' to declare a Team India win. But months of no contact and the difficult calculations of a different time zone meant I buried those thoughts. And then it happened; out of nowhere, a call from a friend from a far-off land to talk about that one thing that connected us. I have no clue why he decided to call *me* of all people after being thrown out of the classroom that day. Looking back, it was one of the most special conversations that I have had with someone around the game.

To think of it, this must be one of the million sweet memories that MS Dhoni was responsible for in the life of his fans, alongside all the victories he's hailed for. Of course, there were moments of frustration too. But the moments that he wowed us with, the times he put a smile on our faces, the days he made us hug a loved one in happiness and hope far outnumber anything. When our long lives come to an end one day, the *shayari* of this *pal do pal ka shayar* will remain an indelible part of our good happy memories that will leave with us. That's how you gauge the impact of sportsmen like Dhoni in the eventual analysis, I feel: not through their wins or losses, not through their runs and averages, and definitely not through the trophies that they managed to win. Their true impact is immeasurable, for the statisticians—despite all the latest advancements in technology—still can't collect and count the good memories that they left a billion people with. Can they?

PART III

The Many Colours of MSD

Auritro Chowdhury
and
Amit Sinha

1

Cricket Khelega?

These two words are a memorable dialogue from Dhoni's biopic which sprung a thousand memes and then some. The question is asked by the character of Keshav Banerjee, played by veteran actor Rajesh Sharma, who is the cricket coach of Dhoni's school team. It is now a well-known fact that Dhoni used to play as the goalkeeper of the school football team and switched to cricket later. If not for that moment, India would perhaps never have the services of, arguably, the best ever wicketkeeper-batsman that the country has ever produced. Two fleeting words that changed the cricketing world.

Talent-spotting is a talent in itself, and one coach or spotter does not a career make. That depends on multiple levels of talent-spotters, coaches and of course a lot of luck. For Dhoni, it was Keshav Banerjee who spotted his cricketing potential and set him on the path to glory. The next man to spot Dhoni's talent was Deval Sahay who joined Central Coal Limited (CCL) in January 1998 as director of personnel. Sahay wanted to build a CCL team capable of competing in the local Ranchi league and started hiring talented cricketers under the company's sports quota. Dhoni had recently scored a double century in an unbroken opening partnership of

378 with teammate Shabir Hussain in the finals of an inter-school cricket tournament and Sahay quickly offered him a job and paid him more than the rest for being 'a match-winning player'.

The next two men who realized the potential of the future Indian captain were then South Eastern Railway coach, Subroto Banerjee (not the former Indian pacer), and then South Eastern Railway divisional manager, Animesh Kumar Ganguly. Ganguly was a cricket connoisseur and on the lookout for talented youngsters. Banerjee told him of such an up-and-coming player on the Bihar team and Ganguly himself bowled at him to test his abilities. Ganguly was so impressed that he offered Dhoni the job and even arranged for him to skip work to attend cricket practice and matches. Even with such an arrangement, Dhoni found it difficult to balance work and cricket and had to ultimately choose one.

Fortunately for Dhoni and Indian cricket, Prakash Poddar and Raju Mukherjee, two ex-Bengal players working with the BCCI as TRDOs happened to watch Dhoni playing during a Jharkhand match. The rest, as they say, is history.

The TRDW was a BCCI initiative formed under the chairmanship of Dilip Vengsarkar in 2002 and was tasked with identifying and locating talented cricketers from beyond the established cricketing centres in the country. The TRDOs would usually travel around the country, watch various matches, both age level and domestic types and fill in a form mentioning the details of the players (name, batter/bowler, right-handed/left-handed, etc.) and their skills (fast bowler, spinner, swing, etc.). There was also a 'recommendations box' at the end of the form and that would almost always remain empty.

It was very different that day; Poddar and Mukherjee were taken aback by what they saw, and the recommendation box was filled in with these words; 'Good striker of the ball; has a lot of power but needs to work on his wicket-keeping. Technically not very good. Is very good at running between wickets.' Once the

TRDOs recommended someone, Vengsarkar would go watch him himself and, suitably impressed, Vengsarkar wrote this about Dhoni; 'There was a lot of talent out there and much of it was flashy. But the deciding factor for me was temperament. If you have that, you will continue to improve . . .' By 2003–04 Dhoni had already made it to the India A team and after that he only kept reaching greater heights.

From 'cricket *khelega*' to being a part of cricket history!

2

Durga Sporting

Mahendra Singh Dhoni, two-time World Cup-winning captain, one of the hardest hitters of the cricket ball, wicketkeeper extraordinaire and former member of Durga Sporting Club! What is that last one, you might ask? Well, it all started in 2001 when Dhoni moved to Kharagpur to take up a job with the South Eastern Railways. Dhoni was appointed as a ticket collector and was offered the job by the then divisional manager (of SE Railways), Animesh Kumar Ganguly, who was looking to build a strong cricket team for his department.

Dhoni had already played domestic cricket by this time and he apparently used to wait restlessly for 2 p.m. to arrive every day so that he would be relieved of his professional duties and quickly head over to play or practise cricket. And unusually for a professional cricketer, he used to do something that was the nightmare of coaches. Dhoni played tennisball cricket as a member of Durga Sporting Club.

Soma, Dhoni's teammate at the tennis-ball cricket club, provided him with a 10X12 tenement to stay in, free of cost. And apart from his work, playing leather-ball cricket and enjoying Thomas's chai and trips to chicken dhabas, Dhoni found the time to play for Durga Sporting Club located in the Golkhuli area of Kharagpur.

The ground at the club was heavily biased towards the leg side and so bowlers would bowl almost on the sixth stump on the offside to keep Dhoni from hitting his legendary 6s. Not that it worked, because he used the helicopter shot, which he had learnt in Ranchi, to keep swivelling those 6s on to the leg side. Durga Sporting Club has a Facebook page, and they are still winning trophies, although one cannot be too sure if it is the same club.

In quaint old Kharagpur, known thus far for a pretty long railway platform and for India's first IIT—Indian Institute of Technology, which produced such accomplished names as Arvind Kejriwal and Sundar Pichai—Dhoni and Durga Sporting Club are the town's tryst with sporting destiny!

3

The Helicopter

Santosh Lal was a decent cricketer born in Ranchi, the capital of Jharkhand, and played a handful of domestic matches representing the state. Lal has very nondescript numbers; 280 First Class runs from 13 innings at an average of just over 21.5 and a couple of half-centuries. Lal's List A and T20 numbers are far more modest: 225 runs from 15 innings at a shade over 16 with one half-century and 44 runs from 5 innings at a strike rate of 81.48, respectively. He also took a combined 23 wickets across formats with his right-arm medium bowling and his bowling averages or economy is nothing to write home about either. Unfortunately, he passed away from pancreatitis even before reaching his thirtieth birthday in July 2013. There is nothing extraordinary or special about Santosh Lal's cricket career and he would have normally been yet another mandatory statistical entry in record books and a footnote in various cricket magazines. But for one small detail that record books usually do not acknowledge. Santosh Lal played in the Jharkhand and Bihar youth teams during the same time as another Ranchi lad—Mahendra Singh Dhoni—and the two were friends. And it was Santosh Lal who taught Dhoni how to play the helicopter shot. A shot that would later become synonymous with Dhoni.

The story goes that Lal taught his friend the shot in exchange for a few *shingharas* (that is what samosas are called in that region of India). Not a bad bargain for the friend at all, given how famous it would make him and how much success it would bring him. Lal and Dhoni had remained friends, and when Lal was suffering and almost on his deathbed, Dhoni arranged for Lal to be airlifted to Delhi. Ironically, bad weather forced them to land at Varanasi and it was too late for Lal when they reached Delhi. The helicopter that would be his legacy had failed him when it mattered the most!

The helicopter shot is basically a bottom-handed wristy flick. The batter uses a heavy bottom-handed grip to generate power and uses his/her wrists to flick the ball away. It is more often played against full-length or yorker deliveries and the shot gets its name because the follow-through of the batter resembles the whirring blades of a helicopter. In the finishing flourish after completing the stroke, the batter circles the bat overhead and all that movement completed in one swift motion reminds the spectator of the motions of a helicopter's blade and thus the name of the shot. The helicopter shot is an unorthodox and unconventional cricketing shot and is a relatively new innovation; it is not a classical shot found in any coaching manual. Its popularity stems from the spectacle surrounding the shot as well as how effective it is against full-length deliveries, especially the yorker. The yorker is a fast, low delivery aimed at the base of the stumps and is also called a toe crusher because it usually hits the batter's toes. It is not an easy ball to hit against, especially for a 6, but with the innovation of the helicopter shot, Dhoni has consistently hit the yorker in the air and even for 6s.

The helicopter shot was not always called that. According to Dhoni's biopic, Santosh Lal called it the *thappad* shot, as it resembled slapping the ball away to the boundary. Dhoni had already been playing the helicopter shot on the international stage for years but right before the 2011 ICC World Cup, Pepsi released a series of advertisements that perhaps for the first time brought the name 'helicopter shot' into popular culture. The advert series aimed to tell the origin stories behind popular cricketing shots and deliveries, and one of them was dedicated to Dhoni's helicopter shot. The mythos created by this particular advert saw Dhoni being trained to operate what is presumably a hay cutter and that leads to the eventual helicopter shot. Commentators and journalists called it various things, often focusing on the result of the shot over the name of the shot itself, but after that Pepsi advertisement, it was ingrained in popular consciousness as the helicopter shot.

Like many cricketing skills, shots or deliveries, if you look hard enough, you will always find someone who had already done it before. And similarly for the helicopter shot, there are numerous videos of it being executed on the Internet—the exceptions that prove the rule, if you will. There is one of Sachin Tendulkar playing a kind of a helicopter shot against England in 2002; he had just completed his thirty-second century and hit a boundary. The commentator calls it 'a simple innovation'. More remarkably, there are a couple of matches where Mohammad Azharuddin hits a shot that resembles Dhoni's helicopter shot very closely. There is one from his innings of 182 against England in 1992–93 where he unfortunately gets out attempting the shot and there is another example from the first innings at Eden Gardens in 1996. Azhar scored 109 from only 77 deliveries and in the middle of a spree of 5 boundaries against Lance Klusener, he hit a couple of amazing helicopter shots. Given that Azhar had always been a wristy player of Hyderabadi vintage and was known for his flick shots, these examples are not really a surprise. However, what is for certain is that neither Sachin nor Azhar played it regularly enough to either be associated with the shot or for commentators or journalists to identify the shot as a unique one and ergo give it a name. The credit goes entirely to Dhoni, as far as the international stage goes, and thus it is Dhoni who is synonymous with the helicopter shot.

Dhoni has been playing the helicopter shot almost ever since he found himself on the international stage. One of the first memories of him playing the shot is from an ODI against England in 2005 where the commentator Laxman Sivaramakrishnan simply acknowledges the boundary. Dhoni went on to hit many in his international career as well as in the IPL before slowing down the shot at the tail end of his career. But perhaps the most famous use of his helicopter shot was against Nuwan Kulasekara at the Wankhede in Mumbai. A nation of a billion and a half people erupted when that helicopter landed in the stands. India had won the World Cup!

4

Hair to the Throne

There is a scene in the Mahendra Singh Dhoni biopic, starring the late Sushant Singh Rajput, where the Bihar team is to play Punjab in the U-19 Cooch Behar Trophy final match of the 1999 season at Keenan Stadium in Jamshedpur. In less than a year, Bihar would cease to have a domestic team, U-19 or otherwise, and a new state, Jharkhand, would enter the Indian Union and take Bihar's membership in the BCCI. Both Bihar and Jharkhand are relatively underdeveloped and poor states (more so then than now), especially when compared to Punjab, which is one of India's richer states. And the scene in question reflects this difference.

The Punjab players—among whom is one Yuvraj Singh, already a precocious talent and identified in cricketing circles as a future star—come in carrying expensive gadgets and looking fashionably dapper. The Jharkhand players are visibly impressed by such glamour. Later in the film, Dhoni points out that they did not lose the match on the cricket field but that his statemates were instead awestruck by their stylish opponents from the north. One can only assume that the moment stuck with Dhoni who, having realized the impact presentation can make, experimented with various fashionable hairstyles throughout his career.*

The styling of hair, in its most basic sense, is an aspect of personal grooming but hairdos have historically been associated with cultures, subcultures and making a fashion statement. Some styles like hair-braiding date back tens of thousands of years (think Queen Cleopatra's gilded ones) and some like the mohawk trace their roots to Native American tribes (although the links are tenuous, and the current style is more an invention of twentieth-century popular culture). Hairstyles usually have a geography and time period associated with them and some cyclically come back in style. A few of the more famous ones from the last century, especially from the world of music and cinema, are Marylin Monroe's blonde bombshell cropped waves, Mia Farrow's pixie cut, Jennifer Aniston's 'Rachel' cut from F.R.I.E.N.D.S, Elvis Presley's pompadour, Einstein's unruly uncombed 'absent-minded scientist', Marge Simpson's blue beehive and arguably the most famous one—the Beatles' moptop! These hairstyles have contributed significantly to the making of these superstars and their legacy.

The modern athlete lives the celebrity life as much as an actor or musician and ergo they spend a considerable amount of time fashioning their own style. George Best of Northern Ireland and Manchester United is often considered the first celebrity sports star. Best wore the same moptops that the Beatles did and since both the music band and Best's rise to fame coincided, he is referred to as the Fifth Beatle. It's not far-fetched then that the athletes who choose the celebrity life or want to stand out frequently take the hairstyle route as they are required to wear team-sanctioned jerseys along with their teammates during their time on the playing field, which is when they are most visible to the public.

---

* Alim Hakim is Dhoni's hairstylist.

Some of the most iconic hairstyles in sports came from the world away from cricket, where players usually wore their hair like the rest of their generation did. Think long and moppy in the seventies and shortish and parted in the nineties. Carlos Valderrama turned up at the 1994 FIFA World Cup in the United States with a magnificent blonde afro that resembled strands of instant noodles. Andre Agassi and Wayne Gretzky were rocking the mullet in tennis and ice hockey, respectively, and Dennis Rodman was lighting up the NBA in a riot of different hair colours. Who can forget the 'goal' cut by The Phenom, Ronaldo, who won the Golden Boot to complement his hairstyle at the 2002 FIFA World Cup. And then there is the man who set the benchmark for all after him, David Beckham. Beckham wore everything from the mohawk to the fauxhawk, shaved head to long flowing locks and cornrows to ponytails. Beckham even reportedly flew his personal barber into Japan and South Korea for the 2002 World Cup.

And then came a boy from little-known Jharkhand, wearing long straight hair, into the Indian team. The 'in' hairstyle for the misguided Indian youth at that moment was the ridiculous 'Tere Naam' cut inspired from the eponymous film that had released the year before Dhoni's India debut. Although two international cricketers were experimenting with coloured hair at the start of the noughties—Collin Miller from Australia, who was seen with electric blue and bright pink hair, and Zimbabwe's big all-rounder Andy Blignaut, who dyed his hair to reflect the colours of the Zimbabwean flag—Indian cricketers before Dhoni had hardly ever strayed from the mainstream.

Dhoni's hairdo was as much a talking point as his explosive batting style at the start of his career, so much so that the then Pakistani president, General Pervez Musharraf, advised him to not cut his long, flowing shoulder-length locks during India's tour of Pakistan in 2004. For a while in 2006, Dhoni had even coloured his long hair dirty blonde and that hair won us our first World Cup in 24 years, in the inaugural T20 edition of 2007, albeit without the blonde dye.

After the T20 victory, Dhoni cut his hair short into something more sober and mainstream. This he wore till the end of the 2011 ICC World Cup, a tournament that India won again that year. The very next day he surprised everybody by turning up with a shaved head, holding the Cup with the Gateway of India in the background. According to *The Times of India*, Dhoni did so to fulfil a religious pledge and offered his hair to the Balaji Temple at Tirupati.

Next up from Dhoni's library of hairdos was his 2013 IPL look, when he turned up to captain Chennai Super Kings with a mohawk that extended almost till his shoulders. By 2018 the pressure of captaining India for so long had begun to show and Dhoni embraced it with style, wearing his hair short and sporting the salt-and-pepper look. Last seen, Mahendra Singh Dhoni was sporting the fauxhawk, paired with a stylish beard looking for a hair to his throne!

5

Super Bowl-Out!

The year is 2007 and India has had a terrible tour of the Caribbean during the ODI World Cup held there. India came into the tournament as the runners-up of the previous edition and boasting a very strong team. India was one of the contenders for the title and was drawn in a group alongside new boys and regional minnows Bermuda and two of its subcontinental neighbours, Bangladesh and Sri Lanka. India was definitely one of the favourites for the two qualifiers from its group. A shocking loss to Bangladesh and another defeat against Sri Lanka meant India had to go home early, despite a thumping win against Bermuda—a match perhaps more remembered for Dwayne Leverock's earth-shaking catch to dismiss Uthappa.

The aftermath saw massive changes in the team and most seniors either opted out or were dropped from the squad which was going to participate in the inaugural T20I World Cup in South Africa later that year. The Indian Board had so far been reluctant to explore the newest form of cricket and the Indian team had consequently only played one T20I thus far. The match against South Africa was played in December 2006 at Johannesburg. It was an easy victory for India although all eleven Indian players were making their debuts and amongst them were six Indians who were playing their first-ever T20 match. Surprisingly, future Indian T20 stars Dhoni and Suresh Raina were amongst those six. If one looked at the scorecard, one would realize that most of the players across both teams were playing as if this were ODI cricket and only Albie Morkel's innings resembled that of a modern T20 innings. India, however, selected a young squad for the upcoming World Cup and the captaincy was handed to Mahendra Singh Dhoni. Seven of the players from that first game went on to make the fifteen-member World Cup squad and Virender Sehwag, Harbhajan Singh and Ajit Agarkar were the three oldest and most experienced (in terms of international appearances across formats) players in that squad.

Dhoni was given an immense responsibility, and this was the first time that he was made a captain in any form of cricket. Thus far the world had only seen a flamboyant batter who could hit hard and hit long. Dhoni was a big-hitting wicketkeeper in the mould of Adam Gilchrist and unlike anything India had seen before. Both Ganguly and Dravid, his previous captains, used him in such roles where he could go in and up the ante with his powerful hitting. Dhoni was a talisman for an Indian team that had been looking for a wicketkeeper capable of batting and he proved to be more than that; he could not only bat but could also put the fear of God in the opposition's mind with his devastating batting. Style, flamboyance, big hitting and standard wicketkeeping were the only aspects of Dhoni that the world and the fans had witnessed and known. Now he was to captain his team in a World Cup, and no one knew what to expect.

Anticlimactically his first match as a captain was washed out. It was India's first match of the World Cup group stages, and they were scheduled to play Scotland at Kingsmead, Durban. Not a ball was bowled as rain poured in, although the rain gods provided just enough of a relief for Dhoni to complete his first act as captain— losing the toss to Ryan Watson.

India's next match and Dhoni's captaincy debut for all intents and purposes was against their eternal rivals, Pakistan. Shoaib Malik won the toss and put India in. India kept losing wickets and looked very uncomfortable, Uthappa scored a half-century and captain Dhoni stayed till the twentieth over and made a decent contribution to guide India to a respectable score. The Pakistani seamers bowled superbly, especially Mohammad Asif who took 4/18 in his 4 overs—an effort that would win him the Man of the Match.

The Pakistan innings stuttered and faltered as well and none of their batsmen got going except Misbah-ul-Haq, who scored a half-century and got run out on the very last ball of the innings, attempting what would have been the winning run. Dhoni had already showed signs of the exemplary captain he was to become in that first match. But there was more to come.

The tournament had a unique rule to resolve tied matches, somewhat adopted from football's penalty shoot-outs: there were going to be bowl-outs. Basically, each team would be given five attempts to aim at unguarded stumps and the team with the most 'outs' or 'hits' would win the tiebreaker. India hit all three of their 'bowls' and won the bowl-out while the Pakistanis missed all three of their attempts.

There were three things that Dhoni had done, two of them conspicuous but not obvious and one that we later came to know during an interview. India was going to go first and Virender Sehwag was handed the ball which seemed odd as he was not a regular bowler. In fact, of the three attempts, only Harbhajan Singh was a regular bowler and Uthappa was the third bowler. Those watching live would have wondered about the choices but given the results they were surely not disappointed with the tactics. Pakistan fielded Yasser Arafat, Umar Gul and Shahid Afridi, all of them bowled either over the stumps or wide of them. One glaring comparison was the position taken behind the wicket by the respective wicketkeepers. While Kamran Akmal, the Pakistani wicketkeeper stood deep behind the stumps in a more or less regular position, his Indian counterpart, Dhoni, came very close right behind the stumps and knelt down, thus making himself big and into a sort of a sight screen for his bowlers to aim at. This obviously worked, given the results.

In a later interview Dhoni revealed that the choice of nominated players was not a fluke. India was aware of the rule and Dhoni the captain wanted to be prepared for any eventuality. The Indian team had started every practice session with a bowl-out practice. The idea was to make things fun while also identifying those guys who would regularly hit the stumps during that session. The smiling and relaxed faces of the Indians during the actual in-game bowl-out is proof of how well their captain's sharp thinking paid off!

6

Keep Calm and Carry On

The British government issued a series of posters in 1939 in preparation for World War II. The copy of the poster read 'Keep Calm and Carry On' and it was intended to raise the morale of the British public in preparation of the threat of predicted air attacks and the upcoming blitz. The poster was evocative of the Victorian British idea of a stoic stiff upper lip, self-discipline and remaining calm in the face of adversity. The 'Keep Calm' posters were lost to time before being rediscovered in the noughties. Coincidentally, the noughties were also the time that the world discovered one Mahendra Singh Dhoni, the personification of 'Keep Calm'!

International and/or professional sport is a cauldron of high pressure, especially if you are playing in a country in which that sport is the most popular one and you are one of the star players or in a position of responsibility within the sport. In the subcontinent that sport is cricket. There has been a popular joke that the position of most public scrutiny in India is that of the Prime Minister and second to that is the position of the captain of the Indian cricket team. It is obviously a flippant joke but there is a sliver of truth reflected in it. The role of the Indian cricket captain is indeed under heavy public scrutiny in a country and region that is heavily invested in the sport. And along with that scrutiny comes immense pressure—a pressure to perform and the pressure of responsibility to deliver results. The same fans that adore you, the same fans that worship you, will turn on you the moment your performance crumbles under pressure. It is a balancing act on an extremely thin piece of thread, perfected only by few.

Dhoni has been one such athlete. Standing unmoved and resolute in the face of any and all pressure. If not for his prematurely greying hair no one would have even noticed that Dhoni also feels pressure. So calm and cool in his demeanour, his expressions hardly change whether he is facing defeat or victory, whether the situation is dire or a walk in the park, whether he has lost half his batting side in an important chase, or his bowlers are having a collective bad day or he himself is having one. We have already written about Dhoni and the art of batting with the tail, and that art is fundamentally based on handling pressure. Forget mere mortals, more accomplished batters than him often give way to the pressure of handling the tail and farming the strike, but not Dhoni.

And this is not just about batting. Dhoni the wicketkeeper as well as Dhoni the captain has built his legacy around these traits. Captain Cool, as commentators often call him, did not even flinch under pressure; his cool calm head saw him and his team through many a tough situation. Dhoni had a bad start to his international career, but he did not let that pressure get the better of him, scoring an amazing century against Pakistan after four failures. A young and not-so-experienced Dhoni had the captaincy thrust upon him and was given a young team by a board seemingly disillusioned with its senior players after their disastrous Caribbean campaign during the 50-over World Cup earlier in 2007. India went into the inaugural T20I World Cup with all the pressure on the young team and their equally young captain. And how did Dhoni handle that pressure? By winning the championship of course.

There is a word they use in Bihar and Jharkhand, where Dhoni is from, and that word is *hotei*. Roughly translated, it means that 'it will happen', the emotion behind it is somewhat like que sera sera—whatever will be, will be. But in Bihar and Jharkhand, it reflects the attitude that we will deal with something when it happens; there is no point worrying about something till it happens. Not just crossing a bridge when one comes to it, but to build one, if necessary, but more importantly, to worry about the raging river beneath in either case. It is said that language shapes the way one thinks and behaves, and evidently that is the case with Dhoni. Brought up in that environment, Dhoni has an inbuilt and innate ability to deal with pressure.

Two of the finest illustrations of Dhoni handling pressure would be the World Cup final in 2011 and the group stage match between India and Bangladesh at the 2016 T20I World Cup when he displayed two very different skills and two very different ways of handling pressure.

It usually escapes people that perhaps the best way of handling pressure is to not let it build up in the first place and that is something Dhoni did during the 2011 World Cup final. India was playing at home; expectations were sky-high, and the opposition was Sri Lanka, who were the runners-up in the previous edition and were an extremely consistent team at this point. It was the swansong of their golden generation and they set a formidable target. In response India lost both their openers by the seventh over. When India lost Virat Kohli at 114, there were still over 150 runs to the target. An in-form Yuvraj Singh was slotted to come in at this juncture, but the captain made a crucial decision. The captain decided to shoulder the pressure himself, went out to bat, steadied the ship and, in the process, did not let the pressure affect his teammates. He stayed till the end, guiding his team to victory.

In the second instance, half a decade later, India was playing another World Cup (but in the shortest format of the game) at home, and they had a bad start to the campaign. Consequently, the

match against Bangladesh took on critical importance. The match
went down to the wire; Bangladesh needed a mere 10 runs off the
last over. Dhoni backed his young bowler, Hardik Pandya, even
when he got hit for two boundaries. Dhoni then quickly moved his
best fielder Jadeja to midwicket and on the very next ball, Jadeja
took a crucial catch there. With one ball left and 2 runs to get,
Dhoni took off one of his wicketkeeping gloves to throw better,
although he finally backed his speed to run to the wickets before
the batsman and effected the match-winning run-out. This man,
under immense pressure, consistently made the right choices! As
Kipling might have said about him—he kept his head even when
the opposition lost theirs.

7

Spirited Away

In the second Test of India's tour of England in 2011, played at Nottingham, the match was evenly balanced after the completion of the respective first innings of each team and India managed a slight lead. England started their second innings well and soon reached 250 at a healthy run rate with Eoin Morgan and Ian Bell batting. Right at the end of the sixty-sixth over, the over just before tea, Morgan flicked Ishant Sharma to deep square leg where Praveen Kumar, the fielder, made a comical but successful attempt to save the boundary. This evidently created confusion in the batters as they had both strolled out of their crease for a chat thinking it was indeed a boundary. The throw quickly came back though, and the bails were taken off with Bell out of the crease and the umpires ruled that as out. Boos reverberated around the ground.

During the course of tea, however, the Indian team, and more specifically Dhoni, had a change of heart and the appeal was retracted. Bell was informed that he was not out and that he could come out and bat again, which he did, added 22 more runs and went past 150 before being caught at slip. The boos from the after session had turned into cheers aimed towards Dhoni and the Indians during the post-tea session.

Rahul Dravid explained the thought behind the decision: 'There was a team discussion during the tea interval, Dhoni and Fletcher convened the meeting, and Dhoni led it. There was a feeling of unanimity that we should reinstate Bell because the spirit of the game was important, and that getting him out in that way would contravene the spirit.' Ian Bell was understandably pleased, stating, 'I didn't know until the last minute that I would be going back out again but the way it's been handled has been fantastic and in the spirit of the game.'

For his role in the incident Dhoni won the ICC Spirit of Cricket Award in 2011. The very next year, Dhoni became the first cricketer in the world to win the AIPS Fair Play award for the same incident. Association Internationale de la Presse Sportive, or AIPS is an international association for sports journalists. Nine years after the incident, Dhoni's exemplary action of recalling Bell won him the International Cricket Council Spirit of Cricket Award of the Decade.

8

O Captain, Please Captain!

India was playing Australia in Nagpur with the Border–Gavaskar Trophy on the line. India had a lead in the series and had to win this match to regain the trophy at the same venue where they had let Australia conquer their 'final frontier' four years ago. Anil Kumble had started the series as India's captain but had retired at the end of the previous—the third—Test of the series. This was after another former Indian captain, Sourav Ganguly, had also announced that he would retire at the end of the series. Dhoni, who had also captained in the second test because of Anil Kumble suffering an injury, was now made the regular captain of the team.

In the forty-fifth over of the fifth day of the last Test, Harbhajan Singh had Brett Lee caught at short leg for a duck. Australia had lost their ninth wicket for 191 chasing a target of 382. The cameras then picked up something unusual; Dhoni had his arms around Sourav Ganguly, and both were seen smiling. Ganguly was then seen instructing the players and setting the field. Mahendra Singh Dhoni had stepped aside to let his first international captain lead the Indian team as captain one last time, before his retirement. Another sweet coincidence was the fact that this was exactly eight years to the day that Ganguly had made his Test captaincy debut against Bangladesh. That was on 10 November 2000.

The television commentor Mark Nicholas was quick to spot the touching gesture by Dhoni. Ganguly brought the field in, and the cameras followed an animated Ganguly, pointing, gesturing and applying various touches to the game. He then handed the captaincy back to his junior after 3 overs. If he had only stuck around for a few more deliveries, he would have captained till the end of the match. Both former and present captain were seen embracing after the match.

Sourav Ganguly later revealed that Dhoni had offered him the captaincy before the start of the fifth day as a tribute to him, but he had refused then. It came as a surprise when Dhoni repeated his request at the final moments of the match and of Ganguly's international career, and this time, he could not refuse the gesture. Apparently, his mind was so focused on retirement he didn't really remember what he was doing, and therefore handed the responsibility back to his protégé!

One of the most heartfelt gestures by one captain to another— by one athlete to another—by one man to his senior! The little things that make the legacy of a great person. The small gestures that make up Mahendra Singh Dhoni—man, cricketer and captain.

9

One Eighty-Three to Bind Them All

Since the turn of this century, India has had seven Test captains, including two stand-ins in Virender Sehwag and Ajinkya Rahane. Of the other five, Anil Kumble had the shortest captaincy career of 14 Tests and his fellow Karnataka teammate, Rahul Dravid, captained in only 25 Tests. Sourav Ganguly took over as captain right after the match-fixing fiasco hit Indian and world cricket and led the team in 49 Tests with a win percentage of a shade under 43 per cent. Mahendra Singh Dhoni then led India in 60 Tests and had a win percentage of 45. Virat Kohli has so far led India in 66 Tests and boasts a win percentage of a shade over 59. These three are by far the most successful Test captains of India (of anyone who has captained over a statistically significant number of 10 Tests).

Ganguly, Dhoni and Kohli have also captained India in a combined 441 out of 996 total ODI matches that India have ever played. That is about 44 per cent of the total number of ODIs. If we look at the numbers since Sourav took over, India has played 567 matches, which means this trio has captained in about 77 per cent of India's ODIs. The only other regular captain during this period was Rahul Dravid although seven others have filled the role when required. They include Anil Kumble, Virender Sehwag, Suresh Raina, Gautam Gambhir, Ajinkya Rahane, Rohit Sharma and Shikhar Dhawan. Ganguly never played a T20I match and of the 153 T20Is that India have played so far, Dhoni and Kohli have in total captained 122 of them. It is, therefore, fair to say that these three have been the most influential and significant captains of modern Indian cricket. Especially since the turn of the new century. Curiously there is a common number that binds the three.

Taunton, 1999. The World Cup group stage match against Sri Lanka. Sourav Ganguly opens with Sadagoppan Ramesh in what is a must-win match for India. Disaster strikes in the opening over as Sri Lankan left-armer metronome Chaminda Vaas castles Ramesh with India's score at 6. In walks Rahul Dravid, who still has not quite shaken off his tag as a Test-only batsman. What follows is 49 overs of carnage. Ganguly faces 26.2 overs and scores a mammoth 183, ably supported by Dravid who contributes 145 of a 318-run partnership. Ganguly did not get much of the strike in the last few overs and at the tail end of the innings had two potential deliveries to hit two 6s to break the then world record individual ODI score of 194 held by Pakistan's Saeed Anwar. Ganguly tried to do exactly that and holed out at deep at the long-on boundary, missing the world record but creating a curious benchmark for future Indian captains!

Six years later in 2005, India is playing Sri Lanka in a bilateral series. The third match is in Jaipur, and Sri Lanka has given India a tough target of 299 to chase down in 50 overs. Ganguly has been left out of the team and Dravid is the captain. Mother of coincidences and Sri Lanka again gets the first wicket on the fifth ball of the first over, just like in Taunton in 1999. And who gets the wicket? Why, Chaminda Vaas, of course. This time it is Sachin Tendulkar who is out though, but the superstitious amongst the Lankans must have heard alarm bells ringing. The captain sends in the precocious new wicketkeeper to bat at no. 3, ahead of himself, in his usual one down slot. Mahendra Singh Dhoni does not disappoint. It is a brazen, bold and audacious innings. Dhoni reaches his century in almost no time and the three other batters to have batted till that point had in total scored only 68 runs. It is his second ODI century. By the time Yuvraj Singh is out in the thirty-seventh over, India have already scored 250 runs and Dhoni's contribution is over 150 of those runs. India finishes the chase with 23 deliveries to spare and India's future captain extraordinaire remains unbeaten. His score? 183!

We have already had the World Cup and a bilateral series, ergo this time it is the Asia Cup. The neighbours have changed as well, the ones from the south have given way to the bitter rivals from the north and west. India is playing Pakistan at Dhaka and is set a more than challenging target of 330. Dhoni has become the captain of the team by now and has already won two World Cups, one each of the ODI and T20I variety. India is again one down in the very first over, Gambhir gone to the off-spinner Hafeez off the second ball of the innings. Dhoni sends in the young sensation who has been lighting up world cricket. Virat Kohli ravages the Pakistani bowlers, hitting 22 boundaries and a 6, and almost finishes the chase, getting out with 12 to win. Obviously, Dhoni hits the winning shot and lest we forget to mention, Kohli scores 183.

A must-mention side note is the one common factor in all three of these matches—a certain someone called Sachin Tendulkar.

All three ascended to the captaincy whether in Tests, T20Is or ODIs within a year or two of scoring this seemingly magical number. Here's hoping to witness another youngster follow on this path, will it be Shaw, Pant or Gill? 183 to bind them all!

10

The Art of Batting with the Tail

Mahendra Singh Dhoni has played 166 of his 297 ODI innings at no. 6 or lower and remained not out a whopping 84 times. The corresponding numbers in Tests are far more human—14 not outs out of 139 innings—in those positions (Dhoni has 16 total not outs in Tests from 144 innings). The former captain has also played 98 T20Is, among which he has remained not out 42 times. But the 21 times he has batted at no. 6 or lower in T20Is, Dhoni has never been out, having scored 387 runs at a strike rate of almost 144. These are some unreal numbers and it has only been possible because Dhoni had the ability to do something that previous generations lacked. Dhoni was an artist batting with the tail; he farmed the strike cleverly and took the game deep. This was unfortunately not always the case with Indian cricket, and just the previous generation of Indian cricketers and fans alike were far too used to the infamous Indian collapses.

Once upon a time in a newly liberalized India, a hopeful generation looked towards their cricket team as yet another avenue to announce their presence to the world, albeit vicariously. And the generation had much to hope from their skilful and talented cricketers. They had Sachin Tendulkar, arguably the best batsman in the world. There was his sublimely talented schoolmate and co-world record holder, Vinod Kambli. Two future Indian greats in Sourav Ganguly and Rahul Dravid were just around the corner waiting to appear in the latter half of the decade, and the middle order had brilliant players in Mohammad Azharuddin and Ajay Jadeja and two world-class bowlers in Javagal Srinath and Anil Kumble.

Yet, there was a perennial problem that the team suffered from, as sure as our monsoons; when it rained, it poured! Perfectly summed up by the old joke oft repeated by Navjot Sidhu during commentary—when one bicycle fell, the entire row collapsed like dominoes.

Sachin Tendulkar was often that first domino, the first bicycle. It was an infamous cliché that millions switched off their telly once Sachin got out, fearing (and knowing) what was coming next. It always followed a pattern. India would be in a good position, then Sachin would get out, triggering a collapse and Jadeja, often alongside Robin Singh, would try to stem the flow and India would contrive to lose despite a good start.

Perhaps the two most shattering examples illustrating such collapses were at Eden Gardens, 1996, and at Madras two years later. India, set a target of 251 at the Eden, were in a comfortable position at 98/1 in the twenty-third over. Sachin was batting at 65 and the World Cup final at Lahore was within reach. A freak stumping, Sachin back in the hut, the ensuing collapse stirred crowd trouble and the match was awarded to Sri Lanka with India finishing at 120/8. Two years later at Chennai, this time in a Test match, India was 254/6 needing another 17 runs to win. Same story gets repeated, Sachin gets out, India folds for 258, snatching defeat from the jaws of victory.

The new millennium brought with it a new brood of players, forged in their then captain's mould—unbowed, unbent, unbroken—to borrow the House Words of the Martells from *Game of Thrones*. Sourav Ganguly ushered in a team of braves and the fans got the first whiff of what was to come in the 2002 NatWest finals when India recovered from 146/5 to chase down a then unthinkable target of 326 with Mohammad Kaif batting sensationally with Yuvraj Singh and then staying with the tail to finish things off.

Dhoni had not yet played for the Indian team at this time but one can only imagine that he was watching the match, and in the next few years would take this one-off miracle and convert it into a regular art form for Team India. Younger Indian fans brought up on watching the Yuvrajs, Dhonis and Kohlis could never imagine the tension and disappointment of the earlier generations of Indian fans. Although one may argue that Kaif and Yuvraj pioneered this, Dhoni perfected it. And with Dhoni at the crease, number of wickets lost and even the (required) run rate became just fleeting statistics. There was hope, built from experience, that Dhoni would and could turn it all around as long as he took the match deep!

In 2013 at Mohali, Dhoni walks in at the end of the twelfth over with India at 76/4. Kohli gets out in the thirtieth over and Jadeja, the last recognized batsman, leaves the crease in the thirty-second over with the score at 154. Dhoni finishes the innings not out and takes India to 303, after putting on a partnership of 76 with Ravichandran Ashwin, another 37 with Bhuvneshwar Kumar and 32 with Vinay Kumar. India lost that match, but Dhoni ensured that India put up a competitive total.

In 2012 at Pallekele, India was setting a target and Dhoni lost Gautam Gambhir, the last recognized batsman, with the score at 213 with 11 overs to go. Irfan Pathan and Dhoni forged a partnership to take the score to 294, which was enough for India to win that match. In Madras 2012, India was 29/5 in a shocking start against Pakistan. Dhoni scored a century and India finished at 227/6, a miracle given the start. Again, in Pallekele, this time in 2017, India found themselves 5 down for 121 chasing a revised target of 231 from 47 overs. Dhoni, struggling for timing, made sure to be with Bhuvi throughout the chase, taking the back seat himself. Bhuvi scored a half-century and Dhoni remained not out, scoring 45 and ensuring yet another Indian win.

Dhoni was a master at batting with the tail and these are just a few examples from ODIs; his Test record was stellar too, more so given that he was a wicketkeeper and he did manage the tail in Tests as well, although not as many times as in ODIs. In the shortest format of the game, his record speaks for itself. With Dhoni at the crease, opposition bowlers knew that there was always going to be a twist in the 'tail'!

PART IV

Words—By Dhoni and On Dhoni

Aakriti Mehrotra
and
Arinjay Ghosh

1

The Words of MS Dhoni

'Maybe you should ask his physio to issue a press release.'

MS Dhoni curtly replied to a reporter when asked about Virender Sehwag's injury in the lead-up to the ICC T20 World Cup 2009. Sehwag had pulled out of the tournament at the eleventh hour due to an aggravated shoulder injury and this statement of Dhoni's caused a lot of speculation centred around a possible rift between the two players. However, to publicly show Team India's unity, Dhoni paraded the entire squad to the pre-match press conference ahead of the opening game against Bangladesh and dismissed all reported claims in two words—'irresponsible reporting'.

'Actually that was the case. Virat used a knife. He stabbed Shikhar, who just recovered out of that then we pushed him to bat. These are all stories. Marvel, maybe Warner Bros. or somebody should pick up this and make a nice movie out of it.'

MS Dhoni used humour to dispel rumours on Christmas Day of 2014 after reports circulated of a falling out between

Shikhar Dhawan and Virat Kohli during the previous Test match. Prior to the fourth morning of the Brisbane Test, Dhawan was struck on the arm in the nets and that gave Kohli—batting in his place—little time to prepare. Kohli was dismissed for 1 off 11 balls and Dhoni admitted to 'unrest' after India's batting collapse that day. That one word would result in the speculation of a heated confrontation between the Delhi boys, who had to be separated by then team director Ravi Shastri.

'I have quite a few cars and bikes in my garage, I don't use all of them always.'

MS Dhoni came up with a unique explanation when quizzed about not using the services of Harbhajan Singh in CSK's victory over Sunrisers Hyderabad (SRH) in the first qualifier of IPL 2018.

'Take whatever you want, don't call me again.'

In a podcast, Suresh Raina recalled an incident from India's tour of Ireland in 2018 when MS Dhoni, humble as he is, played the role of the twelfth man. But soon enough, he would regret his benevolence as his mate Suresh Raina, kept calling for new gloves and bat, prompting Dhoni to run on to the field, leaving behind the warmth of the dressing room. In a bid to stay away from the Irish cold, Dhoni brought out an entire kit bag and asked Raina to make his mind up one last time. The southpaw obliged but not before asking Dhoni to complete a final round trip to get a fresh grip for the bat handle. Safe to say MS played an important role in Raina's half-century in that second T20.

'Lambu tune mujhe Test match mein chod diya' (You left me midway in my last Test match).

Ishant Sharma recalled an emotional moment from MS Dhoni's last Test match. The fast bowler was suffering from severe pain in the knee and taking multiple injections to keep bowling until tea on Day 4 when he gave in. He would later be stunned to know of Dhoni's decision, courtesy of the above stated exchange, and had he known of the retirement at the time, says he would have kept fighting the pain to bowl.

'I have taped the fingers of both [Virat Kohli and Ishant Sharma] of them. Now, they won't be able to lift them. It'll be interesting to see if they can repeat what they did.'

Both cricketers, Kohli and Ishant, had flicked their middle fingers at different points of India's tour of Australia in 2012. While Kohli did it during the Sydney Test match, Ishant kept it only slightly more discreet, brandishing a similar gesture on his way back to the team bus after a session of go-karting. On these incidents, Dhoni was questioned, and he came up with the hilarious response.

'If Rohit doesn't get out he will certainly get 250 today.'

MS Dhoni tweeted this at exactly 5 p.m. IST on 13 November 2021 after Rohit Sharma scored the second of his third ODI double centuries. India was playing Sri Lanka at Eden Gardens in the fourth ODI of the five-match series which India had already won. Then captain MS Dhoni was resting in that particular bilateral meet and his tweet turned out to be a spoiler as Rohit Sharma made sure everything he touched reached the boundary en route to a record 264.

'When you give Sir Ravindra Jadeja 1 ball to get 2 runs he will win it with 1 ball to spare!!'

As MS Dhoni's tweet suggests, Ravindra Jadeja had won a game, scoring 2 runs off zero legitimate deliveries. What transpired is perhaps as comical as the tweet itself. CSK needed 2 runs off 1 ball to win versus Royal Challengers Bangalore (RCB) at Chepauk Stadium. R.P. Singh ran up and bowled a short delivery outside off stump affording Jadeja enough room to swing his arms. The all-rounder, however, could only manage a top edge, which Ravi Rampaul safely reverse cupped at third man. Virat Kohli led RCB into celebration only for the camera to pan towards the umpire who had his right arm outstretched to signal a no-ball. Jadeja and Chris Morris had crossed, which meant that CSK scored 2 runs—1 off the no-ball and the other was added on Jadeja's account—and won the game with the solitary ball to spare.

'To point out that this is the particular thing I learnt from him is very difficult. I think in the opportunities I got to bat with him I learnt to read the game.'

MS Dhoni is famed for his superior ability to remain one step ahead of any game of cricket. Thus, it speaks volumes of the legend of Sachin Tendulkar that Dhoni would credit the Little Master for his ability to pace an innings, especially in ODIs. Dhoni said this following the retirement of Tendulkar.

'He's still my first Test wicket.'

In six and a half words, MS Dhoni left everyone in splits, including the commentators on air. During an IPL game in 2017 between Pune and Mumbai, Kevin Pietersen, on commentary, asked mic'd up Manoj Tiwary to tell Dhoni he was a better golfer than the wicketkeeper. To that yorker, Dhoni responded with a verbal helicopter that knocked everyone off their seats in laughter.

'You did not go to your best ball under pressure.'

In the Champions League T20 of 2010 held in South Africa, R. Ashwin conceded 23 runs in a super over loss to the Victoria Bushrangers. David Hussey took a heavy toll on the off-spinner, hitting him for three 6s. Dhoni's reaction, however, was one that perhaps set him apart from the pack. The captain simply advised Ashwin to trust himself and bowl his best ball under pressure—in this case it was the 'carrom ball'. CSK went on to win the tournament and Ashwin was one of the best bowlers.

'We surprised Ishant Sharma on his wedding like this and so was the case for Suresh Raina.'

Mandeep Singh narrated an incident when MS Dhoni surprised him by paying a visit to his marriage reception in December 2016. The IPL 2012 emerging player of the year award winner said he had invited Dhoni more out of hope than expectation as the two were not close friends. Despite that, Dhoni took time out of his schedule to board two flights and drive for a further two hours to reach Jalandhar before the groom arrived.

'Aur de isko (Give him more).'

MS Dhoni asked Suresh Raina to build the psychological pressure on Umar Akmal as India applied the squeeze on Pakistan's run chase in the semi-final of the ICC World Cup

2011. The southpaw narrated this incident on a talk show referring to Dhoni's clever ways of showing emotions when the cameras were not focusing on him. In this particular instance, Umar Akmal complained to Dhoni that Raina was using unparliamentary language. When asked, Raina replied to his captain denying it and said he was fizzing in throws towards his end while tempting him to hit a shot in anger— all within the lines of decency.

'If this catch is dropped, I cannot imagine what will happen.'

MS Dhoni was asked to recall the exact two moments India won the two World Cups under him at a press meet ahead of the release of his biopic. Happy and uncharacteristically jovial, Dhoni recalled the match-winning incident from the ICC T20 World Cup 2007. He said, when the ball went up in the air, he saw Sreesanth at short fine leg uncomfortably gyrate before settling underneath the ball and taking the famous catch—Dhoni even mimicked Sreesanth's body movements at the event while spelling out what was on his mind at the time. He even said that when he saw the replay, his heart started beating fast due to the frame which made it seem that the ball was travelling for a boundary.

'I think in the middle overs there was some very irresponsible cricket by some of the most experienced international cricketers, so I think definitely we need to have a look.'

MS Dhoni was naturally—yet uncharacteristically— emotive after the defeat against the then Kings XI Punjab in Qualifier 2 of IPL 2014. CSK were well in the game after 6 overs in the chase of 227 runs, courtesy of an unprecedented assault by Suresh Raina. Fresh from smashing 33 runs off Parvinder Awana, Raina had to walk back, run out due to a miscommunication with Brendon McCullum, who set off for a single and then refused the run. Raina was found short at the non-striker's end to finish his magical innings at 87 off 25 after 6.1 overs. The comment was perhaps directed at the Kiwi who scored 11 off 16. The remaining overseas batters—Dwayne Smith and Faf du Plessis—were dismissed for 7 off 11 and 0 off 1 respectively.

'If Watson tries to dive, he may injure his hamstring.'

When CSK won the IPL in 2018, it was on the back of stellar performances from experienced players. One of them was Shane Watson, who jumped from no. 16 to 5 on the top run-getters list for the season courtesy of an unbeaten 117 in the final. In the post-match press conference, MS Dhoni gave an honest assessment of his team's shortcomings citing fielding as one of the weaker points. He further cited that everyone within the group was very aware of where they stood in their careers and had no illusions about their respective games.

'That's what it is, you want to bluff the batsmen, you want to confuse the batsmen.'

MS Dhoni revealed his conversation with Dwayne Bravo post a victory against RCB at Sharjah in IPL 2021. The CSK skipper said that he often argues with his 'brother' Bravo on the number of slower balls the latter should bowl. Dhoni opined that everyone now expects Bravo to take the pace off and hence, the all-rounder should bowl 6 normal pace deliveries to surprise the batters. The reason being that the slower ones were originally meant to bluff the batter and since he primarily bowls them, the bluff should be to use the quicker ones now.

'Imran bhai, welcome. This is my room and you are more than welcome anytime.'

Many players have narrated tales of MS Dhoni always keeping his room's door open for teammates to visit, have a conversation, play video games and just hang around. In a 2020 interview, Imran Tahir revealed how Dhoni eased his nervousness in their very first conversation when the two met while playing for Rising Pune Supergiants in IPL 2016. Tahir went on to add that he still visits Dhoni's room because of the stock of tasty mangoes the CSK captain keeps.

'Yuvi has always been a trump card for me. He was the perfect individual to have in the side.'

MS Dhoni narrated how important Yuvraj Singh has been for the success of the Indian cricket team during his peak years as a leader. He called Yuvraj the perfect all-rounder at a cricket summit. He further heaped praise on the southpaw for relishing big games and performing in those matches which mattered the most.

'I got to know about it quite early, even Yuvi was not aware about it and [it] came as a shock for me.'

MS Dhoni spoke about getting to know about Yuvraj's illness and could not believe his friend and teammate was diagnosed with cancer. At the same time, he said that in his heart Dhoni was sure Yuvraj would fight out of it because of his mental strength.

'I never said anything.'

Harbhajan Singh was speaking at a cricket conclave about an altercation with Kumar Sangakkara from back in the day in the presence of the Sri Lankan. After joking that he would not say anything about the then Marylebone Cricket Club president, Bhajji went on to state that both players were trying to win a game for their respective teams but off the field, everything is forgotten. The off-break bowler, though, did add that Sangakkara started that particular incident before saying that the constant chirping of wicketkeepers are the starting points of most arguments. That is when MS intervened to plead his innocence.

'Eventually, the team does what Virat Kohli decides.'

Ahead of the ICC World Cup 2019, MS Dhoni had appeared before a gathering of employees of a brand he had signed with as an ambassador. Here MS was asked whether the team followed then captain Kohli's lead or his. To which he replied while every member of the team is encouraged to think about the game and help the captain with inputs, eventually it is the captain who takes the final call. Dhoni went on to add that wicketkeepers can play the role of an informal vice captain as given their proximity to the pitch and batter, they are able to see the nuances from close.

'After playing three years of IPL with Murali, I knew if in the first few deliveries I can step out and take singles through mid-off, I will have the upper hand.'

Members of the Indian cricket team had gathered for a function after winning the ICC World Cup 2011, and MS Dhoni was naturally quizzed about promoting himself ahead of the eventual Player of the Tournament Yuvraj Singh. Dhoni was quick to answer that it was then coach Gary Kirsten who had floated the idea and at the time, the captain had asked for some time to ponder. A quick visit to the washroom later and Dhoni had made up his mind. And as they say, the rest is history.

'Which player hits so many 6s? Everyone's parents are watching—who embarrasses bowlers like this?'

CSK's return to IPL in 2018 was emotional for everyone associated with that franchise and their first match back at Chepauk Stadium was perhaps as perfect as it could be for the cricket-loving Chennai crowd. KKR was visiting town and Andre Russell was having one of those games where he converted every ball into an incident. CSK would eventually chase down the target but not before the big Jamaican had plundered as many as eleven 6s. In a show with the official broadcasters, Dhoni was asked to recall that game and he exclaimed that it was one of those helpless situations where he just wanted the overs to finish. He went on to add—in jest—that poor Bravo had well-wishers who were watching and Andre Russell should have considered that before launching such a vicious attack on his international teammate. Russell scored 88 off 36 balls hitting one boundary and eleven 6s.

2

Dhoni in the Words of Others

'Dhoni is very impressive both on and off the field. He is a very cool-headed guy.'

—Andrew Flintoff in 2009,
speaking as a Chennai Super Kings player

'He [Mahendra Singh Dhoni] reminds me a lot of both Ricky [Ponting] and Steve [Waugh]. They have similar personalities, strong personalities. They love the team and the camaraderie of the team. For me, he has all the ingredients [to be successful].'

—Matthew Hayden in May 2009

'I think it's really important and significant that MS Dhoni has won a World Cup and a Champions Trophy. That World Cup for me, that's a real big milestone. I have mentioned it before we have played loads of cricket in the one-day format and I just feel that when it comes to being ready for a World Cup, you not only got to have a good leader but you also need to have a calm strong player in the middle order like he has.'

—Matthew Hayden on the Star Sports show
Cricket Connected in 2020, naming MS Dhoni as
India's most impactful player of the decade in ODIs

'Dhoni is my hero. We talk a lot about Sachin Tendulkar, Virender Sehwag, but this boy has as much talent as anyone in the game. He is an unbelievable talent. He has good technique and strikes the ball very hard.'

—Kapil Dev in 2006, at the launch of the Golf Masters 2006

'One way to look at your cricketing career is through the prism of statistics. You have been one of the most successful captains, instrumental in taking India to the top of the world charts. Your name will go down in history as being one of the world's batting greats, among the greatest cricketing captains and certainly one of the best wicketkeepers the game has seen.

Your dependability in tough situations and your style of finishing matches, particularly the 2011 World Cup Final, will forever be etched in the public memory for generations. But the name Mahendra Singh Dhoni will not be remembered merely for his career statistics or specific match-winning roles. Looking at you as just a sportsperson would be injustice. The correct way to assess your impact is as a phenomenon!'

—Excerpt from Prime Minister Narendra Modi's letter to MS Dhoni after the cricketer announced his retirement in 2020

'One of the biggest compliments I ever received was when my fans told me they would pay to watch me bat. I am willing to do the same for Dhoni.'

—Adam Gilchrist in 2008 at an event of the University of Wollongong

'I can easily pick him as one of the players to be watched in the 2007 World Cup. He is unorthodox but very effective and at times murderous. He is difficult to bowl to because he has this ability to even hit the good balls with a jab shot. He is equally good in horizontal and vertical bat shots. He is safe behind the wickets and can be compared to Adam Gilchrist though the Australian has proved himself as the best after years in commission.'

—Inzamam-ul-Haq in 2006

'The calm with which Dhoni brought to a conclusion both India's victories, at Adelaide Oval and the MCG, was yet another reminder of what a cool, calculating finisher he is in ODIs. He only has one challenger as the best finisher in the game—Australia's Michael Bevan—but Dhoni's remarkable longevity and frequency of success surely gain him the nod. Nobody has Dhoni's nerve for finishing off victories. Many times I've thought, "He's left it too late this time", only to be amazed as he produced a couple of powerful shots to bring India a nail-biting victory.'

—Ian Chappell in 2019 in his column in ESPN Cricinfo

'When Dhoni first started to play ODIs for India that long flowing locks that we call it in the Caribbean, he looked like a maverick. He looked like someone who came out there just to destroy whatever comes in front of him and he pretty much did that. Throughout his career he hit 229 6s (in ODIs). When you think of those numbers you must be thinking he must have played for 40 years to have hit so many 6s and 4s. But that is the nature of the man. As he grew some grey around his temple area then he had to tone it down a bit and he was lot more controlled with his batting. Anyone watching MS Dhoni in the middle would know he was always in control, unflappable, never ever he looked out of control. What a career this man had, a fantastic one. This man made almost 5,000 Test runs and remember, he's not a pure batsman, he's a wicketkeeper. Over such a long career, to be able keep wickets and do such a fantastic job is commendable.'

—Michael Holding in 2020, on his YouTube channel

'He reminds me of my great captain Imran Khan. Both have staggering self-belief and they have such faith in their players, it is difficult to comprehend it from outside. I will give you the example of Mansoor Akhtar, who played [19 Tests] because Imran believed in his ability. Once they back a player, they back him all the way.'

—Mushtaq Ahmed, former Pakistan leg-spinner then spin bowling coach of England, just before the Champions Trophy in England in 2013

'I hadn't heard about him [Dhoni] until he got into the Indian team. I saw him for the first time in Bangladesh during a one-day tournament. I was having a discussion with Sourav and told him that this guy has something special in him and has the ability to hit the ball. However, hitting the ball at first-class cricket level and hitting it at the international level are two different things. He had hit two boundaries in that [practice] match, and I told Sourav, "Dada, he has that jhatka *[whip] in his hand which he uses while hitting the ball." It was something special to see. It was his first outing with the Indian team. But the way he was hitting the ball, one could make out he was someone special.'*

—Sachin Tendulkar in August 2020,
after Dhoni announced his retirement

'When I first met Dhoni in 2005, I was taken by his strength and the fact that he hit balls into parts of the field that others couldn't. Short balls that most pulled through midwicket, MS hit straight back past startled bowlers. His back-foot, short-armed punches down the ground were also a signature shot but what impressed me most of all was his ability to clear boundaries at will. I saw more potential than a brute in the dying overs. I could see that his decision-making and his reading of a game could make him one of the most dangerous finishers in the game. As Rahul Dravid and I began to reshape the way India played one-day cricket, we could see that Dhoni was going to be a key component in becoming one of the most dangerous teams either setting or chasing a target.'

—Former India coach Greg Chappell in
August 2020, after Dhoni announced his retirement

'I didn't really watch the India–England Test series, but Dhoni has the respect of all other playing nations. I've found him to be a really strong leader.'

—Glenn McGrath in 2013

'He has been absolutely the heartbeat of CSK, there's no doubt about it. Whether it's performances, guidance or leadership . . . you run out of things to say about him. His longevity also has to be mentioned and appreciated . . . to play 200 games and still have a desire to do well and perform well is a testament to his attitude towards the game and the franchise. I think the franchise has grown and MS has grown with it, so it's a very good relationship and great fun.'

—Stephen Fleming in 2021 after CSK
celebrated Dhoni's 200 games at the franchise

'Thank you for demonstrating how self-belief can help achieve in sports and life. Rising from a small town to being the hero of the nation, your calculated risks and calm demeanour will be missed by Team India.'

—Kamal Haasan in August 2020,
tweeting after Dhoni's retirement

'He [Dhoni] is the best captain I have played under. He is very sharp and always alert. He reads the situation well and is open to sharing ideas. He always has discussions with bowlers, batsmen and senior players separately.'

—Sachin Tendulkar in 2011, two days
after India won the Cricket World Cup

'A few days later IPL started, Chennai Super Kings were playing their first match and I was at the ground. I met MSD and said, "Look in this world if I've got a couple of minutes left, I'm gonna ask someone to put that shot on because I'd love to see that shot and say goodbye to this world. Because that would be a fantastic way, I'd go with a smile on my face". That's exactly what I had said to MSD and he was of course pretty modest about it. He smiled and didn't say anything.'

—Sunil Gavaskar recalls a meeting with Dhoni in IPL 2011

'He was an every man's leader to his team, authoritative but yet down to earth enough and approachable to the members under him. That whole sense of confidence and self-belief he had was unobtrusive in that you never felt any level of significant arrogance. I think wearing your leadership so lightly is a good thing. History will remember him kindly for that. As a cricket brain, the shorter the formats became, the more you saw the computer-like cricket brain behind many of his decisions. But yet, he was able to be instinctive. Just the marriage of that allows us to remember his international journey as a significant one in India's chapter of leadership and world cricket as well.'

—Ian Bishop in 2020, speaking in a video for
the ICC after Dhoni announced his retirement

'If I am looking at MS Dhoni as captain, he is one of the greatest of all time. The reason for this is his incredible calmness under pressure. This calmness is absorbed by his playing group and it allows them the freedom and allows the game to be played in the way it should be played—that's to have fun and that's very much the Dhoni way. Tactically, he is brilliant, he always appears to be one of those captains who is an over or two ahead of the game when it comes to decision-making. He empowers his players to just play with their gut which is a central part of his being as a leader.'

—Tom Moody in 2020,
speaking after Dhoni's retirement

'Yaar main toh usko apna pajama bech ke bhi kharid lun, wo aaye toh auction mein. (Brother, I can even sell my pajamas to buy Dhoni. He has to come for the auction for that.)'

—Shahrukh Khan in 2017, talking
about wanting to buy Dhoni for KKR

'He [Dhoni] is probably the best player in the world in those situations, in these conditions. He does it time and time again. He's incredibly hard to bowl at and with that extra man in the circle, it's very, very hard to stop on these flat wickets. You're always going to have hindsight,

but probably one batsman you don't want an off-spinner bowling to is Dhoni. We've seen him a number of times and with a spinner at the end, it's very hard to bowl to him.'

—Former England captain Alastair Cook describing
bowling to MS after his counter-attacking 72 from
66 balls late in India's innings set the stage for their
127-run victory in the second ODI in 2013

'I remember before one big game against RCB at Chennai, the crowd was rocking and we had the little huddle before we went out to play. MS pulled the team in and said, "Right guys, big game today against RCB, but the fair-play award is really important to me. We've got to make sure we play the game in the right spirit so that we get full points on the fair play." I remember looking at him like: Are you serious? This is a massive game and we have to win it. But he was very big on playing with the right spirit and he wanted us to be known as a team that was very good with results but also a team that was very fair.'

—Excerpt from Michael Hussey's interview with
ESPN Cricinfo after Dhoni announced his retirement

'He was such a cool captain on the outside, but from the inside such an aggressive player. He was such a "shrewd", you could say, captain— the way he handled the team, the way he just developed the team and changed the team from seniors [senior players], brought up some juniors. He changed the whole culture of the team, the whole face of Indian cricket—a wonderful servant of the game.'

—Misbah-ul-Haq in 2020, speaking after
Dhoni announced his retirement

'You guys are funny. No, I would play MS Dhoni in my team every day of every year. He can be 80, in a wheelchair, and he would still play for my team. He is fantastic I mean look at his record. You want to drop a guy like that? You can go ahead by all means. I wouldn't.'

—A.B. de Villiers in October 2018

PART V

Dhoni in Numbers*

MS Dhoni in International Cricket

2004 to 2019

ODI Cricket

- Mahendra Singh Dhoni made his international debut for India at Chittagong (now Chattogram) on 23 December 2004 in the ODI match against Bangladesh. He then became the 157th player to appear in an ODI for India.
- He had the misfortune of being run out for a duck off the very first ball he faced in international cricket (in the above match). [The only other Indian debutant dismissed 'run out' for a duck was Roger Binny against Australia at Brisbane on 6 December 1980. However, in Binny's case, he was run out without facing a ball!]
- In his fifth match for India, he made 148 (123 balls, 4 sixes, 15 fours) in the ODI match against Pakistan at Visakhapatnam on 5 April 2005.
- It was then the highest by any Indian ODI batsman against Pakistan.

Highest Individual Scores for India against Pakistan in ODIs

Score	Batsman	Venue	Date
183	Virat Kohli	Mirpur	18 March 2012
148	**MS Dhoni**	**Vizag**	**5 April 2005**
141	Sourav Ganguly	Adelaide	25 January 2000
141	Sachin Tendulkar	Rawalpindi	16 March 2004
140	Rohit Sharma	Manchester	16 June 2019

- It was also then the highest by an Indian keeper in ODI cricket, bettering the previous best of 145 by Rahul Dravid against Sri Lanka at Taunton on 26 May 1999.
- It still remains the highest by any keeper against Pakistan in ODI cricket.

Highest Individual Scores by a Wicketkeeper against Pakistan in ODIs

Score	Batsman	For	Venue	Date
148	**MS Dhoni**	**India**	**Vizag**	**5 April 2005**
131	Brendon McCullum	New Zealand	Abu Dhabi	6 November 2009
128	A.B. de Villiers	South Africa	Johannesburg	17 November 2013
128	Jonny Bairstow	England	Bristol	14 May 2019
116*	Jos Buttler	England	Dubai	20 November 2015

- He blasted an unbeaten 183 (145 balls, 10 sixes, 15 fours) against Sri Lanka at Jaipur on 31 October 2005.
- This score still remains the highest by a wicketkeeper in all ODI cricket.

Highest Individual Scores by a Wicketkeeper in ODIs

Score	Batsman	For	Against	Venue	Date
183*	MS Dhoni	India	Sri Lanka	Jaipur	31 October 2005
178	Quinton de Kock	South Africa	Australia	Centurion	30 September 2016
176	Liton Das	Bangladesh	Zimbabwe	Sylhet	6 March 2020
172	Adam Gilchrist	Australia	Zimbabwe	Hobart BO	16 January 2004
170*	Luke Ronchi	New Zealand	Sri Lanka	Dunedin Univ	23 January 2015
170	Shai Hope	West Indies	Ireland	Dublin	5 May 2019

- It was then the highest by any batsman while batting second in an ODI match.

Highest Individual Scores by a Batsman While Batting Second in ODIs

Score	Batsman	For	Against	Venue	Date
185*	Shane Watson	Australia	Bangladesh	Mirpur	11 April 2011
183*	MS Dhoni	India	Sri Lanka	Jaipur	31 October 2005
183	Virat Kohli	India	Pakistan	Mirpur	18 March 2012
181*	Ross Taylor	New Zealand	England	Dunedin Univ	7 March 2018
180*	Martin Guptill	New Zealand	South Africa	Hamilton	1 March 2017
180	Jason Roy	England	Australia	Melbourne	14 January 2018

- He also appeared in three ODI matches for Asia XI against Africa XI in June 2007. It was the only side he represented other than India in international cricket.
- He also has the distinction of registering a three-figure score (139 not out) for Asia XI at Chennai on 10 June 2007.
- His 139* is the highest individual score for any Asian XI side in ODIs.

Highest Individual Scores by a Batsman for Asia XI in ODIs

Score	Batsman	Against	Venue	Date
139*	MS Dhoni	Africa XI	Chennai	10 June 2007
107	Mahela Jayawardene	Africa XI	Chennai	10 June 2007
88	Sourav Ganguly	Africa XI	Chennai	9 June 2007
75*	Rahul Dravid	World XI	Melbourne	10 January 2005
66	Mohammad Yousuf	Africa XI	Bangalore	6 June 2007

- During the above knock, he and Sri Lankan Mahela Jayawardene put on 218 runs, which was then an ODI record for the sixth wicket, until it was surpassed in January 2015.

Highest Sixth-Wicket Partnerships in ODIs

Partnership	Batsman 1	Batsman 2	For	Against	Venue	Date
267*	Grant Elliott	Luke Ronchi	Australia	New Zealand	Dunedin Univ	23 January 2015
218	Mahela Jayawardene	MS Dhoni	Asia XI	Africa XI	Chennai	10 June 2007
188	Tatenda Taibu	Stuart Matsikenyeri	Zimbabwe	South Africa	Benoni	8 November 2009
177	Shehan Jayasuriya	Dasun Shanaka	Sri Lanka	Pakistan	Karachi	30 September 2019
165	Mike Hussey	Brad Haddin	Australia	West Indies	Kuala Lumpur	18 September 2006
165	Craig McMillan	Brendon McCullum	New Zealand	Australia	Hamilton	20 February 2007

- His tally of 10,773 career runs, makes him the fifth Indian to aggregate 10,000 runs in ODI cricket.

Indians with Most ODI Runs

Runs	Indian Batsman
18426	Sachin Tendulkar
11867	Virat Kohli
11363+	Sourav Ganguly
10889+	Rahul Dravid
10773+	**MS Dhoni**

+ Tally includes runs for other sides also

- In ODI cricket, only Kumar Sangakkara (13,341) has scored more runs than Dhoni as a keeper.

Most ODI Runs as a Wicketkeeper

Runs	Keeper-batsman	For
13341+	Kumar Sangakkara	Sri Lanka
10773+	**MS Dhoni**	**India**
9410+	Adam Gilchrist	Australia
5835	Andy Flower	Zimbabwe
5762	Mushfiqur Rahim	Bangladesh

+ Tally includes runs for other sides also

- His batting average of 50.58 makes him one of the only 10 ODI batsmen, with a minimum of 1000 runs, to have a career average exceeding 50-plus in ODI cricket. He is the second Indian in that list after Virat Kohli.
- Among batsmen with 5,000 or more runs in ODI cricket, his batting average of 50.57 places him in the fifth position.

Highest Career Batting Average in ODI Cricket (Minimum 5000 Runs)

Average	Batsman	Runs	For
59.33	Virat Kohli	11867	India
53.58	Michael Bevan	6912	Australia
53.50	A.B. de Villiers	9577+	South Africa
51.05	Joe Root	5922	England
50.58	**MS Dhoni**	**10773+**	**India**

* Tally includes runs for other sides also

• His batting average in successful run chases in ODIs is the highest for any batsman with an aggregate of 1000 or more runs.

Highest Career Batting Average in Successful Run Chases in ODI Cricket (Minimum 1000 Runs)

Average	Batsman	Runs	For
102.71	**MS Dhoni**	**2876**	**India**
96.21	Virat Kohli	5388	India
86.25	Michael Bevan	1715	Australia
82.77	A.B. de Villiers	2566	South Africa
77.68	Joe Root	1942	England

• His wicketkeeping dismissal tally of 444 is the third highest in ODIs.

Most Wicketkeeping Dismissals in ODIs

Dismissals	(Cts+Sts)	Wicketkeeper	For
482*	(383ct+99st)	Kumar Sangakkara	Sri Lanka
472*	(417ct+55st)	Adam Gilchrist	Australia
444*	**(321ct+123st)**	**MS Dhoni**	**India**
424*	(402ct+22st)	Mark Boucher	South Africa
287	(214ct+73st)	Moin Khan	Pakistan

* Tally includes dismissals for other sides also

- He is the only keeper in ODI cricket to claim over 100 stumpings.

Most Stumpings in ODI Cricket

Sts	Cts	Wicketkeeper	For
123	**321**	**MS Dhoni**	**India**
99	383	Kumar Sangakkara	Sri Lanka
75	132	Romesh Kaluwitharana	Sri Lanka
73	214	Moin Khan	Pakistan
55	417	Adam Gilchrist	Australia

- His six dismissals against England at Leeds on 2 September 2007 is an ODI record for the most dismissals by a keeper in an ODI match. However, he shares this record with nine other wicketkeepers.
- His tally of 200 matches as captain is the third highest in ODIs.

Most ODI Matches as Captain

ODIs	Captain	For
230	Ricky Ponting	Australia
218	Stephen Fleming	New Zealand
200	**MS Dhoni**	**India**
193	Arjuna Ranatunga	Sri Lanka
178	Allan Border	Australia

- His tally of 110 matches in won ODI games as captain has been surpassed only by Ricky Ponting in ODI cricket.

Most ODI Victories as Captain

Won	Captain	For
165	Ricky Ponting	Australia
110	**MS Dhoni**	**India**
107	Allan Border	Australia
99	Hansie Cronje	South Africa
98	Stephen Fleming	New Zealand

- In ODI cricket history, he remains the only player to appear in the maximum number of ODI matches as both a captain and wicketkeeper. From 2007 to 2018, he appeared in a record 200 ODI matches in this dual role, when the next best is just fifty matches.

Most ODI Matches while Captaining and Wicketkeeping in the Same Match

ODIs	As captain-keeper	For
200	**MS Dhoni**	**India**
50	Sarfraz Ahmed	Pakistan
46	Andy Flower	Zimbabwe
45	Kumar Sangakkara	Sri Lanka
39	Alec Stewart	England

- Under his captaincy India won the World Cup title in India in 2011.
- Also, under his leadership, India won the ICC Champions Trophy in 2013.
- During his ODI captaincy India became the #1 ODI side in the ICC rankings for the first time for 12 months from January 2013 to January 2014, then again for one month in September 2014 and then for half a month in November 2014.
- He was run out for 50 in his final international match, which was the World Cup semi-final against New Zealand on 10 July 2019.

- He thus became the only player in international cricket to be run out both off the very first ball he faced and also the last ball he faced.

Test Cricket

- MS Dhoni made his Test debut at Chennai in December 2005 against Sri Lanka. He then became the 251st player to appear in a Test match for India.
- He got the opportunity to first step into the ground as a Test player only on the fifth day of the match just before lunch. The first three and half days of the Test match were washed out because of rain! However, he managed to make 30 runs on debut.
- In his second Test match he made an unbeaten 51 at Delhi against Sri Lanka.
- In his fifth Test match he made his maiden Test century—148 against Pakistan at Faisalabad in January 2006 (he had made the identical score for this maiden ODI century against the same opponent in April 2005 at Vizag, which was also in his fifth ODI match!).
- His 148 is the highest among the scores of the five Indians who made their maiden Test century against Pakistan.

Indians Registering Their Maiden Test Century against Pakistan

Runs	Batsman	Venue	Month, Year
148	MS Dhoni	Faisalabad	January 2006
128	Ravi Shastri	Karachi	January 1983
112	Yuvraj Singh	Lahore	April 2004
110	Deepak Shodhan*	Kolkata	December 1952
102	Irfan Pathan	Bangalore	December 2007

* Was making his Test debut

- He made his highest score in Tests, 224 (365 minutes, 265 balls, 6 sixes, 24 fours) against Australia at Chennai in 2013, which made him the first and the only Indian keeper to register a Test double century.
- His 224 is the third highest score by a Test wicketkeeper.

Highest Individual Scores by a Test Wicketkeeper

Runs	Wicketkeeper	For	Against	Venue	Month, Year
232*	Andy Flower	Zimbabwe	India	Nagpur	November 2000
230	Kumar Sangakkara	Sri Lanka	Pakistan	Lahore	March 2002
224	**MS Dhoni**	**India**	**Australia**	**Chennai**	**February 2013**
219*	Mushfiqur Rahim	Bangladesh	Zimbabwe	Mirpur	November 2018
210*	Taslim Arif	Pakistan	Australia	Faisalabad	March 1980

- His 224 was also then the highest by an Indian Test captain before Kohli surpassed him in 2016.

Highest Scores by an Indian Test Captain

Runs	Captain	Against	Venue	Month, Year
254*	Virat Kohli	South Africa	Pune	October 2019
243	Virat Kohli	Sri Lanka	Delhi	December 2017
235	Virat Kohli	England	Mumbai WS	December 2016
224	**MS Dhoni**	**Australia**	**Chennai**	**February 2013**
217	Sachin Tendulkar	New Zealand	Ahmedabad	October 1999

- His Test career tally of 4876 runs is the most by an Asian keeper in Tests and third highest by a wicketkeeper after Adam Gilchrist (5570) and Mark Boucher (5515).

Most Test Runs as a Wicketkeeper

Runs	Keeper-batsman	For
5570	Adam Gilchrist	Australia
5515	Mark Boucher	South Africa
4876	**MS Dhoni**	**India**
4540	Alec Stewart	England
4404	Andy Flower	Zimbabwe

• His Test tally of dismissals of 294 is the fifth best by any keeper in Tests and the best by an Asian.

Most Wicketkeeping Dismissals in Test Cricket

Dismissals	Cts+Sts	Wicketkeeper	For
555+	532+23	Mark Boucher	South Africa
416	379+37	Adam Gilchrist	Australia
395	366+29	Ian Healy	Australia
355	343+12	Rodney Marsh	Australia
294	**256+38**	**MS Dhoni**	**India**

+ Tally includes one match for ICC World Test XI

• His 38 stumpings is the joint third best in Test cricket. He and Syed Kirmani have the same number of stumpings.

Most Wicketkeeping Stumpings in Test Cricket

Sts	Cts	Wicketkeeper	For
52	78	Bert Oldfield	Australia
46	173	Godfrey Evans	England
38	160	Syed Kirmani	India
38	**256**	**MS Dhoni**	**India**
37	379	Adam Gilchrist	Australia

• In April 2009 at Wellington he became only the second Indian keeper after Syed Kirmani to claim six dismissals in a Test innings. Later, Wriddhiman Saha and Rishabh Pant equalled this Indian Test record.

- In December 2014 at Melbourne, he became the first Indian wicketkeeper to claim nine dismissals in a Test match. Later, both Wriddhiman Saha (10) and Rishabh Pant (11) bettered Dhoni's efforts. Incidentally, the Melbourne Test was Dhoni's final Test match. This means that Dhoni had become the first wicketkeeper in Test history to claim eight or more catches in his final Test match (Pakistan's Sarfaraz Ahmed claimed 10 dismissals at Johannesburg in January 2019, which has been his final Test match to date).
- Has captained India in 60 Tests, the most by an Asian player and the sixth most by any Test captain.

Most Tests as Captain by Asian Players

Tests	Captain	For
60	MS Dhoni	India
56	Arjuna Ranatunga	Sri Lanka
56	Misbah-ul-Haq	Pakistan
55	Virat Kohli	India
49	Sourav Ganguly	India

- In Test cricket history, he remains the only player to appear in over 50 Test matches as both a captain and wicketkeeper. From 2008 to 2014, he appeared in a record 60 Tests in this dual role.

Most Tests as Captain-Keeper

Tests	Captain	For
60	MS Dhoni	India
28	Mushfiqur Rahim	Bangladesh
19	Tim Paine	Australia
18	Gerry Alexander	West Indies
16	Andy Flower	Zimbabwe

- During his captaincy, India in December 2009 became the #1 Test ranked side for the first time in their history. India held on to this position until August 2011 for 21 months.

T20 International Cricket

- Dhoni made his T20 international debut in India's inaugural T20I match against South Africa at Johannesburg on 1 December 2006. His player number is #2 among others who appeared in a T20I match for India.
- Like he did in his ODI debut in December 2004 (a golden duck!), he was dismissed for a second-ball duck (silver duck) in his T20I debut!
- His maiden 50 in T20I cricket came quite late in his sixty-sixth innings on 1 February 2017, more than 10 years after his T20I debut.
- By not scoring a 50 in his first 65 innings he holds a record for a batsman with most innings before a maiden 50 in T20I cricket.

Most Innings to Register Maiden T20I 50

Innings	Batsman	For	Start	Achieved on
66	MS Dhoni	India	1 December 2006	1 February 2017
63	Tissara Perera	Sri Lanka	3 May 2010	16 March 2018
62	Kevin O'Brien	Ireland	2 August 2008	15 February 2019
42	Gary Wilson	Ireland	2 August 2008	20 January 2017
38	Chamara Kapugedera	Sri Lanka	15 June 2006	6 April 2017
38	Mohammad Nabi	Afghanistan	1 February 2010	12 March 2016

- His 98 T20I appearances are the most for India after Rohit Sharma.
- His 91 dismissals are the most by a keeper in T20I cricket.

Most Wicketkeeping Dismissals in Test Cricket

Dismissals	Cts+Sts	Wicketkeeper	For
91	57+34	MS Dhoni	India
63	43+20	Denesh Ramdin	West Indies
61	32+29	Mushfiqur Rahim	Bangladesh
60	28+32	Kamran Akmal	Pakistan
54	26+28	Mohammad Shahzad	Afghanistan

- His 57 catches and 34 stumpings are also the most by a keeper in T20I cricket.
- He has captained 72 T20I matches, the most by any player in this format.
- His 42 victories are the most by any captain in T20Is.
- Under his captaincy India won the inaugural World T20 in South Africa in 2007.
- During his T20I captaincy India became the #1 T20I side in the ICC rankings for the first time in March 2014 and during various stages until May 2016, which cumulatively totalled 228 days.

* * *

Postscript

Mahendra Singh Dhoni

Born on 7 July 1981 at Ranchi in Bihar (now Jharkhand)

Major teams: India, Bihar, Jharkhand, Chennai Super Kings (CSK), Rising Pune Supergiants (RPS)

Role: Right-hand bat and wicketkeeper
Bowling: Right-arm medium (occasional)

He is the only captain to win all three ICC tournaments—World T20 (in 2007), Cricket World Cup (in 2011) and Champions Trophy (in 2013).

MS Dhoni in International Cricket

Format	Span	Mts	Inns	NO	Runs	HS	Ave	SR	100	50	4s	6s	Ct	St
Tests	2005–2014	90	144	16	4876	224	38.09	59.11	6	33	544	78	256	38
ODIs	2004–2019	350	297	84	10773	183*	50.58	87.56	10	73	826	229	321	123
T20Is	2006–2019	98	85	42	1617	56	37.60	126.13	0	2	116	52	57	34
Total	2004–2019	538	526	142	17266	224	44.96	79.07	16	108	1486	359	634	195

MS Dhoni in Domestic/International Cricket

Format	Span	Mts	Inns	NO	Runs	HS	Ave	SR	100	50	Ct	St
First-class	2000–2014	131	210	19	7038	224	36.84	56.64	9	47	364	57
List A (50 ov)	2000–2019	423	364	99	13353	183*	50.38	84.93	17	87	402	141
T20s	2006–2019*	317	283	117	6621	84*	39.88	135.62	0	27	170	83
Total	2000–2019	871	857	235	27012	224	43.43	87.72	26	161	936	281

Major Tournaments

Tournament	Span	Mts	Inns	NO	Runs	HS	Ave	SR	100	50	Ct	St
Ranji Trophy	2000–2005	27	46	3	1575	128	36.62	72.77	3	8	70	11
IPL	2008–2018	190	170	65	4431	84*	42.20	137.82	0	23	98	38
Champions L	2010–2014	24	23	8	449	63*	29.93	141.19	0	1	14	11

MS Dhoni's Record as Captain in International Cricket

Format	Span	Mts	Won	Lost	Tie	Drawn/NR	% win
Tests	2008–2014	60	27	18	0	15	45.00
ODIs	2007–2018	200	110	74	5	11	55.00
T20Is	2007–2016	72	42	28	0	2	58.33
Total	**2007–2018**	**332**	**179**	**120**	**5**	**28**	**53.92**

- Dhoni won the IPL titles for CSK as captain in 2010, 2011 and 2018, and CSK were runners-up in 2008, 2012, 2013, 2015 and 2019.
- Dhoni has also won the Champions League (CL) titles for CSK in 2010 and 2014.

Acknowledgements

Through his long career, the subject of our book shone the brightest when the chips were down. As if by destiny, this book on MS Dhoni too came together under the most difficult of circumstances. The first wave of the Covid-19 pandemic had wrought havoc; nobody was quite sure whether there was even a future in the offing and what kind of future it would be. Yet, we stuck to the task, channelling our inner MSD time and again and learning from him on how not to give in to the most challenging of circumstances. And every time that we seemed close to the elusive finishing target, yet another tragedy would rock one of us back on our heels.

We finally managed to get here thanks to some very special people who took it upon themselves to see us through.

Premanka Goswami from Penguin, the guiding light behind the book who suggested the book, bought into the format, and encouraged and supported us at every step. From the same organization, Aparna Kumar and Binita Roy helped shape the book in its final form as we inched closer to the finish line. From the marketing team of Penguin, it was Ahana Singh who helped put together a marketing plan. While we tried to pull off a Dhoni with a few tense moments towards the end, these people ensured that there was never any dearth of support.

Veena Venugopal was a huge source of support at a very difficult time. My son Vivek Bhattacharjya also took on a whole lot more at home to make sure I had the time complete this manuscript.

Our contributors for the essays on Dhoni, each one of them, who agreed without hesitation deserve a special thanks. Lakshmipathy Balaji gave us time between practice sessions on a Zoom call from the UAE; Deep Dasgupta, one of our most prolific commentators, found the time to put together a special piece; Sharda Ugra managed to sneak hers in between international assignments; Jeet Banerjee agreed to put pen to paper to tell a story that few know and his lovely wife Malavika put her own sure finishing touches to the story. Kamal Sharma, that tireless chronicler of Indian cricket, graciously gave us access to his photo archives, and my old friend Mohandas Menon churned out his statistics as effortlessly as he supports the commentatory team on a telecast.

Jaideep Mukherjee, another old friend and fellow quizzer, who put in serious scholarship in order to give Dhoni's Ranchi connection the perspective it deserved. And his support systems, Salil Kumar Sanyal, Dilip Kumar Sengupta, Lata and Debashis Sanyal, Paromita Ghatak, and Parnika Sen, for sharing their memories and insights of working, studying and living in Ranchi. Gouri Majumder and Swapna Mukherjee, for their recollections of teaching at Jawahar Vidya Mandir, Ranchi. Like J.S. Munda and M.S. Dhoni, Jaideep's other half, Adirupa, is Ranchi-born and forged of that steel—this would not be possible without her. He has also written in the hope that many like his son Nikhil will get a glimpse of what being from Ranchi and playing for India means.

Auritro Chowdhury, who took strike during a particularly difficult time and managed to keep the book going when it was in danger of going under. And Aniket Mishra who responded to my cry for help by playing a brilliant finishing knock with terrific support from Arinjay Ghosh and Aakriti Mehrotra.

And finally, my co-author Amit Sinha, who wrote most of this book and brought a lens to Dhoni's cricket which was absolutely unique and personal, and yet universally relatable. His was the most difficult journey of all.

This book is his triumph.

Joy Bhattacharjya
June 2022

Contributors

Lakshmipathy Balaji

Fast bowler Lakshmipathy Balaji made his test debut against New Zealand in Ahmedabad and spearheaded the Indian pace attack in a historic series win in Pakistan in 2005 before a serious injury cut his test career short. He made an inspiring comeback, making it to the ODI team in 2008, and was a star bowler for Dhoni's CSK, champions in 2010, and KKR's champion team in 2012. He is currently a bowling coach with CSK.

Jeet Banerjee

Jeet Banerjee is the founder and managing director of Gameplan Sports, one of India's leading sports management firms. An integral member of the original Kolkata Knight Riders think tank, he has worked with some of the leading athletes worldwide including MS Dhoni, Vivian Richards and Steve Waugh. He is also a co-founder of the Kolkata Literary Meet, and organizes India's largest chess tournament, the Tata Steel Tournament

Auritro Chowdhury

Auritro Chowdhury earned a diploma in Sports Management from IISWBM, Kolkata, and an MSc degree in Sports Business Management from Sheffield Hallam University. He has worked on the Commonwealth Games, Delhi, the Hockey and Cricket World Cups as well as the IPL and the Indian Super League (ISL). A passionate quizzer, he voraciously consumes books, videos and publications on sports, history, geography, popular culture and literature.

Deep Dasgupta

Wicketkeeper-batsman Deep Dasgupta announced his arrival to Ranji Trophy cricket with a century on debut for Bengal. He soon made his Test debut against South Africa at Bloemfontein and also scored a Test century against England. He was one of Bengal's most successful captains, leading them to consecutive Ranji finals in the 2000s. Deep is currently one of India's most respected cricket commentators, a valued voice on the game in both Hindi and English.

Aakriti Mehrotra and Arinjay Ghosh

Aakriti Mehrotra and Arinjay Ghosh are talented young sports professionals. Aakriti is a Media and Communications Manager at FIFA and Arinjay is the Communications Manager, LOC, FIFA U17 Women's World Cup India 2022.

Mohandas Menon

Mohandas Menon gave up a flourishing corporate career to make a profession of his first love, cricket, and became India's first full-time cricket statistician. From his early days at ESPN Star Sports in the late 1990s, Mohandas has been one of the most regarded and reliable cricket statisticians of this era. He has worked on international cricket for over two decades, and Cricket World Cups since 1996.

Jaideep Mukherjee

Jaideep 'Jai' Mukherjee has made a career out of following his passions—first as a cricketer and quizzer in his teens, then for the next three decades in the media and in higher education; in the development sector for the UN; and presently for the UK's largest children's charity, where he is a director for learning and development, heading their corporate university. Understanding sport and society, and how the two influence and impact each other continues to fascinate him. He has published on this in academia and media, and worked in managing the delivery of several international sporting events in Singapore.

He lives in Hertfordshire just outside London where his family and he can play and watch sport. Jai's links with Ranchi run deep, and he intends his contribution to the book as a celebration of the place and its most famous son.

Kamal Sharma

Kamal Sharma is a veteran sports photographer who has been capturing Dhoni in his many moods right from his very first major tournament. Kamal has covered international cricket for three decades, displayed his pictures in many exhibitions and was also one of the only Indian photo journalists on ground in New York during the 911 terrorist attacks.

Sharda Ugra

Sharda Ugra has been a sports journalist for over three decades. She began her career with Mumbai tabloid *Mid-Day* before stints at *The Hindu*, *India Today* magazine and ESPN India. She has written and spoken about Indian sport in conferences and publications at home and overseas. She worked with former New Zealand captain John Wright on *John Wright's Indian Summers*, his memoirs of his years coaching India and with Yuvraj Singh on *The Test of My Life*, an account of recovery from cancer. She was a fellow of the Australia India Institute, University of Melbourne in 2013.